In Memory of

Dr. James Chin
Nyack Faculty
1997 – 2015

View from the Urban Loft

View from the Urban Loft

*Developing a Theological Framework
for Understanding the City*

SEAN BENESH

RESOURCE *Publications* · Eugene, Oregon

VIEW FROM THE URBAN LOFT
Developing a Theological Framework for Understanding the City

Resource Publications
An Imprint of Wipf and Stock Publishers
199 W. 8th Ave., Suite 3
Eugene, OR 97401
www.wipfandstock.com

ISBN 13: 978-1-61097-514-8

Manufactured in the U.S.A.

To those who are being drawn to the city.

Contents

Foreword

D R. SEAN BENESH AND I are neighbors in a global village. Although we live in different countries, we are members of a "tribe" that is "plugged in" to a virtual *community*. Social media have become our "tribal circle." We connect in chat *rooms*, breathe the same air in the *blogosphere*, and can be easily spotted by the fact we possess the clear tribal markings identified by the great cultural anthropologist Christian Lander in *Stuff White People Like*.

Every once in a while, we might even be in the same city during "tribal gatherings" such as a Catalyst conference or at a meeting of the Congress for New Urbanism.

Even as the world hurtles towards urbanization at an ever-increasing pace, some have argued that communications technology has made the city and its public squares obsolete. Historically, community meant not only the people you did life with, but the physical context (within a reasonable walking radius) that you did life in. Today, we throw "community" around quite a bit to describe the virtual connection that technology provides.

Sean and I have never met. However, we have both come to the conclusion that when you divorce *community* from *place*, you inherently lose something in the translation.

God has placed on both of our hearts a passion and love for *ecclesia* and the city. God has been leading us both along a journey in the re-reading of his meta-narrative from the garden to the city and discovering at every step along the way that he is a God of *community* and *place*. Our triune God models community. From a "good" start in the Garden of Eden to the Promised Land, from Jerusalem to the City of Heaven, God has designed and used place to facilitate vertical connections with him and his creation, as well as horizontal connections, or community, between us. It seems that his "dwelling among us" and the redemption of people and place are one of the key aspects of the Incarnation and of our shared Christian faith.

The divorce of community from place in our society mirrors a neo-Gnosticism within the church, which creates a Berlin Wall between the spiritual and the physical. Sean boldly confronts this heresy that has taken root at both ends of the evangelical spectrum. For example, there's an "old-school" perspective that since "it's all gonna burn," the material world can be reduced to simply the place where we discover and choose personal fire insurance and then go on to become insurance salesmen ourselves. Among the "cooler" circles of many of my hipster urban church planter friends, it is common to hear an anti-"bricks and mortar" bent. If catacombs and homes were good enough for the first-century church, it is good enough for them. This is fine if we accept that *ecclesia* is simply a one-to-two-hour-a-week event that can happen in borrowed space. But if Christ-centered community is something more than a weekly gathering, then redemption of place and community re-enter the equation.

What we need is a theology of place.

View from the Urban Loft is a seminal work in this effort.

Winston Churchill once said "we shape our buildings; thereafter they shape us." The same can be said of our cities. Understanding the context that we move, breathe, and live in can be more difficult than it would seem at first glance. The challenge can be akin to trying to describe the ocean to fish.

The ocean that the majority of our species swim in is the city, whether we know it or not. However, both caffeine-addicted Portland urbanites and anti-urban "married with children" suburbanites often share a mistaken definition of the city. It is often limited to urban core areas such as its central business district and the adjacent tier of high-density mixed-use residential neighborhoods. While such districts clearly exhibit the characteristics of "urbanity" (density in form, diverse in use, human in scale), international definitions of "urbanized area" and "city" reach far beyond these "core" zones to encompass multiple zones of various densities before ending at the agricultural zones or natural features which define their perimeter.

As an architect of *ecclesia* and an urban designer, I have found that the ministry and community spaces should be soil-specific. As Paul models on Mars Hill, the best missionaries are cultural anthropologists who take the time to understand the context in which they are communicating, and tie God's story into the story of the city space. One of the most influential recent urban planning innovations—the urban-to-rural transect—is helpful in understanding this context. This ecological concept, which describes changes in habitat along a cross-section, moves us beyond the notion of land-use zones, to help us to see cities as inclusive of the urban core (T-1 Zone) as well as the urbanized fringe (T-3 Sub-Urban Zone).

Missionaries and church planters such as my client and friend Rick Warren have done good cultural anthropology at the fringe, which I call "autopia." New urbanist design has figured out how to mitigate the movement and storage of the car, while creating satisfying, human-scaled neighborhoods and town centers. Much of our work at this urban periphery has been involved with the idea of redeeming suburbia. Concepts that used to stand in opposition to each other such as "city" and "sprawl" are being turned upside down. Recent research by the Brookings Institute revealed that a majority of the nation's poor in the 100 largest metropolitan areas lived in the suburbs. The "married with children" demographic that suburban America was built for now comprises only 10 percent of U.S. households. I've joined missiologist Alan Hirsch on an initiative called "Future Travelers" which is taking many of the fastest-growing suburban mega-churches on a learning journey towards responding to these shifts and moving away from the "Christian country club" campus model. For example, mega-church parking lots are being re-planned and redeveloped as human-scaled mixed-use community centers with *ecclesia* as an "anchor tenant." This looks different in each city and transect zone. At Austin Stone Community Church, this meant building a "For The City" center on an abandoned motel site which incubates business and non-profits that have a heart for Austin, rather than a traditional campus. We've broken ground on a village commons at Granger Community Church. Future phases include an artisan village linking the commons to the community retail center at the corner of their parking lot. Other additions to the recipe of what was once a single-use mega-church typology include single-room occupancy housing for homeless, lifelong learning centers, sports, performing and creative arts, food banks, and postmodern piazzas.

Just as the lens through which we see suburban soil requires adjusting, Sean highlights the need for changing our lenses if we're to view the city in its entirety and the heart of the city differently. No longer the 9-to-5 central business district, nor the catch-basin of a city's poorest residents and immigrants, "downtown" is emerging as a viable choice for aging boomers, empty-nesters, "cultural creatives," and even families choosing diversity and density over "autopia."

I appreciate the humble stance with which Sean asks some foundational questions. Is God interested in redeeming both people and places? What is a city? What is a good city? Why should it matter to us? What gives him credibility in my book isn't his DMin and solid urbanist library, but the fact that he's asking these questions outside the ivory tower, as an immigrant in the midst of a world-class city in the throes of globalization, international immigration, and densification. He's asking these questions as his wife and kids are stranded at a transit station with groceries, as buses packed full of passengers pass them by.

Chris Seay once told me that he believes real estate development can be one of the most incarnational acts we take on. We are image bearers of the Creator and have been tasked with cultivating creation and creating culture, rather than just critiquing it. We can either continue to stamp out unsustainable development "products" (strip malls, tracts, industrial "parks") that isolate, or we can cultivate human habitats where we get out of our steel cocoons (the car) and rub shoulders with our fellow denizens of the city. We each choose our mission field. Some are on a rescue mission to those plugged into the suburban matrix of social isolation and deadening commutes medicated by media. Some are joining God in redeeming those liminal spaces. Some are performing open-heart surgery on the heart of their city. All should be humbly praying for and seeking the welfare of the city where God sent us. Good cities facilitate relationships and thus stories. In cities, not only is history being made, but his story is being told.

Mel McGowan
President, Visioneering Studios
Irvine, California

Preface

VIEW FROM THE URBAN *Loft* emerged from one simple question: How do I understand the city? Trying to answer that question has sent me on an expedition like a treasure hunter in search of finding that which is precious. Except in this case, the riches lie in the context of the city which more than half of the world's population now call home. Like any endeavor or experience that is of preeminent value, it is worth further research and consideration. As I've come to fully immerse myself in the city, I am constantly on a quest to add meaning to what I see and take in on a daily basis. Tonight over *biryani* we sat and listened to the stories of two families' journey from south Asia to Canada and to Vancouver. They too are grasping for meaning, a framework of understanding, and answers to help them understand life in this global village they find themselves in. Walking the two blocks home in the coolness of the Vancouver summer night, I reflected on the magnetic pull the city has on people. I've given my life to this magnetic pull in seeking to understand it, the various dynamics at hand, and the belief that cultivating a deeper theological grounding in terms of the city is in my opinion, the path the church needs to continue to follow. As I see it, the city is much more than a collection of people, roadways, glass, steel, and concrete towers . . . it is now the center stage in the drama of humanity where God is at work.

Far from indulging in theological abstractions, I wrote this book to help me understand the city, how God has shaped its history and future trajectory, and how I am to live accordingly. My hope is that as a result of my own personal quest, which you will find poured out on the pages to come, we as the church can learn to embrace and love the city, to note where God is at work, identify the mystery behind the formation of cities, and how we're to live in them today. This book seeks to enlarge the scope and framework of how the church's longing for city-wide transformation can unfold in the city.

Although essentially a theological book, and since the context is indeed that of the city, I spend considerable time relying heavily on the various academic disciplines of history, urban planning, transportation planning, architecture, sociology, economics, and so forth to inform and buttress deeper theological reflection. Rather than seeing these as competing disciplines, I instead examine them within a theological framework to try to discern their underlying values and assumptions. This is akin to having a Bible and a book on community development theory open in front of me at the same time, and so allowing one to inform the other. The Bible would inform me on what community development can look like from a divine perspective or template, while a book on community development would help me to identify those instances where this phenomenon took place in Scripture, as in the book of Nehemiah.

This book starts off with a theological reflection on what cities are, with my own story of urban migration woven into themes that are examined. How do we even look at cities? With what perspective? As gifts of God or as accursed places? These are but a few of the questions that are asked from an urban backdrop. We long to see redemption and the transformation of cities, but what exactly do these even look like? How do we know when these have truly happened or not? I look at common perceptions of city-reaching and city transformation, and begin enlarging the scope of what it can and should look like. But in order to see cities transformed, it is imperative that we begin understanding their attributes. Parallel to the theological questions being asked is a deeper exploration of the nature of cities from the historical development of various city-related words to popular word usages that all coalesce into our understanding of cities today.

The next section of the book is like going on an archaeological excursion as we seek to uncover the dusty origins of cities. I lay a theological framework over back-to-back accounts of the formation of ancient cities as found in Genesis and in the *extra-biblical* material. Given thousands of years of hindsight, we're able to offer theological reflection on these early events in light of divine intention and the trajectory of cities. Next comes a tracing of the urban thread that begins in Genesis, makes a few stops along the way, and continues right up to the time of Jesus in the first century. I then note how this shapes and forms the backdrop for the emergence of the early church and its urban trajectory. Most may be surprised to discover that even only a cursory analysis of urban themes in Scripture reveals a depth of theological meaning for the city that informs even modern-day city-dwellers. Again, while the tone and nature of the book are certainly theological in nature, I do not follow a rote or systematic approach. Admittedly it is neither comprehensive nor exhaustive. My own cultural biases, leanings, and context informed much of the hermeneutical process.

After establishing the parameters of what cities are, their historical development, as well as urban themes, blueprints, and templates found throughout Scripture, the book makes a decisive shift in direction. It transitions from looking backward to looking around and then to looking toward the future. Chapter 10 is a key transitional pivot in the book. Again, this is all born out of my attempts to begin understanding the city which I live in. As I walk the streets of the city and interact with people in my neighborhood from all over the world, I'm drawn to explore such topics as the importance and theology of place and the built environment, the various layers or perspectives in looking at the city, and what it all means.

Lastly, I turn my attention to the future of cities and church planting and ministry within this context. As cities expand and densify comes the need to think biblically, theologically, and strategically about high-density city contexts, walkable neighborhoods, bike-friendly cities, and pedestrian-oriented church planting. How does urban form dictate the how of mission? Do we continue to apply generic templates across the city in terms of church planting and missional engagement or how do we learn from the city and adapt accordingly? This all pushes us again towards this idea of a transformed city and what that looks like. More than the norm of gentrification, what does a transformed city look like that includes the redemption of urban places and urban people?

I invite you into the exploration process with me. God has a plan for our cities and we have the incredible privilege of living in these places, following where he is at work, and collectively dreaming and planning for a better future through transformation.

Acknowledgments

THERE ARE MANY PEOPLE who deserve acknowledgement and thanks because this book would not be a reality if it weren't for them, their support, and encouragement. On a personal and family level I'm grateful for my family . . . Katie, Grant, Camden, and Seth. It has been a fun adventure of a lifetime living in the city together as we seek to understand God's heart for the city and how we're to live accordingly. Many times whether reading Bible stories at bedtime, talking as we walk and longboard the neighborhood, or partaking in "Dollar Drink Days" at McDonald's where seemingly the entire global village known as Edmonds Town Centre congregates, we share and discuss what we're learning, how the gospel is transforming our lives, and what God wants us to do in this city. These have been the best days of my life!

I'd like to thank my good friend and editor Frank Stirk. He's a master craftsman at what he does as a writer and editor who's taken this manuscript and made it into something special. Over and over he's helped refine and refine again the points I'm making and where I am going in my arguments. It has been an absolute joy and privilege working together on this as we've both learned lots about the city and God's heart for it. I could not have done this without you!

We've had some special friends who've walked alongside us in our time here in Vancouver as we collectively dreamed about the city, church planting (Ion) and doing campus ministry (Red Couch) in this context, and how we can support and encourage one another. Kelly and Jeanne Manire, Nathan and Amy Laughlin, and J. J. Johnson (*le sofa rouge!*) have been an incredible blessing to me and my family. Stephen Harper was a huge encouragement to me always as we talked about many things—seminary education, writing books, CFL football, college football, and most importantly, about life. Thanks for always being a Skype call away!!! We're grateful for many others who've blessed us immeasurably in more ways than they could even imagine: Cam Roxburgh and Dan Bennett of

Southside Church and Forge Canada demonstrated their love and care for me and my family. We count it a privilege to live just blocks from Southside Church (ETC) as they brought us into their neighborhood family. Paul and Nancy Ingold have impacted our lives as they breathed into us anew the depth of the gospel and its transformative effects on our lives. Thank you all!

I'd like to thank Dr. Steve Booth at the Canadian Southern Baptist Seminary and College who took a risk to allow us to pioneer new classes here in metro Vancouver. Along with that thanks to the students of these courses who drank way too much coffee with me as we talked together about the city (Conrad, Ken, Nathan, Kelly, Stephen M, Stephen H, Wayne, Soe, and Yong). These classes and theological discussions about the city provided the fuel for this book. Thanks guys! Thank you to other instrumental people in the WestCoast Baptist Association family for your encouragement and support: Ray Woodard, Don Springer, Janet Campbell, Gary and Carol Oaks, and so many more. Thanks to Mike Parry, FCC, and the SEMO BSU for their love, support, encouragement and blessing us with, in the words of Cousin Eddie as spoken to Clark W. Griswold, "the gift that keeps on giving" (Trader Joe gift cards). Thanks to all of the baristas at the ETC Starbucks for their kindness and innumerable free drinks.

Lastly, I'd like to thank you the reader as well. Happy reading!

Introduction

Excerpt from my blog The Urban Loft (www.theurbanloft.org)
July 4, 2011 | Burnaby, BC, Canada | "The Urbanity of the Bible"

I UNDERSTAND THAT WE have made the Bible many things that it never was meant to be. We've reduced it to bullet-point formulas for a myriad of things from how to live a happy life, how to be a good leader, the keys to a better marriage, financial success, and so on. As a result, advocating for an urban framework for understanding the Bible might appear to be simply another in a long list of ways we've made the Bible fit our agenda. There are many unworthy things in centuries past and present that we have justified "under the banner of God." Point well taken.

Robert Linthicum, in his book *City of God, City of Satan* makes the statement: "It comes as a surprise to us all: the Bible is an urban book! It is hard for us to appreciate that the world of Moses and David and Daniel and Jesus was an urban world."[1] In theology as well as cultural exegesis we stress the importance of context. Context is indeed everything. In missiological terms, context sets the parameters for how the church is to engage its community with the good news. This is normative thinking. If we hold true to this way of thinking, then we must consider the context of much of Scripture. Much of the biblical drama was played out not in sleepy little villages and farms, but in the city, from Ur of 2000 B.C. with a population of 25,000 to first-century Rome with a population of around a million inhabitants. What's the hold up then? "If the Bible is such an urban book, why do we not see it that way? It is simply because we approach the Bible from an essentially rural theological perspective. When we read the Bible, we are thinking: 'country' instead of 'city.' We see what we read through 'rural glasses.'"[2]

1. Linthicum, *City of God City of Satan*, 21.
2. Ibid., 22.

Linthicum points out that once we get beyond the apostle Paul, John of Damascus, and Augustine, then the majority of the other influential leaders in church history were mostly rural people. Aquinas, Luther, and Calvin were essentially more rural than urban. "Only Calvin, among later theologians, attempted theological formulation for an urban environment—and the Geneva of his day numbered only sixteen thousand!"[3] What would happen if we read Scripture within an urban framework? What would we see? What have we missed in our own lives by not donning this crucial contextual lens? All of a sudden what we then find throughout the pages of the Bible is hope and help for our cities today. We would also find that Scripture has much to say about the topic of the city. For example, a third of the Psalms were city-based and cities were the location and context where most of the events in Scripture unfolded. Maybe it is time we put on some new glasses . . . .

3. Ibid., 23.

1

Theological Questions Painted
on an Urban Canvas

THE ORANGE GLOW FROM the street lights reflecting off the low-hanging clouds casts an odd color in the night sky. I look out my kitchen window and I'm struck by what I see. Below the clouds, sleek steel-and-glass towers protrude into the heavens. They look like enormous Christmas trees with patterned lighting as some windows are lit while others are dark. Distant sirens—is it police, fire or ambulance? I can never tell—break the silence as I'm jolted back into the here and now.

From my vantage point, I see traces and evidence that New Urbanism is alive and well in this city with residential and commercial life all mixed together amidst bustling pedestrians, bulky transit buses hastily picking up and dropping off passengers, and the familiar nearby sound of the Skytrain pulling into and leaving the station. This is my neighborhood and this is my city. As I daily walk the streets and interact with local residents, I've become acutely aware of the reality that not only am I living in one of the most multicultural cities in the world, but that my own neighborhood is the number one landing place for immigrants in all of western Canada. But that's okay, for I too am an immigrant.

Growing up in the American heartland, the whole idea of being an immigrant was almost, well, foreign to me, other than knowing that in the first part of the twentieth century, my family came to Iowa via New York from what was then Bohemia. This particular area in Iowa was settled by a number of Bohemian immigrants who chose it because it reminded them of home. It also provided them soil rich for farming. Several generations removed, I grew up knowing very little of Bohemian or Czech culture, other than eating some of their national delicacies at my grandparents' house or going with them to the polka dances in the town hall. When we moved to Canada, all of a sudden the whole issue of being an immigrant was thrust upon me as I became one, just like my ancestors before me.

Through a series of events and promptings, we felt God was leading us to move to Vancouver, BC to not only plant a church but plant our lives as well. My first visit to Vancouver a few years ago was a shock, as I began to see the enormous difference between Canadian cities and American cities, not only in the built environment but more so in regards to demographics. Like a typical American, for some reason everything north of the 49th parallel was a big blank spot on the map that conjured up images of ancient mariners who thought the world was flat and simply dropped off at some point into oblivion. In my imagination, that was right at the Canadian border, because I had no idea of what took place north of that line other than it was a land of Mounties, igloos, snow, and hockey—the Great White North. When we finally settled on Vancouver as the city we felt God was leading us to, I knew we needed to live in an urban setting. Through a whim and a prayer with hundreds of people praying for us, we landed in Edmonds Town Centre in Burnaby.

One of the most prominent shaping influences of Vancouver in general and our neighborhood in particular is immigration. The common theme here is that most people are foreign-born and in that respect we fit right in. To find someone who was actually born in Canada or whose parents were born here seems like an anomaly. It is a community of contrasts with many of the more affluent living in high-rise residential towers, driving expensive cars and dressing like they walked out of fashion magazines. The vast majority of the people living in these towers are Chinese. Just across the street in low-rise apartments is a whole different world. The immigrants there are from all over, ranging from Turkey to Iran to Romania to India to Sudan. I see Muslim women in full head and face coverings toting their pull-along carts walking to the grocery store, or eastern European guys huddled around, laughing, smoking, and wearing Capri pants. I watch as a Sudanese dad walks his little son to school dressed in a little mini-suit looking cute and studious. It is a neighborhood of contrasts whether in reference to ethnicity, variety of languages spoken, or socio-economic status. It is akin to what Darrin Patrick writes in *For the City*, "Real life in an urban context isn't neatly segregated into distinct cultural communities. Instead, everyone is thrown together, living on top of one another, and there are endless cultures, subcultures, and tribes in any given city."[1]

As an immigrant family, we sit in this weird world of paradoxes. Apart from some church planters that we know here, we've yet to meet another American in the city, although I know they're here somewhere. While we immigrated from the middle class in the US, it is a whole new scenario here. We were once proud homeowners, had two cars and the like, while our kids went to a great suburban school that was one of the highest-ranked schools in the metro Tucson area and very homogeneous. Now I find myself as an underfunded church planter (through my own ineptitude at fundraising) living in a high-density urban neighborhood, car-less, and officially low-income.

Why do I bring this all up? Out of self-pity? No, to give you context. We've been on a whirlwind adventure where we've had to adapt to a way of living that never would have come on our own accord. The anxieties of being have-nots all of a sudden puts us in arm's reach of all the other immigrants around us as we walk everywhere or take transit, shop in thrift stores, and learn to live in a multicultural community. This past week I went to breakfast with my oldest son Grant at our neighborhood McDonald's. As we were talking about living here in Canada this past year, he went on to say, "You know, Dad, by far this has been the best year of my life." As crazy as it all sounds, I wouldn't trade any of this for the world.

Most mornings I walk the three blocks over to our local Starbucks where I try my best to find a lone table near an outlet to work, plan, read, and write. While I attempt to drown out the background noise by donning headphones, I can't help but overhear what is taking place all around me. To my right sits the same middle-aged man from the former Yugoslavia. He proudly tells me so. I watch in fascination all morning as there is a constant stream of people coming in and out to talk with this man who must be one of the community leaders of this ethnic group. He also speaks seven languages. Sometimes there are ten people huddled around him listening, laughing, and drinking coffee. To my left sit two young Chinese women, each with their laptops opened in front of them while texting on their phones and talking to each other all at once. I soak all of this in as I steal glances out the big windows to watch pedestrians

1. Patrick and Carter, *For the City*, 73.

hurry to their destination as the gentle rain has turned into a downpour. All around me are more of these high-density residential towers looming above the streetscape. I begin to ask myself a question which turns into a blog entry . . . what makes a city great? What is the purpose of the city? And what does God think of the city?

I'm definitely not the first to ask these questions and more, but they form in my thinking and brew in my imagination like the drip coffee I smell wafting through the coffee shop. What does make a city great? In an attempt to get my mind not only around this city in particular but cities in general, I've spent considerable time reading book after book related to various subjects ranging from urban planning, architecture, transportation, New Urbanism, Canadian urbanism, the social sciences, and more as well as sitting in lectures on various urban topics in search for the answer to that question. Over 2,500 years ago, the Greek historian Herodotus also asked that question as he surveyed the urban landscape and the rise and fall of cities around him. "The critical questions of Herodotus's time still remains: What makes cities great, and what leads to their gradual demise?"[2]

What then qualifies as greatness? Is it simply the built environment with appealing aesthetics, plentiful green spaces, and movements like transit-oriented development? Does greatness rise and fall on transportation? If a city has ample (or thorough) public transit, walkable neighborhoods, and a high per capita of people who cycle to work, do these make a city great? Maybe greatness is found in culture and in the people themselves. Are great cities more or less homogeneous? If they are diverse, then is the social capital particularly high across ethnic and linguistic lines? If one is looking at this from a spiritual standpoint as a follower of Christ, would the argument be that greatness then means more people are Christians and there is a bumper crop of new churches being planted across the metro area, whether urban or suburban? Does that make a city great? Is there such a thing as a great city apart from a strong Christian presence? Do there need to be more Christians and churches for greatness to happen?

More often than not, theology is associated with a "landed status" in regards to thought and theological reflection. Theologies purport a finalized feel about the topics at hand as if to say, "OK, we've nailed this down. It's done. The book is now closed on this topic." My hunch is that

2. Kotkin, *The City*, xxi.

a theology of the city is more or less like an open-source theology in that as the decades and even centuries move forward, more people will be making their own contributions. As the sciences expand and archaeology uncovers new (or old) insights from antiquity, theological reflection continues to have a shaping effect on how we view all things urban in the Bible. A quick perusal through church history will reveal that at times theology played a reactionary role as Christians were confronted with issues that had not previously been thought through. We saw this from the very beginning of the church as it wrestled with various questionable influences, whether they be Judaizers in the church or Gnostics. In the next chapter, I will extrapolate insights from a key second-century church leader as he personally confronted and wrestled with Gnosticism. What happened is that these struggles had a refining effect on the church as believers worked hard at nailing down in writing just what they believed, why, and even how.

It is this reaction to the changing tide of culture that has indeed influenced Christians throughout the centuries. While the church was birthed in some of the largest urban centers of the first century AD, so that being a Christian became synonymous with being an urbanite, something changed along the way. While from the beginning, cities have always possessed dysgenic features, certain features were accentuated with the growth and evolution of the global city. As the Industrial Revolution quickened its pace and people flocked to the city in hopes of a better life, a brighter future, and simply jobs, it also introduced a whole litany of social ills that tore a rift in urban life. As living conditions became crowded, unsanitary and deplorable, there was an involuntary reaction of revulsion by many with even the church being a prominent voice of disdain in that regard. Even though the church began and grew as an urban movement, the Industrial Revolution shook that notion to the core as many Christians began rejecting the city.

But more recently, this attitude has changed yet again. Like a global seismic shift, there have been sweeping changes that are in some ways reconfiguring the very nature of the city and even how people view it. As people flock to the world's urban centers, it does more than simply expand the built environment. There is a transformative change. "Cities are changing *everything*. They are transforming ecology, economics, politics, and social relations everywhere, for better or for worse, depending on different approaches to city building."[3] As cities one by one remove the industrial city or manufacturing city moniker from their persona, in its place are new adjectives like the creative city with a creative or knowledge-based economy. One of the side-effects is that cities throughout the world are experiencing one enormous gentrification project. Once neglected and depleted city cores are going through a flowering renaissance as people move back into the city. Through media and widespread travel, urban life is now within the reach of most people. For many, the city holds appeal, houses aspiration, and is the place where dreams are realized. Not only that, but institutions of higher learning are scrambling to offer new tracks, degrees, or concentrations in urban studies, urban planning, urban ministry, and the like. Revolutionary? Indeed. The church is waking up to this global phenomenon. More books on the subject are being written, the city is at the core of numerous conversations, and many denominations and mission organizations have made a decisive shift to focus on urban centers. Along with this has come the need to offer more theological reflection in regards to the city.

What is God doing? Is he behind global urbanization? What does Scripture teach us about the city, God's plans or intentions for it, and what are we to do about our involvement in it? Others within the church and outside the church are asking similar questions about the shaping effect of urbanization and the continued rise of the global city. "How does the increasing concentration of people and human endeavor in cities change our world?"[4] These are just a few questions that will be explored throughout this book. With a myriad of questions formulating and circulating, maybe a foundational one to ask is this: how are we to view the city? To put it another way: as those of us who are Christians (followers of Jesus), how are we to view the city and with which lens?

The way in which we view cities in general and our own in particular has a shaping effect upon us. That view, vantage point, or lens will dictate and shape the degree of our involvement in the city. If our primary assumption is that cities are evil, a detriment to overall faith, and in opposition to God, then more than likely we'll find ourselves aloof, disengaged, and uninterested. If we are indeed involved, it may be more or less on the spiritual plane alone and that's the extent of it. On

---

3. Brugmann, *Welcome to the Urban Revolution*, ix.
4. Ibid.

the other hand, if we see cities as something altogether different, it may inform us and shape our thinking in ways we didn't know possible.

Is the city a gift, a curse, or something neutral? Did cities simply "happen" somewhere in the ancient Near East thousands of years ago and we're still living in this accidental happening now in the twenty-first century? Was God's intention all along for us to be a rural people wearing blue jeans, listening to country music, and sitting atop a John Deere tractor with a can of Skoal in our back pockets? Pick up an armload of books addressing the subject of the city from various scholars and academics, and immediately one will be struck by the divergence of thinking. Much of my own thinking, logic, and reasoning about the city has been shaped by such authors and scholars. It is my contention that the city, though plagued with many social ills and broken on numerous fronts, is still at its core a gift from God. I would even venture to say it is the result of divine intention.

I've had the privilege of sitting under Dr. Ray Bakke's teaching and influence as a student at Bakke Graduate University in Seattle. I vividly remember the first time I came across his contention that the city is a gift of common grace from God to mankind. Like a typical evangelical, my thought process always defaulted to city involvement taking the form of evangelism or church planting. The city was like an untamed tiger to be fended off and tamed, whip in hand. My thinking was greatly challenged and stretched when I read, "We Christians are the only people who can truly discuss the salvation of souls and the rebuilding of city sewer systems in the same sentence."[5] This all ties back into Herodotus' question of what makes a city great. In recent history, certain segments of Christians would assess a city's greatness in terms of how many Christians and churches it had. The rationale was that if we see enough people come to faith in Christ and the number of churches being planted escalates exponentially, it will have such an overwhelming effect upon the city whereby urban renewal and community transformation would simply be a by-product. The city will then be made great.

If that's true, then logically the healthiest cities in the US would be located in the South where there is a high proportion of people who identify themselves as Christians as well as a high density of churches, including innumerable mega-churches. Are such cities—Dallas, New Orleans, Atlanta, among others—truly marked then by societal transfor-

5. Bakke, *A Theology as Big as the City*, 34.

mation because they have so many believers? Do these cities model what it means to live in racial harmony? Is the social capital among the various ethnic groups elevated because the Gospel is so readily available and so many people follow Jesus? What about the built environment? Are the cities in these areas the most aesthetically beautiful and appealing? Are the arts flourishing? Is the economy noticeably stronger? Is public education on the leading edge nationally? Can we say that these cities are model cities because of their higher proportion of Christians and churches compared to other cities?

To be fair, the answers to those questions will vary depending on the city. But I would argue that a city can possess the highest possible standards of living but that these still may have little to no effect upon the fabric of urban life. Too often we're good at giving pat answers to difficult situations where evangelism is the cure-all for everything from failing marriages, financial troubles, bad breath, and body odor. Without doubt, Christ is the central point in our lives. The Gospel indeed has the potential and the power to not only transform individual lives and families, but the ripple effect can indeed influence neighborhoods and cities. But in order to do so, we need to reorient our thinking. What makes a city great? What then is our role in city-building?

What would happen if we viewed the city as a gift of common grace from God to people? Later on in the book, I will go exploring into the origins of the city by examining the biblical texts as well as archaeological evidence in a side-by-side manner to look for divine intention. But for now let's tease out some thoughts, ideas, and some biblical principles for this notion of cities being a gift of common grace from God to us. Theologian Wayne Grudem defines common grace as "the grace of God by which he gives people innumerable blessings that are not part of salvation."[6] Grudem goes on to offer numerous examples of common grace and even the reasoning behind it. One of these gifts of common grace to mankind is in the societal realm: "[God's] grace is also evident in the existence of various organizations and structures in human society."[7] Part of those structures or organizations are the very ones that govern and protect our urban centers. "[Human] laws and police forces and judicial systems provide a powerful deterrent to evil actions, and these are necessary, for there is much evil in the world that is irrational

6. Grudem, *Systematic Theology*, 657.

7. Ibid., 661.

and that can only be restrained by force, because it will not be deterred by reason or education."[8]

It is not a great theological leap to indeed make the case that cities are gifts of common grace from God. Sometimes we fail to realize the scope of God's love and care for humanity. We usually divide people into two teams: those in Christ and those apart from him. This reflects Jesus' teaching on wheat and tares (weeds). However, we can sometimes take the analogy too far by saying that nothing good can come from those who are apart from Christ, which is entirely untrue. God uses those who love and follow him as well as those who don't to still accomplish his purposes in the city. If we're to make sweeping broad statements based upon a cursory glance at the whole of Scripture, we'd have to conclude that God loves and favors the orphan, the widow, the immigrant, the poor, and the rest of those who are marginalized. God does indeed love and care for all, but he has a special place in his heart for them. We see this in the way he established the Old Testament law to include setting the trajectory for an urban existence that would give preferential treatment to these people. Fast forward to the New Testament and we notice that Jesus was about the same thing. As we look at our cities, we find many organizations, institutions, and non-profits which are close to the heart of God as they care for the marginalized and the overall city.

As a way to practically attempt to love and serve the city, I began volunteering at the North Shore Neighbourhood House in North Vancouver. I was immediately humbled by the tireless efforts of the staff and the hundreds of volunteers who serve the least, the broken, the elderly, and the young. In regards to common grace, they serve as a gift to the city. God is loving and blessing those who come in contact with the Neighbourhood House. This is only one example of many in our cities. "Other organizations in human society include educational institutions, businesses and corporations, voluntary associations (such as many charitable and public service groups), and countless examples of extraordinary human friendship. All of these function to bring some measure of good to human beings, and all are expressions of the common grace of God."[9] Not only is the city a gift of common grace as a whole, but so also are other such things as institutions, organizations, and governments. Grudem poses a great question: "As you look around

8. Ibid.
9. Ibid.

the place where you are at this moment, can you name at least twenty different examples of common grace that you can see? How does that make you feel?"[10]

One of the challenges facing Christians in the West is to step outside of our individualistic worldview. This has ramifications even for how we view the city and our involvement in it. We can grasp the reality of individual sin, whether it is in our own lives or in those around us. We can readily spot abuse, unhealthy behaviors, gossip, infidelity and the like. But one of the perspectives we struggle with is systemic sin in a city and its overarching influence on those who live there. "Understanding the nature of evil in the city requires examining the primary systems that make a city function and then analyzing these systems biblically."[11] When we view the city through the lens of individualism and focus solely on the spiritual, we lose sight of the broken systems all around us. As the world rapidly urbanizes, it has a collateral effect upon city systems. "Rapid urban growth in the past 50 years has meant that managing the built (or human) environment, while coping with environmental pollution (especially waste) and degradation, has become a significant challenge in the cities of developed countries and has overwhelmed many cities in the developing world."[12] Does the redemption of cities go beyond the scope of saving individuals? Is God calling those of us who love, follow, and worship him to do more?

There needs to be a place in the church where we elevate and emphasize the "physical" right up alongside the "spiritual" activities that take place. That dichotomy is a product of Western thinking as we compartmentalize everything from worldviews to our underwear and sock drawers. In contrast, what would happen if we viewed *everything* as spiritual or sacred? That the way we treat the barista at Starbucks is just as indicative of our relationship with Christ as how much time we've spent reading the Bible, praying, and fasting? When we focus on what we deem spiritual and exclude the physical, we end up missing out on huge swaths of possible urban venues to be involved in that go beyond being pastors, church planters, or missionaries. Do we struggle, then, with an undercurrent of a scaled-down Neo-Gnosticism? What if more Christians became urban planners and viewed it as a high calling on

10. Ibid., 666.

11. Linthicum, *City of God City of Satan*, 47.

12. *Global Report on Human Settlement 2009*, xxv.

par with vocational ministry? People in these positions of influence indeed have a lot of say in how cities and neighborhoods develop and unfold. They wield much influence as they work with architects and developers designing common spaces for all to use that could actually elevate a neighborhood's social capital. Through the built environment alone there could be spaces of interconnectivity where relationships are formed. These planners could work with those in transportation to create bike-friendly communities which foster health, or to ensure safer streets, and more thorough public transit access for those who don't have the luxury to own a car. In many ways, urban planners can have more say, more influence, and in their day-to-day decisions can have a greater impact on a neighborhood than a church. On the other hand, the lack of good urban planning can have a negative impact on cities which means more social ills for the church to struggle against. Something seemingly simple like better planning could actually help make a city great, reduce relational tension, and overall make cities a better place in which to live. When it is absent, it has a devastating effect upon cities and their inhabitants. "High levels of urban growth in the absence of adequate planning have resulted in spiraling poverty, proliferation of slum and squatter settlements, inadequate water and power supply, and degrading environmental conditions."[13]

One of my personal goals throughout this book is to do my best to keep concepts and ideas out of the ivory tower of academia. As one who holds a doctorate, I highly value education and it has been transformative in my own life. As various concepts I've studied over the years began taking root within me, I couldn't help but to change, whether it was a deeper understanding of the finished work of Christ on the cross or the transforming power of the Gospel in culture. I've also had enough schooling to have ploughed through my share of uninteresting theological tomes that make root canals seem fun. While this book is indeed a theological work, I want it to be grounded in the common and everyday life. As a result, I do most of my writing at the intersections of life in our neighborhood whether Starbucks or, as crazy as it sounds, at our local McDonald's. The entire community shows up here at some time or another, whether it is the homeless, the hookers, the mentally ill, the elderly, the young, and so on.

13. Ibid., 26.

Welcome to the beginnings of exploring a theology of the city. We cannot address the notion of this topic unless we're thoroughly rooted and grounded in the city in our everyday life. Again, that mindset dictates my practice of where I do most of my writing. Not in a secluded mountain cabin, or tucked away in an office or den, but instead in a public environment where the global urban village surrounds me. Interruptions become commonplace whether it is the wheelchair-bound man who sometimes yells at me across the room at Starbucks because he has some conspiracy theory about Genesis 3, or helping an immigrant sitting next to me fill out a job application. This is the intersection where theology becomes grounded in the common and the mundane.

I understand that most theological works, like baby food, come "pre-chewed" (or blended) and ready for consumption. This book invites you into the chewing process where we can collaborate and work on this together; thus my reasoning behind asking lots of questions. Asking questions sends us into further inquiry and theological reflection about God's purpose and intent for our cities, whether throughout history, in today's world, or our future trajectory. These then are the theological questions painted on an urban canvas. Let's journey together.

2

Parameters of City-Reaching

IT REMINDED ME OF a scene right out of a Jason Bourne movie, only this one was real with, in some cases, real life-and-death implications. There were about thirty of us clustered together in a second-storey room in a dense urban center in a distant city. I was the outsider. The others? They were in some ways an advanced group of global urban workers receiving last-minute training before heading off into the cities of the world. Some in their new locations will be able to be open and expressive about their faith, while others will enter various countries where, as "humanitarian workers," they will not be able to wear their faith on their sleeves. It was indeed an exciting time to come and share.

I had three hours to talk about the layers, lenses, and perspectives of the city (which I'll address later on in the book). One of the tensions that came out was in regards to impacting and influencing a city. What is our role in the city as those of us who follow Christ? For many decades in the West, we've been taught that our primary role is deemed to be spiritual in nature—that if the city or neighborhood we're in is on a crash course of degradation and blight, our responsibility is to gather people and point them to eternal life post-mortem. What about now? Is it our primary call to populate heaven while urban neighborhoods around us struggle, contort, and writhe in pain and agony?

There is a lot of buzz and conversation going on today about city-reaching and city-building. Many mission organizations and denominations are refocusing and redoubling their efforts on the city, not only in North America, but globally. Even within my own denomination, the same is true and change is in the air as a massive shift takes place to reorient mission around the leading urban centers both here in North America and overseas. Yet when it comes to city-reaching, there are still key pieces missing when it comes to how we view cities, what city-reaching looks like, and between the spiritual dynamic of cities and their physical dimensions.

If we're going to talk about what makes a city great as well as how to reach it, it would be helpful to begin putting some parameters around it to guide our thinking. If you've ever sat in a church planter's network meeting, whether with those in your tribe or a city-wide gathering, inevitably at some point the conversation turns to "reaching this city." What is interesting to note is that most of us do not have the foggiest notion of what we mean by it, myself included. It sounds impressive as we talk about the wide scope of the city and our dreams and desire to see it "impacted by Jesus." When pressed, I'd venture to say that most of us would fumble with what exactly we mean by a city being reached. I know I would. If we would be cornered for an answer, more than likely we'd default to speaking in terms of the number of churches being planted, the number of baptisms, and overall church attendance. Logic would tell us that if we're seeing people won to faith in Christ resulting in baptisms, new churches being planted in both suburban and urban settings alike, and church attendance on the rise, we are well on our way to seeing this city "won for Jesus." The purposeful usage of quotation marks is not to mock or downplay what goes on in our circles. Instead, I'm highlighting our own vocabulary and wonder out loud what we even mean and if we know where we're going. Again, what makes up the framework in our thinking when we speak in sweeping generalizations about city-reaching or even city-building?

Before I begin defining the parameters of city-reaching, it would be helpful to take a step back into early church history. One of the struggles that hampers us is our own cultural blind spots. When we begin stepping outside of our own culture, we often become aware of topics or truths found in Scripture that were either underdeveloped in our thinking or altogether missing. This is even one of the reasons behind the writing of this book: to make a case for an urban theological framework. For me, this is all too relevant, as I spent the first three-fourths of my life in Christ thinking that God simply loved sheep, shepherds, and the countryside. Besides, Jesus always seemed to tell farm stories. However, over time I began to see the thread and even the perspective of the urban nature of the biblical story that I had missed before. Did the Bible change? No, but my lens did.

Often when we share our faith, what we're really doing is asking people to go through two conversions.[1] The first conversion is to God through the reconciling work of Jesus Christ. This conversion is beautiful, burden-lifting, transforming, and awe-inspiring. The second conversion is into our Christian subculture. This can be confusing, burdensome, and frustrating, especially if one has come from a completely unchurched background or from some other world religion. Because we live in, love, and serve in today's global cities, we begin asking ourselves questions as we interact with people from around the world. Is the Westernized version of Christianity in alignment with the Bible? Are we asking people to follow Christ as much as our own cultural norms?

The reason I bring that up isn't to assault the Christian subculture that I myself am a part of. It is simply to bring to attention possibly how culture affects the way we interpret our faith and Scripture itself. It also carries with it implications on how we view the city and the transforming work of Christ. It goes back to the whole topic of lenses and how we view Scripture from a cultural vantage point. This seems to have been a problem that has plagued the church since the first generation after the Apostles. How can I not interpret Scripture, cities, or anything else for that matter, than from my Westernized evangelical worldview? I'm a slave to culture no matter how much I think I come to Scripture or even a fuller understanding of the Gospel with no biases. "There is no cultureless gospel. Jesus himself preached, taught, and healed within a specific cultural context. Nor is it the case that the gospel can be reduced to a set of cultureless principles. The message of the reign of God, the gospel, is always communicated with the thought constructs and practices prevalent within the cultural setting of the church in a specific time and place. But when truly shaped by the Holy Spirit, this message also points beyond its present culture's thought forms and customs to the distinctive culture of God's reign proclaimed by Jesus."[2]

The second-century writings of Irenaeus and his theological perspectives intrigue me. They offer a case study in theological and cultural perspectives, hammering out theology in the face of opposition, and challenging how we are to view the city. What also intrigues me is the foundational differentiation between East and West in terms of theo-

1. Although I don't particularly like the word *conversion* I'll use it for the sake of discussion.

2. Guder, *Missional Church*, 114.

logical perspective as influenced by culture. As one growing up in the West, all I knew was the Westernized forensic (legal) view of salvation as advanced by many of the Reformers. To me, salvation was always "Jesus and me" and was very privatized, individualistic, and almost consumeristic. Last night, I was talking with my wife about all of this and what I was processing. I told her that sometimes our theological perspectives are like a pie. Could the East and the West be both halves of the same pie? While I cannot at this point separate myself from my Western perspective, I feel like I've only been served one half of the pie. At times reconciling an Eastern versus a Western view on salvation may at times be paradoxical. To me it's a tension I'm willing to live with, because what it does is expand my thinking in regards to city-reaching.

As one born around AD 120,[3] it is well worth noting that Irenaeus was still very close to the original grassroots movement of Christianity. He was tutored by Polycarp who was himself mentored by the Apostle John. We can almost say that Irenaeus was a grandson of the Apostles.

Irenaeus' theory of redemption really challenged my thinking and opened up my eyes to the another slice of the pie with direct application to how I view the city and what we mean by city-reaching. Basically, in his view, the Incarnation itself is redemptive. "The Incarnation of Christ also provides insight into the effect of the gospel."[4] Yet for us in the West, most of what happened in Jesus' life between birth and the cross doesn't hold too much weight. While we love and adore baby Jesus, we in the West tend to follow Paul's teaching more than Jesus'. It can be argued that most of us almost identify more with Pauline teaching and thinking rather than with Jesus. According to David Bosch, the Incarnation is a doctrine under-used and underdeveloped among those in the West: "Protestant churches, by and large, have an underdeveloped theology of the Incarnation. The churches of the East, Roman Catholics, and Anglicans have always taken the Incarnation far more seriously – albeit the Eastern church tends to concentrate on the Incarnation within the context of the pre-existence, the 'origin', of Christ."[5] In Irenaeus' theory, the Incarnation and life of Jesus are just as much a part of the mystery of redemption as is his death. That's why Irenaeus fought tooth and nail with the Gnostics who sought to debunk the Incarnation, because refut-

---

3. Olson, *The Story of Christian Theology*, 68.

4. McAlpine, *Sacred Space for the Missional Church*, 18.

5. Bosch, *Transforming Mission*, 512.

ing it would cause the whole soteriological house of cards to tumble. Uphold the Incarnation and salvation is upheld. For Irenaeus, the Incarnation was transformative. "Such an affirmation would amaze and refute all Hellenistic philosophical and Gnostic dualisms that separated God from his world."[6]

Still another slice of the pie that Irenaeus brought forth was the proposition that all of humanity was affected by the fall of Adam and all of humanity is affected by the Incarnation of Christ. According to this viewpoint, the Incarnation began the process of redeeming mankind as a whole. "In a literal sense the entire human race is 'born again' in the Incarnation."[7] According to historian Roger Olson, salvation didn't become really "Jesus and me" until the time of the Reformation.[8] What then of the first fifteen centuries of Christian faith? If salvation wasn't privatized until the Reformation and if in some way humankind was born again at the Incarnation, then what do we make of it? Are the last five hundred years then the only years that count? Did we finally get educated and smart enough to figure out salvation? Was everyone else in church history ignorant theological Neanderthals? Is it then possible to hold on to seemingly paradoxical truths and yet at the same time be right? Irenaeus' view of the impact of the second Adam (Christ) really is foreign to us in the West. Was he right or is it simply the case of filling in the other half of the soteriological pie?

The basis of Irenaeus' thoughts derive from Romans 5. In Paul's discussion of justification, he draws a comparison between Adam and Christ:

> Therefore, just as through one man [Adam] sin entered into the world, and death through sin, and so death spread to all men, because all sinned—for until the Law sin was in the world, but sin is not imputed when there is no law. Nevertheless death reigned from Adam until Moses, even over those who had not sinned in the likeness of the offense of Adam, who is a type of Him who was to come. But the free gift is not like the transgression. For if by the transgression of the one the many died, much more did the grace of God and the gift by the grace of the one Man, Jesus Christ, abound to the many. The gift is not like that which came through the one who sinned; for on the one hand the judgment

6. Ladd, *A Theology of the New Testament*, 278.

7. *The Story of Christian Theology*, 75.

8. Ibid.

arose from one transgression resulting in condemnation, but on the other hand the free gift arose from many transgressions resulting in justification. For if by the transgression of the one, death reigned through the one, much more those who receive the abundance of grace and of the gift of righteousness will reign in life through the One, Jesus Christ. So then as through one transgression there resulted condemnation to all men, even so through one act of righteousness there resulted justification of life to all men. For as through the one man's disobedience the many were made sinners, even so through the obedience of the One the many will be made righteous.[9]

What Christ did by his Incarnation, life, death, and resurrection also washed over humanity. Adam and Jesus Christ were not mere individuals but instead, according to Irenaeus, the "fountainhead of humanity." That is why his theory has been called the "theory of recapitulation," from the Latin *capitus* which means "head." *Recapitulatio* literally means "reheading" or "providing a new head." It's the idea of Adam as the head of humanity in sin being replaced by Jesus as the redemptive head of humanity. Adam brought death to all of humankind and Jesus Christ brought life and light to all of humanity.[10] "In a literal sense, the entire human race is 'born again' in the Incarnation. It receives a new 'head' – a new source, origin, ground of being – that is unfallen, pure and healthy, victorious and immortal."[11]

Part of the way in which the theory of recapitulation works is that it assumes a solidarity of humanity in both sin and redemption.[12] In other words, what Adam did in the Garden and what Jesus did in his earthly life affected all of humanity, since they both are "heads" of humanity. "When Irenaeus wrote that in Jesus Christ, God 'recapitulated the ancient formation of man,' he meant that in the Incarnation, the Word (Logos) took on the very 'protoplast' (physical source) of humanity—the body of Adam—and lived the reverse of Adam's course of life that resulted in corruption."[13] So in order to reverse the devastation wrought by Adam, Jesus had to be born and live among us to transform us. Irenaeus said

9. Romans 5:12–19.

10. *The Story of Christian Theology*, 73–74.

11. Ibid., 75.

12. Ibid.

13. Ibid., 76.

that Adam was "reborn" of Mary in some mysterious way.[14] Throughout Jesus' life, he reversed the effect and disobedience of the first Adam at every juncture.

This theory is seemingly walking the tightrope between orthodoxy and heresy. It would be easy to misconstrue Irenaeus' theology as Unitarian. A casual glance at this would lead one to believe that simply by Jesus' Incarnation, all of mankind is "saved" and reconciled to the Father. This was not Irenaeus' teaching. We need to step back from the details to look at the bigger picture. He was writing to ward off the onslaught of Gnosticism that denied the humanity of Christ. According to Irenaeus, if there was no Incarnation, then Jesus really wasn't human, and redemption was impossible. The Incarnation is foundational. "The confession of Jesus as God come in the flesh is a biblical test of orthodoxy."[15] So in a real way, then, everything does rise and fall on the Incarnation. If Christ was truly to be the second Adam, the new fountainhead, then he needed to add humanity to his deity. "When God came into our world in and through Jesus, the Eternal moved into the neighborhood and took up residence among us (John 1:14)."[16]

For Irenaeus, the life that Christ lived was vital. There's a direct parallel between Adam and Christ in the Temptation. Adam was tempted by Satan and gave in to sin. Jesus was also tempted by Satan, but did not give in. This is a big part of the redemption story for Irenaeus, because Jesus undid what Adam did in regards to the Temptation. All of this then adds value to the life that Jesus lived. The ramifications of his Incarnation go far beyond just the finished work on the cross. Jesus not only died for us, but he showed us a new way to live. Wayne Grudem points out this practical implication of the Incarnation in our lives: "Our goal should be to be like Christ in all our days, up to the point of death, and to die with unfailing obedience to God, with strong trust in him, and with love and forgiveness to others. Jesus had to become a man like us in order to live as our example and pattern in life."[17] Mankind's decision is then to choose which "head" we will follow. Will it be Adam and his path of sin and destruction, or will it be the second Adam (Christ) and choosing him through faith and repentance? This, in turn, dispels any supposed

14. Ibid.

15. Driscoll and Breshears, *Vintage Church*, 15.

16. Hirsch, *The Forgotten* Ways, 132

17. Grudem, *Systematic Theology*, 542.

connections to Unitarianism. While Irenaeus upholds the necessity and redemptive nature of the Incarnation, his teachings still involve mankind having to choose between one or the other Adam.

Salvation, though defined in forensic terms and advanced by the Reformers, is also, according to Irenaeus, something much bigger. The two halves of the pie might be simply defined as individual and corporate salvation. Both are true and yet each on their own is lacking. While the Reformers may camp out on a privatized faith, theologians in the East view redemption beginning with the Incarnation. The Incarnation is not only vital in terms of redemption, but even as an overall model and template for how we're to live now in our cities. "If God's central way of reaching his world was to incarnate himself in Jesus, then our way of reaching the world should likewise be *incarnational*. To act incarnationally therefore will mean in part that in our mission to those outside of the faith we will need to exercise a genuine identification and affinity with those we are attempting to reach."[18]

I like being exposed to ancient thinkers who didn't have the luxury of formal theological education. I like that Irenaeus was mentored by one of the Apostle John's protégées. I like the passing on of a raw faith. I can appreciate Irenaeus wrestling with what he knew without the formality and theological categories that we have today. I enjoy how his passion for clear theological reflection arose not out of ivory towers but instead in the trenches of controversy that threatened to tear apart and bury the new church and faith. In a similar way, as we're confronted with the ever-growing prominence, presence, and influence of the global city, all of a sudden we're left scrambling to figure out how to respond. It may not all be neat and tidy at the get-go, but as time goes on, we'll continue to refine and wordsmith our thinking.

There are several reasons why the historical look at Irenaeus is relevant to this chapter in a theology of the city. First of all, it opens our eyes to the corporate ramifications of salvation when it comes to the whole city. I'm not making the theological jump to say that because of the Incarnation that the city is "saved." What Paul is writing in Romans 5 has enormous implications as we consider the scope of Jesus' life and then death on the cross. Romans 8 even makes the case that all of creation is longing for redemption. That's odd, because if redemption is only "Jesus and me," then why would God's creation long for it as well? It goes back

18. *The Forgotten Ways*, 133.

to the idea of recapitulation, in that one man, Adam, brought sin and death into the word. Now Jesus, the second Adam, brings healing and restoration. "For the creation was subjected to futility, not willingly, but because of him who subjected it, in hope that the creation itself will be set free from its bondage to corruption and obtain the freedom of the glory of the children of God. For we know that the whole creation has been groaning together in the pains of childbirth until now."[19]

In what ways is the redemptive work of Christ pertinent and applicable to viewing the city as well as our involvement within it? Should our default position then simply be about populating heaven, or do Romans 5 and 8 give us direction and insight to hold out some hope for the city? If creation longs to be free from its bondage, does that also apply to the city? Is this all part of God's global and universal urban renewal plan? In their book, *Urban Ministry: The Kingdom, the City and the People of God*, Harvie Conn and Manuel Ortiz write: "And with his coming came the inauguration of God's urban renewal plan."[20] Adding to that thought, author Stephen Harper refers to how an understanding of the Incarnation forms our thinking to help us pay attention that God is already at work among us. "Understanding the literal ramifications of the Incarnation means that we must keep in mind and realize that God is at work in the world and in the lives of individuals before we arrive on the scene."[21]

The second insight we glean from Irenaeus is that he gives us an example of creating theology on the fly to deal with an issue that was plaguing the church. As stated above, it was no small feat for Irenaeus to do what he did to ward off the assault of Gnosticism on the church. It took a lot of courage as well as theological insight and savvy to hammer out a theology on the anvil of life and in the trenches. He wasn't privy to the sophisticated theological systems we have in place; instead he did it in the heat of battle against a powerful and yet subtle heresy. This is inspiring and even encouraging for me, as in a very minute way, I can identify with attempting to hammer out a theology on the fly and on the anvil of life. My context is the city and all of the issues that go with the territory. Some are responding by withdrawing and separating altogether from the city. Even if they have to live in the city they cling to the edge of the city away from its "evils." Some take on a more confrontational

19. Romans 8:20–22.

20. Harvie and Ortiz. *Urban Ministry*, 122.

21. Harper, *They're Just Not That Into You.* chap. 2.

role and posture against the city. They are good at pointing out sin, giving people an earful, and still see the city as evil as the great whore of Babylon. Still others mindlessly assimilate in the city and lose their sense of identity and calling to be salt and light and bearers of the Gospel. The best posture is to recognize indeed the state of the city, but also to see the larger picture—*that the city is a gift of common grace and even a place that longs for redemption.* It is the Incarnation which forms and shapes our involvement within cities. "The Incarnation must therefore inform the way we engage the complex multicultural world around us."[22]

Constructing a theology of the city is truly on-the-fly as we're confronted with the challenges and great joys of living in the global city. Like Irenaeus, over the ensuing years, decades, and centuries, others will be able to look back on our work and spot our shortcomings, blind spots, as well as the need for better wordsmithing. But that is the nature of things. For me, I'm thrust daily into theological reflection as I watch the city all around me. I see hope and pain, blessing and cursing, bondage and freedom, and new life and decay. It drives me back to Scripture in search of a theology of the city. I continue to revisit the Gospel, and while it has transformed me and continues to transform me, I wonder how it extends beyond my life into the city.

Lastly, Irenaeus and his theological perspectives give credence to the words and lifestyle of Jesus as a model for urban mission. Irenaeus demonstrates that the actual life of Jesus really did matter. Jesus showed us not only how to live in the way he modeled life, but his teachings are meant to be adhered to and followed. Messages like the Sermon on the Mount, for example, have enormous practical ramifications in the city (and everywhere else). The way Jesus gave preferential treatment to the despised, the lowly and the broken models for us how we're to live. We don't have to guess at all what God thinks about certain things or how he'd react to others, because Jesus, being God himself, showed us. This was at the forefront of my thinking this morning as I pushed a wheelchair-bound man to his bus stop. As I was walking out of Starbucks to head home, he flagged me down as he and his wheelchair were burdened with groceries which made it difficult for him to maneuver. I was glad to help. At the same time, my wife Katie was at a bus stop in a different part of the city on the way to work spending time talking with a barefoot

---

22. *The Forgotten Ways*, 135.

prostitute, offering her grace and compassion. Jesus' Incarnation and life serve as a template even in the little things.

To bring this whole thought process and conversation into city-reaching pushes the parameter of the definition as well as the enormity of the scope outward. Do we still only believe at this point that our contributions to city-reaching or urban renewal are only through evangelism and church planting? Do we now have the beginnings of a better framework to see that it is so much more? City-reaching then can be defined as *extending both saving and common grace to the city*. That's it. Let's unpack it. Sometimes the best definitions are the simplest ones that we can remember.

To say we're extending *saving grace* to the city means that we're still serious about Jesus' last words on earth before he ascended. He admonished his disciples to go throughout the world teaching people the ways of Jesus that they too in turn would follow him. A disciple is a learner. We also know that the term *disciple* is packed with soteriological meaning in that not only are people following Jesus as a great teacher but also as Messiah and are repenting of their sins, seeking forgiveness and redemption, and are washed clean by the shed blood of Christ. "Jesus is our justification who takes away our sin and gives us his righteousness as a gift by exchanging places with us on the cross so that we can be justified in the sight of God."[23] This is paramount in any context. Sometimes we simply must conclude that some things are just broken because of sin, sinful people, systemic evil. "For in understanding both the nature of a city's goodness and its evil can we truly hope to understand the city into which God called us, his people, to minister."[24] People need to come in contact with the transforming power of the Gospel. This can take the form of church planting, evangelism, and discipleship, regardless of how formal or informal the process is. This could also be classified as spiritual activity as it deals with the realm of the mystical, the invisible and the internal. This perspective also recognizes that the saving work of redemption in Christ does have ramifications and application to the whole city and not just for the individual person.

Extending *common grace* to the city is the recognition that already the city is a gift of common grace from God, but that we still have a role to play in it. A key verse in this line of thinking would be Jeremiah 29:7:

23. *Vintage Church*, 21.
24. Linthicum, *City of God City of Satan*, 40.

"But seek the welfare of the city where I have sent you into exile, and pray to the LORD on its behalf, for in its welfare you will find your welfare." This goes beyond the scope of what we normally deem as spiritual, even though there's the reality that everything is spiritual and sacred. This is upholding and valuing all of the various ways people engage in city life whether as a teacher, a lawyer, a police officer, an architect, a social worker, a doctor, and so much more. It is also recognizing that extending common grace is just as vital as offering saving grace. As followers of Jesus, we can no longer divorce the two. Peter alludes to this in one of his letters to the believers in the Jewish Diaspora, "Keep your conduct among the Gentiles honorable, so that when they speak against you as evildoers, they may see your good deeds and glorify God on the day of visitation."[25] The good news is that God is glorified both in people coming to saving faith in Christ as well as when the needs of the poor are served in a gentrifying neighborhood. "If in our being the church, the world *sees* God's reign, and by our doing justice, the world *tastes* its gracious effect, then the call to all on the earth to receive and acknowledge that reign begs to be expressed."[26]

Welcome to the initial foray into a theology of the city. This is such an exciting time in human history to be alive as now over half of the earth's inhabitants live in the city. Through urbanization and immigration, the very fabric of urban life is currently being altered. I see and experience this daily. A walk through my neighborhood is like walking the halls at a UN summit. This kind of collecting and reshuffling of humanity has continued and will continue to cause the church to wake up, respond, and jump into the city by extending both arms of grace. This is only the beginning.

25. 1 Peter 2:12.
26. *Missional Church*, 107–108.

3

What is a City?

As our car sped down the interstate highway, I could see the distant faint orange glow in the sky warning me that I was getting close to the city. My stomach churned and every impulse inside me wanted to turn the car around. I longed for a night sky that wasn't discolored an eerie orange from the city lights. Who ever decided to make all of the street lights in the city orange in the first place? At this time in my life, I was in college and I simply hated cities. Big, small, it didn't matter. All I knew was that as I drove towards Omaha, the rays of orange lights reached out from the city into the night skies as if they were tentacles from a giant deformed leviathan. That's what cities were to me.

I'm not too sure where these feelings came from. I never had any painful experience as a child of being abandoned in a city with no help or directions. I wasn't sure what exactly constituted a city, because all I know was that Marshalltown, population 30,000 at the time, was a 30-minute drive from where I grew up and that I never really enjoyed going there. It felt like a big city to this small-town Iowa boy. As a child and youth, I never took the time nor had the awareness to analyze my feelings. Did my distaste come from something I saw on television? Was it growing up in a household where my Dad preferred country and polka music that set the course for my thinking? Did the inner recesses of my psyche pick up all of those country music lyrics about tractors, trucks, rural living, farming, dogs, blue jeans, and sleeveless cowboy shirts? All I know was that when driving across the state or country, I couldn't help but literally resist the city.

When I arrived on campus as a college freshman, I jumped into the deep end. I volunteered to help out at a church in North Omaha. I learned quickly that this was in the African-American part of the city and every stereotype I had seen on TV came racing across my mind. I wasn't prejudiced, just ignorant and naïve. I drove to the church one night and I was terrified. I vividly remember pulling my car up to an intersection and realized that for the first time in my life, I was a minority. Sure enough, I found my way to the church and sat in on a midweek service. I talked with some of the leaders afterwards about helping with the youth. I knew quickly that helping this church was not in my immediate plans. I'm not too sure what my excuse was for not coming back, because I never did. I didn't like cities, I was terrified of them, and didn't really understand them . . . or want to. I wasn't yet ready or prepared to begin learning about the city or exploring it, even though our college campus was in the inner city just a mile or two from the downtown core.

What is a city? I posed this question recently to my *Theology of the City* class one night and we spent the next hour attempting to define what "city" and "urban" mean. We all sat around a table in a small room, as we did every Tuesday night, together defining and exploring a theological framework for understanding and living in the city. This book stems from those many nights as a class in theological reflection, biblical exploration, and looking at the modern city. The collection of those who were taking the class was broad, ranging from seminary students to guys who already had their Master's or doctorates. The ethnic make-up of the class was also a good reflection of the city. We'd converge together once a week from all over the city, drinking the free coffee donated by Starbucks and talking. For our city discussion that night, I had Conrad stand at the front with a big sheet of paper and marker in hand, writing down everyone's responses. What was immediately noticeable was how it was one of those activities where it was much more difficult than we initially realized. There were lots of descriptions thrown out, but the bottom line was that it was challenging to come up with a concise definition. What is a city? How do we put parameters around it to define it? Go ahead and try it . . .

The answers given that night were varied, ranging from population density, the built environment, culture, systems, and so much more. We quickly realized that *city* or *urban* is often easy to point to and yet difficult to clearly define. It is one of those things where you know it when you see it, you can feel it, and say, "Look! There's one!" But to define it? What makes it even more challenging is that even from nation to nation, various governments define *city* differently. For example, over

80% of Canadians and Americans live in cities. University of Calgary Professor of Sociology Harry Hiller plainly states, "The city has increasingly become the container in which most Canadians now live their lives."[1] In the United States, the definition of "city" varies from state to state. In some places, a community of 296 inhabitants is called a city.[2] That doesn't seem like a city, does it? How can it and San Francisco or Montreal all be defined as cities? If you Google the word "city," you'll find all kinds of interesting definitions:

1. People living in a large densely populated municipality.

2. City is a German rock band, formed in East Berlin in 1972, best known for the song *Am Fenster*.

3. A center of population, commerce, and culture; a town of significant size and importance.

4. In Canada, any of various large urban municipalities within a province.

5. A center of population larger or more important than a town or village.

All of a sudden, this activity is not as easy as it at first seemed. This is where a theology of the city begins to rely on other disciplines to develop a more comprehensive understanding. How can we have a theology of a city if we don't understand what a city even is? As we will see later, what we find out about cities in Scripture is vastly different from cities today. Not only that, but ancient cities from the time of Abraham stand in stark contrast to the cities around the time when Jesus came onto the scene. We should not look at cities in these eras through our contemporary understanding of cities. "To move from the cities of the ancient Near East to those of Jesus' day is to take a large leap. Cities, after all, change and adapt in function as the social systems of which they are a part change. Scholarship is learning that we cannot judge the Bible's preindustrial cities by industrial city models."[3]

Now back to the first question: what is a city? There is little doubt about the prominence and importance of cities, not just in biblical times,

1. Hiller, *Urban Canada*, xii.

2. Wikimedia Foundation Inc., "City."

3. Conn and Ortiz, *Urban Ministry*, 116.

but throughout history. Tracing the development of cities over the past several thousand years is an interesting endeavor as cities rose and fell like the tide. Urban development was widespread from Europe to the Middle East to Asia and so on. What we do know is that when cities entered the scene, they began changing everything. "One of the most significant transitions in human history was from a hunter-gatherer society to an agricultural-urban society—the Neolithic revolution as it is known to science."[4] Not only was that transition significant, but many held up the city as not just a common space where people lived in proximity, but as a great invention. "The city is the most significant invention in the history of the world; indeed, it is the mother of all other inventions. The city may well be humankind's greatest achievement; it is certainly the primary engine of change."[5] I have to agree with that statement on many levels. So much innovation and creativity is housed and fostered in cities as well as in their natural by-products. If necessity is indeed the mother of all inventions, then living in cities does nothing but create necessities. How do we feed everyone? What do we do with our trash? How do we ensure basic requirements like healthcare or education? How will people get from Point A to Point B? And how do we get them there fast and cheaply? How comprehensive do we make this system? And this is only the tip, the very tip, of the iceberg. To begin putting parameters around defining a city is to begin by looking at the semantics of the word and trace its development.

The word "city" comes from a variety of words in different languages and cultures that paint an intriguing backdrop as well as place some great markers or parameters around the term.[6] While Ur is the name of the ancient Sumerian city located in modern-day southern Iraq situated on the banks of the Euphrates, it is also the root word of various terms related to the city. From "ur" we get *urbane*. Urbane can be defined as "having the polish and suavity regarded as characteristic of sophisticated social life in major cities."[7] We also get the word *urban*. Urban appears to cover the overall topic of the characteristics of living in the city or city life. Whereas urbane and urban were very similar, over

4. Newman, Beatley, and Boyer. *Resilient Cities*, 41.

5. Boyce, "The Nature of Cities."

6. I give credit to Dr. Ron Boyce, adjunct professor at Bakke Graduate University, for bringing up the development of the words for city in his paper "The Nature of Cities."

7. Dictionary.com, LLC, "Urbane."

time their meanings separated until urbane carried with it the idea of sophisticated manners and styles of expression.[8] Urban by definition was more focused on the characteristics of living in the city. However, the term "urban" has been adopted by modern culture and it carries a very broad meaning. For example, if you were to go to urbandictionary.com and search for *urban*, there would be all types of entertaining (and at times inappropriate) answers: "adj.: a word used in substitution to 'ghetto'. Often used to refer to something that is not proper and lacks social standing. Can also be used to describe a place that is overly dark. e.g., Man, that club is a little too urban."[9] Urban, as the word developed, now carries all sorts of meanings. In some contexts it is used to describe the physical characteristics of a city, usually in high-density areas. It also can be used to describe decayed inner city neighborhoods, clothing styles, music genres, and the like.

This trend also parallels the development of cities. Cities and neighborhoods are birthed, grow, mature, decline, and are reborn over and over. Is it any wonder that a city defines the term *urban* based upon its (or a neighborhood's) life stage? In context, urban Detroit conjures up images of degraded inner-city neighborhoods and hollowed-out buildings with an abundance of poverty and unemployment. On the other hand, urban Vancouver can mean, more or less, life associated with living downtown and the ensuing characteristics of hip, trendy, modern, and sophisticated.

Another ancient word in regards to naming and placing parameters around the word *city* is the Greek word *polis*. A polis "is a city, or a city-state. The word originates from the ancient Greek city-states, which developed in the Hellenic period and survived (though with decreasing influence) well into Roman times."[10] From *polis* we get various off-shoots that flesh out the field of meaning of the word and our understanding of cities. "Derivatives of *polis* are common in many modern European languages. This is indicative of the influence of the *polis*-centred Hellenic world view. Derivative words in English include policy, polity, police and politics."[11] Each descriptor conjures up images of city life. As the term *polis* entered the Roman world, it became the Latin word *civitas*, which

8. Ibid.
9. Urban Dictionary, LLC, "Urban."
10. WordIQ, "Polis."
11. Wikimedia Foundation Inc., "Polis."

is "A body of people constituting an organized community; city-state."[12] From that foundational word we also get other derivatives, such as civic, civil, citizen, civilization, and even city in Old French. Each word conjures up an image of city or urban life. Life in the city is assumed to be marked with civility and advancement. This also aligns with the proposition made earlier in this chapter of the city being the mother of all inventions.

So what do we see when we bring these thoughts and ideas together? *Ur, polis,* and *civitas* help us to begin to better understand the scope of the city. It seems reasonable to conclude from these words that cities are created places where civilized people are purposely gathered to live together in proximity with one another. Life in this "collection" is marked by civility, there are policies (and police) in place to ensure equity, technological advancement, and there's a higher level of sophistication of social life here that is not characteristic of rural life.

Having grown up in small-town America, I can personally attest to this reality of the overall culture of city or urban life. Not that my life before moving to the city was marked by lawlessness, incivility, and a complete disregard of personal hygiene, but in many ways the city shapes us into its own image. In rural Iowa, no one would think twice about watching a rusty old pick-up truck pull up to the pump at a gas station. Out of the truck emerges a middle-aged farmer with pork-chop sideburns wearing a Pioneer Seed hat who came into town after a long day's work to fuel up his truck, grab some cheap food, and head back out of town. It would not be an uncommon sight to see this same guy covered with mud, straw, and manure. As he steps out of his Chevy truck, he spits the contents of his mouth out onto the ground and then cleans his lip and cheek of chewing tobacco. From the other side of the pump, the pungent smell of cattle manure begins drifting over. Such sights and even smells are normative and familiar. No one at the gas station would even consider for a moment that the scenario unfolding is anything but common everyday life. This is not a cheap-shot at farmers, but to simply point out how the words like *ur, polis* and *civitas* have indeed shaped our understanding of what takes place in the city. I now live in the city and don't even have a car now. If I would happen to be at a gas station and saw this same scene play out in front of me here in urban Vancouver, it would be out of place and noticeable.

12. Wikimedia Foundation Inc., "Civitas."

There is no denying that cities carry a higher level of social sophistication. That sophistication level also varies greatly from city to city and region to region. I always noticed the stark contrasts when we lived in Tucson, Arizona. I had to do a fair amount of travel to various cities. The more I traveled, the more I noticed marked differences between Tucsonans and other urban dwellers. For example, travellers in the Atlanta airport were a completely different lot than those in the Tucson airport. In Atlanta, I would see an innumerable amount of sharply-dressed businesspeople in lots of gray, cool blue and black suits and outfits. Shiny shoes, well-groomed hair and expensive cologne or perfume all went along with their perfectly matched carry-on and travel bags as they sipped Starbucks coffee. When I would fly from Atlanta, land in Tucson and walk through the airport, it was as if I was teleported to a new world. From grays, cool blues, and blacks to now almost all earth tones heavily favoring browns along with shorts and sandals rounded out the attire of many Tucson airport travellers. People moved a lot slower and the overall culture was incredibly casual. It was desert-life-meets-southern-California-meets-Mexico. While living in Tucson and Arizona, I dressed and even acted the part. Lots of shorts-and-sandal days. You rarely saw men wearing ties. My closet was full of shirts that were brown, green, tan, white, and more brown. To "dress up" would be to put on some blue jeans . . . with sandals.

When we moved to Vancouver, BC, everything changed again. Last week, I spoke at a second-generation Korean church. In classic Vancouver fashion, the overwhelming majority of those there preferred the sophistication of wearing black. The guys' hairstyles were short, suave, and definitely well-maintained with trendy glasses, which added to the overall swankiness of the crowd. Was this abnormal? No, it is Vancouver. All of my earth-tone-driven Tucson clothes have been replaced with a closet consisting mostly of black- and gray-collared shirts. I rarely see people out in public who didn't spend considerable time primping and getting ready, even for just a quick trip to the grocery store or meeting a friend for coffee.

So even among cities there are varying degrees of sophistication. In a global city such as Vancouver, one can readily spot the influences of Europe and Asia. I've begun noting in my own mind how members of a particular culture dress as a way of tracking who's who in my city. Those from eastern Asia (China, Korea, and Japan) have an incredibly high level of sophistication, incredible fashion taste, and dress the part. Again, black is the color of choice. Eastern Europeans dress differently from Western Europeans. Afghanis, Ethiopians, and Sudanese each dress a certain way. The white Canadians in my neighborhood also dress a certain way. Again, this is all part of living in the city and its influence on those who live there. In other words, while the ancient words of *ur, polis,* and *civitas* provide the basis for our understanding, they still are not adequate for how we define cities today. All of these factor into the complexities that make up cities. As Stephen Harper notes in *They're Just Not That Into You,* "The world that we live in now is one that boasts myriad cultural expressions all contained within a complex social matrix."[13]

Far from being simply an academic subject, addressing a theology of the city forms and shapes us here and now. A summary of these various words are not merely to add to our knowledge-base, although that is indeed foundational and important, but to continue forming and shaping our lenses and assumptions as we approach the city. Rather than reducing everything to templates and models, the goal is to stimulate our thinking, to open the door for further discussion and exploration, and to draw us back into the city as a whole and your city in particular. Whether one lives in Kuala Lumpur, Addis Ababa, Toronto, Curitiba, or Budapest, these words (*ur, polis, civitas*) are relevant. What does change from context to context is culture and the unique expression of urbanism. One of the benefits of living in a global village and a neighborhood that is reflective of inhabitants from most continents is that it offers me the opportunity to observe how cities have influenced people before they came to Vancouver and how their new city is shaping them now. In our short time here I've seen, in particular, several people from eastern Europe who dressed a certain way when they first arrived here only to have changed their wardrobe to fit Vancouver a year later. The city does shape us. "Cities are not just entities or objects but that they are something that is experienced."[14]

The city forms us into its own image and those who resist tend to stand out. The challenge comes in regards to how much of a city's culture, lifestyle, values, ideology, and worldview do we take on and adopt? "The proliferation of subcultures within most societies only increases

13. Harper, *They're Just Not That Into You.* Preface.
14. *Urban Canada,* xiii.

the enormity of the challenge in understanding culture and interpreting its impact."[15] In taking on an incarnational posture, where is the dividing line between adapting too much or too little? Changing fashion is the easy part and so is supporting the local sports teams, although both are foundational. In the same way that we cannot fully understand Jesus' time on earth without understanding his Jewish roots, how are we faring in understanding our own cities? Again, in the adaptation process, what do we take on and what do we dismiss? While I've come to fully embrace the Canadian Football League since moving to Vancouver, I've made the choice not to adopt Vancouver's philosophical secularism as my world-view lens. Even though I dress in a way that is akin to Vancouver, as well as learning to pick up certain local mannerisms and pronunciations and vocal intonations, I must consciously and proactively battle against the materialism that finds its most extreme expression in cities. Toronto author Jeb Brugmann states it plainly when he writes, "People don't move into cities as blank slates."[16] We each bring with us to the city our own cultural influences, but we must also choose wisely which of the city's potential influences on us that we will want to either accept or reject. Difficult? Yes. Necessary? Absolutely.

Developing a theological framework for understanding the city goes far beyond merely quoting a few Bible verses here and there or tracing the development of the first-century church in the urban centers of the Roman Empire; it is about living in the city as followers of Jesus. We study, we learn, and we process so we can incarnate ourselves on the local level to proclaim and embody the good news of the Kingdom of God. This has been the process of Christians since the beginning of the church. "Virtually since its inception, the church, either by choice or necessity, has grappled with the degree and manner in which it should engage the culture of its day."[17] The good news is that the Kingdom offers us a better alternative—how to live in the city the way God intended. Eric Swanson and Sam Williams write in *To Transform a City*, "Kingdom work involves aspects. It involves introducing people to the King (Jesus), and it involves bringing his perspective, his values, and his generative structures into the world in which we live."[18] I agree wholeheartedly.

---

15. McAlpine, *Sacred Space for the Missional Church*, 14.

16. Brugmann, *Welcome to the Urban Revolution*, 85.

17. *Sacred Space for the Missional Church*, 12.

18. Swanson and Williams, *To Transform a City*, 77.

This Kingdom has a King and his name is Jesus. As we saw in the previous chapter, we must extend both saving grace and common grace to the city. "It is within the concrete context of culture that the gospel is embodied."[19] That's why we study and develop a theology of the city.

19. *Sacred Space for the Missional Church*, 13.

4

The Scope of the City

W E'VE ALL BEEN THERE before. The junior high dance. For most of us, it was that awkward experience that still elicits years later a cold sweat as we drift off to sleep at night. What made it odd and awkward were several factors converging at once. First of all, puberty was just leaving the starting blocks and everyone's body was going through massive changes that felt like creepy mutations from an *X-Men* movie. Whether it was acne, deeper voices for the guys, or leg hairs, we were noticing the rampant changes in our bodies which stirred up deep insecurity. At the same time, we began becoming more interested in the opposite sex. That girl who used have an annoying laugh or that guy who once threw pencils at the girls all of a sudden seemed to become attractive. At first, this was a weird phenomenon as we wondered if a spell had been cast on us or not, but as we grew accustomed to it, we realized how much fun it was. Lastly, the pecking order became more defined. As some guys grew taller, thicker, and stronger, or girls began the progression into womanhood faster than others, they seemed to rise to the top of the social food chain. For the rest of us, we were left as bottom-dwellers catching any scrap of attention that fell in front of us.

Cities are no different. The more I journey into the discovery of a theology of the city and how cities are shaping the fabric of the world's population, economy, and even ecology, it all reminds me of a junior high dance. For a small select few, life at the top of the global city food-chain is a sweet place to be . . . New York, Paris, London, Tokyo. There is a competition to see who is going to be in this elite mix of cities, although currently that list seems pretty exclusive. The twentieth century found the cities, like a junior high schooler, going through massive changes, mutations if you will. University of Connecticut sociologist

Mark Abrahamson writes, "The formerly major industrial cities that were most able quickly and thoroughly to transform themselves into the new post-industrial mode became the leading global cities—the centers of the new global system. Cities that lagged in this transformation process have typically experienced high unemployment, out-migration, neighborhood deterioration, and related problems."[1]

These changes resemble the sifting and sorting of a junior high dance. The handsome guys and beautiful girls get the attention and only grow in popularity. Mind you, in regards to cities this is warranted. For example, in the economic hierarchy, New York leads the top pack with London, Paris, and Tokyo and in the next lower tiers are found other cities such as Frankfurt, Chicago, Hong Kong, Zurich, etc.[2] When looking at the Global Cultural Industries Hierarchy, the list again is almost identical, except for such cities as Los Angeles or Sydney moving up in the top tier.[3] There are clear winners and, unfortunately, clear losers. Maybe not losers per se, but cities that may not, at least in our lifetime, ascend to the top. Again like the sorting of a junior high dance, this reveals the large chasm and even inequality between the elite group at the top and everyone else, and especially those at the bottom. They, unfortunately, lose more than simply a popularity contest. "When there is a high degree of inequality in a city or nation, it can be difficult to maintain civic order and security, seek justice, provide needed welfare, and so on."[4]

The result is a new competition among cities for economic dominance. This is driving the playing field. As I alluded to in my book, *Metrospiritual*, in reference to the Creative Class reorienting our cities, "In some ways it is the new arms race for U.S. and Canadian cities and global cities alike. Whoever rebrands and reinvents themselves first and bolsters their creative economy to make it favorable to draw and retain this class wins."[5] There is a fast and furious competition for cities that are not at the top to scratch and claw to try to get there. Branding is no longer something companies like Nike, Starbucks, or Apple do; cities are also in the branding and marketing business. "Specifically, cities have to

1. Abrahamson, *Global Cities*, 4.
2. Ibid., 89.
3. Ibid., 159.
4. Ibid., 95.
5. Benesh, *Metrospiritual*, 20.

'brand' themselves so that they stand out; they have to create an image and a clearly defined appeal to attract investment."[6]

It was an exhilarating and interesting phenomenon to have experienced the Olympics from the perspective of a host city. While the world's spotlight shone down on Vancouver during the 2010 Winter Olympics, it created more tension here than those watching the Games from afar simply weren't aware of. There is no denying that Vancouver is an amazing city, both in its built environment and in its natural surroundings from the ocean to the mountains. It is a postcard-worthy city. A model city indeed with the marketability to host the Olympics. Hundreds of millions of dollars were spent on the event, including a lot of investment by the City of Vancouver. Why? The answer is branding. Marketing. Attracting investors and new businesses. Unfortunately, there were many losers on the local level as the city sought to put its best foot forward. For example, at a time when public schools were closing and teachers' jobs were being cut because of budget deficits, many millions of dollars were spent on a modern streetcar that ran for about a mile and was only used for roughly a month during the Olympics and Paralympics. Afterwards, the streetcar was put on a boat and shipped back home to Belgium. It reminded me of many people who will go into significant debt over a wedding, because no one wants the embarrassment of such a big showcase event coming off looking cheap or second-rate.

"Cities around the world are in competition with one another to attract and serve knowledge workers in the new economy and professional and managerial classes through entertainment districts and the arts, loft and luxury condominium developments in downtown core, and high-tech industrial parks on the exurban fringe."[7] Branding and marketing are all part of our cities today. Cities are more than merely places where people live in proximity to each other. They are much more than a network of roads, buildings and businesses. Cities have a persona, almost a personality of sorts. Not only that, but they also are like a product to be sold, promoted, branded. They are to be experienced. Exploring the parameters of what a city is then becomes crucial.

So what then is a city? According to the open source encyclopedia, Wikipedia, it is "a relatively large and permanent settlement. Although there is no agreement on how a city is distinguished from a town within

6. Hern, *Common Ground in a Liquid City*, 111.
7. Hiller, *Urban Canada*, 212.

general English language meanings, many cities have a particular administrative, legal, or historical status based on local law."[8] That is rather generic. It is like reading your "fortune" in fortune cookies and taking everything you're told, including the lottery numbers, to heart. It applies to such a wide gamut that everyone who reads a fortune cookie is a winner. It is the same with most or many definitions of a city. What is a large settlement? In tracing the rise and fall of cities, why is permanence a prerequisite and how long does a city have to be in existence to be a city? Again, it all comes with the challenge of clearly defining what a city is, because even among large cities on the same continent there are such discrepancies. Los Angeles has redefined suburban sprawl and its central city skyline elicits mere yawns when compared to other large cities. On the other hand, cities like New York and downtown Vancouver are defined as cities by their densities. The only thing that is dense about L.A. are the number of NBA Championship rings that coaching legend Phil Jackson has on all his fingers . . . and thumbs.

Maybe the best way to define a city is to place parameters around it. Do you remember taking essay tests in high school and college? Even if you didn't know the answer, you'd at least score points by meandering, wandering, and waxing eloquently until you happened to stumble upon the correct answer. What is a city? Well, let's do the same until we come up with the answer. When it comes to describing and labelling cities, there are different directions we can go which will help flesh out our overall understanding. In this discussion, there are such terms as *town*, *metropolis*, *conurbation*, and *megalopolis*. While some of the names may sound like Transformers or cartoon superheroes, they are actually great descriptors to understanding the dynamics of the city, what we mean by the city, and all that it entails.

A *town* can be defined as "a human settlement larger than a village but smaller than a city."[9] That definition seems to fit. A town is not a quaint little village or a hamlet, but neither is it a city. It fills the niche of that nebulous somewhere in-between. Years ago during the NBA playoffs, when the Los Angeles Lakers were battling with the Sacramento Kings, Phil Jackson commented to the effect that Sacramento was simply a sleepy little cow town which elicited a passionate response from Sacramento fans and residents. With a metro area of about 2.5 million

8. Wikimedia Foundation Inc., "City."
9. Wikimedia Foundation Inc., "Town."

people, it is anything but—and yet almost every other city in North America feels that way compared to Los Angeles. Sacramento could be classified a *metropolis*. "A metropolis is a large city, in most cases with over one million living in its urban area. Big cities belonging to a larger urban agglomeration, but which are not the core of that agglomeration, are not generally considered a metropolis but a part of it. A metropolis is usually a significant economic, political and cultural center for some country or region, and an important hub for regional or international connections and communications."[10] Cow town? Not likely. But Phil "the Zen Master" Jackson had a way of getting under the skin of the opposing players, fans, and coaches. It's all part of the mental games he plays. In comparison, the City of Los Angeles is at the core of a *conurbation* which is "a region comprising a number of cities, large towns, and other urban areas that, through population growth and physical expansion, have merged to form one continuous urban and industrially developed area. In most cases, a conurbation is a polycentric urban agglomeration, in which transportation has developed to link areas to create a single urban labor market or travel to work area."[11] In other words, there may very well be small towns that make up a larger city (or conurbation). What makes this tricky is that in these cases, what we deem as a town may in fact be more urban than rural in character and culture. Again, the water gets muddied, but we're at least getting somewhere. Examples of a conurbation would be the New York Tri-State Area or the Greater Los Angeles Area. Both are made up of various cities, counties, and even states.

Lastly, there is the term *megalopolis* or mega-region, not to be mistaken for one of Godzilla's foes from yesteryear. Because of the rapid pace of globalization, it has had a somewhat reorienting effect upon nations and in particular cities. In many ways, nations are led by their cities which continue to expand and densify their ever-growing and spreading global network. Cities are more closely linked to one another than their host nations. These are truly the emerging global cities. "A world city or global city is a city that has a heightened position as a command and control centre in the global economy."[12] In my city of Vancouver, although we're here in Canada on the West Coast, we are intrinsically linked not

10. Wikimedia Foundation Inc., "Metropolis."
11. Wikimedia Foundation Inc., "Conurbation."
12. *Urban Canada*, 13.

only to neighboring Seattle as part of a larger mega-region (Cascadia), but we're also tightly woven together with Asia (Pacific Rim). To understand Vancouver, one must understand our relationship with Hong Kong, Beijing, and so on. The connecting force at play is economics.

Here is a good working definition of a *megalopolis* or mega-region: "A mega-region is a large network of metropolitan regions that share several or all of the following: Environmental systems and topography, infrastructure systems, economic linkages, settlement and land use patterns, and culture and history."[13] University of Toronto professor of economics and author Richard Florida defines a mega-region as, "Mega-regions are more than just a bigger version of a city or a metropolitan region. In the way a city is composed of separate neighborhoods, and like a metropolitan region is made up of a central city and its suburbs, a mega-region is a new, natural economic unit that results from city-regions growing upward, becoming denser, and growing outwards and into one another."[14]

We can now begin piecing together this assortment of data to construct a more comprehensive view of the city. The goal in this chapter (as in the final chapter) is not to present new theories or to purport to offer new ideas in urban geography but to simply pause, assess what's taking place around us, apply some labels, sort through definitions, and allow this to begin shaping our understanding of the city. A city is a complex invention to behold. Like a finely-tuned piece of machinery, there are numerous components all moving simultaneously in unison. When we begin "looking under the hood" of a city, we begin to see some of these parts like neighborhoods, villages, municipalities (towns and suburbs), metropolis, conurbation and, lastly, how they all fit into a mega-region.

So what is a city? Although it is challenging to always articulate what we see with our eyes and imagination, we now have a little clearer picture. Cities have changed dramatically and will continue to do so at a frenetic pace. Although we're on the subject of cities, I have not even mentioned cities located in developed nations versus developing nations. Often the differences in the urban fabric as well as the poignant needs at hand are in some ways similar, but in many ways they stand in stark contrast with one another. Regardless of context, we must begin asking ourselves: how do we develop a theological framework for un-

13. Wikimedia Foundation Inc., "Megaregions of the United States."
14. Florida, *Who's Your City?*, 42.

derstanding the city? How can we develop a theological framework if our knowledge of the city is lagging behind? This isn't to say we need to get post-graduate degrees in urban geography or urban planning, but as those of us who are passionate about following Christ, we should consider studying our culture which includes cities.

For me, the transition to even beginning to want to understand or comprehend cities didn't come until much later after college. Somehow God in his sovereignty didn't allow us to settle down in rural Nebraska where I had applied for several youth ministry jobs after graduation. Looking back, it was almost as if he carried us not only out West but into more cities. God began this continual migration from rural to urban when I first went to college. I am certain of that. So when did it all begin to change for me? After living in larger cities for seven years, we took a two-year hiatus to a small town in northern California. Katie and I kept talking about moving back to the small town since college days. However, once we were there, we realized that seven years in the city had changed us. I vividly remember the day when it all began to sink in.

I was the program director for a camp that our church and several others put on each year in the summer. As youth pastors, we'd take turns being the camp director and in this particular year, it was my turn. Our worship band made the drive up from southern California, and for them it was refreshing to get away from Los Angeles. The only people in proximity to the camp were either ranchers or pot growers. One night as I was hanging out with the band, and probably raiding the fridge in the camp kitchen, we were chatting about L.A. One of the guys turned to me and said, "Sean, what are you doing up here in the boonies? You belong in the city." For the first time, I realized that I had made the switch somewhere along the way. I was no longer at home in rural settings. The city was my home, even though I still had some trepidations. I simply didn't understand it. Six months later, I was back in the city.

The most crucial turning point came two years after that event when I accepted the role of being a church planting strategist for metro Tucson. They had turned to me a year into our church plant, after our denomination had searched far and wide to find someone to fill the position. That decision changed everything for me.

I don't remember receiving a job description and I know there wasn't really any training. My charge was, "Sean, go out and get churches planted, but you can't plant them yourself." It was the best thing that could have happened to me. All of a sudden, my attention was turned to the city as I felt this overwhelming responsibility to put my arms around it, jump in with both feet, and make a difference. For the first time in my life, something switched within me in regards to the city. No longer was I afraid, apprehensive, or even aloof. I was driven, passionate, and desperate to figure Tucson out, what makes cities tick, and how to understand them. Everything changed from that day forward.

Now that we've begun placing the parameters around what a city is and what sets it apart, let's push the discussion forward even more. We can now more clearly articulate what a city is based upon in terms of its historical and linguistic development as well as certain specific terms like metropolis, conurbation, and so on. How then do we view the city in regards to its overall nature? Is the city merely a collection of concrete roadways and towers of glass and steel? Are we to look at cities as complex and cold pieces of machinery working like clockwork with many moving cogs, wheels, and parts? Or is there a way to view the city that takes in its more organic nature? This is the idea that cities in many ways are like living breathing organisms that grow, age, and wither only to become healthy again. Not only that, but are cities as a whole spiritual entities?

First, we'll take a look at the organic nature of the city. It just might help our own thinking and understanding of the city to see it in such a light rather than as a machine. Machines don't have a soul, a collective will, or even an overarching spirituality. If we look at the city as a whole, it does indeed resemble some kind of living organism with various parts and systems. The roadways and transit systems are like the blood vessels carrying vital nutrients (people and goods) to all of the different parts of the body (city). The transportation corridors are vital for the overall health of a city. Like a heart that is clogged from too much cholesterol, a congested city can lead to disease. "Congestion weakens urban economies over the long run, undermining them to the point that they eventually erode and die with disastrous consequences to our national economy."[15] Something as simple as getting from Point A to Point B can become an arduous task if the overall transportation system (cars, buses, light rail, walkability, bicycling lanes) is not efficient or practical. It is even proven to cause damage to a city's economy. "A speedy and efficient

15. Staley and Moore, *Mobility First*, 4.

transportation system may be more important than ever in the context of today's globally competitive, information-based service economy."[16]

Transportation more or less reflects a living system in the city. Most often it is not something we even think about unless something bad happens like a traffic accident on the freeway or when the Skytrain is halted for some reason. As I mentioned earlier, as a family we've been on an adventure in the whole transit jungle where entire days are based around how to "quickly" get from Point A to Point B. Usually the night before any day trips across the city, I take time plotting out my course for the day on Google, which tells me which bus to catch and when, where I need to make a connection, and so on. Sometimes I can get where I need to go faster than if I had a car, while other days I'm wishing I could simply drive. Last week, I had a meeting way out on the suburban fringe of Langley which took an hour and fifteen minutes to get to on transit. Right after the meeting, I had to trek all of the way across the city to North Vancouver on transit which took over two hours for another meeting. When that meeting was over, I sluggishly jumped back on transit for another hour-plus to get home. In the course of that one day, I rode on six different buses, the Skytrain twice, and made eleven exchanges or transfers. For two hours of meetings, I had spent over four-and-a-half hours simply getting there and back. Cities shape us in ways which go beyond the pervasive culture, be it fashion, worldview, or values. Transportation issues have also shaped me, as I explain in *Metrospiritual*. It has even crept into the values of our church as I continuously think about such things as creating a walkable, bike-friendly, and transit-oriented church. Transportation has been probably the most blogged-about topic on my blog www.theurbanloft.org in the last six months and the focus of the bulk of my reading.

Traffic and congestion is an organic issue, not mechanical. It affects the entire metropolitan area. Not only is this a problem in the U.S. and Canada, but it is a major issue in nearly every city in the world. It's a problem that plagues cities on every continent. In nations where cities are exploding with growth, it is a real everyday struggle. "Chinese cities are choking with congestion, and few cities exemplify the practical challenges transportation planners face more than Beijing. Eight hundred

---

16. Ibid., 38.

thousand new people officially move to the Chinese capital each year, and thousands move illegally."[17]

Other cities, such as Amsterdam, continue to push for a bike-friendly city. To combat auto congestion, "their goal is to provide a healthy non-polluting alternative for short trips, particularly in their jewel-like cities, which they want to protect from the ravages of huge volumes of motor vehicle traffic."[18] They've succeeded in that 27 percent of the trips in the city are by bike.[19] Part of being a resilient and healthy city is responding in an appropriate way that maximizes all the city has to offer in ways that are good for the environment and urban dwellers.

If the city is like a human body, then we can begin to look at the other systems that are essential for health. What is the brain of the city? Where can we find its heart and soul? Can a city as a machine create a neighborhood's funk and vibe? Who creates it? Developers? Government officials? Urban planners? "A funky, vibrant city can only be made by everyday people."[20] That's been one of the struggles in urban planning circles. Too much planning and master-planned communities leave a city feeling sterile. For all of Vancouver's beauty in its built environment in the downtown core and other urban areas, one of the criticisms is its sterility. As local author and lecturer on urban issues, Matt Hern, explains, "The real question I want to ask here sits near the intersection where aesthetic and political arguments meet: How can Vancouver develop some funk, some flavor? How can we densify without being sterile and choreographed?"[21] Where is the balance between a city that is too master-planned and one that is rampantly sprawling with haphazard squatter developments? Some advocate for a more chaordic middle ground in urban development where urban planning provides the basic structure but the rest is given ample freedom for creative expression. This is moving closer to recognizing that a city's nature is truly organic.

In our modern culture, there is a definitive development in our thinking and imagination that blurs the line of where the organic ends and the machine begins. For example, take the ever-famous robot figure popularized in Hollywood film, TV shows, and other media. Fifty-plus

17. Ibid., 135.

18. Mapes, *Pedaling Revolution*, 65.

19. Ibid.

20. *Common Ground in a Liquid City*, 69.

21. Ibid., 67.

years ago, robots in films and on TV looked like square toasters with legs and arms. Fast forward to robots in the movies of today and many take on the form, shape, and personification of living organisms like we saw in the famous *Matrix* series. Automobiles went through a phase of being square and boxy only to become more streamlined. We're attempting to make what is mechanical less sterile and more "flesh and blood." On the other hand, it is as though we're attempting to regulate and coerce the organic to be more regulated, planned, and mechanical in terms of predictability. Modern-day professional athletes are on rigid diet and exercise programs in order to squeeze every drop of potential from their bodies. Athletes are commended for "clockwork precision" whether as a quarterback or pitcher. In movies from the 1950s, cities were predominantly viewed with the cool rigidity of a machine. This even spawned innumerable futuristic movies where the post-apocalyptic city of tomorrow looked like the inside of a computer or piece of machinery.

Cities are changing. As a whole, many are trying to shed the heaviness of the industrial city moniker and replace it with warmth, attractiveness, vibrancy, resiliency, and liveability. The industrial city indeed was like a machine with people slavishly tramping their way each day to work in unsafe, substandard, and unsanitary factories. They were like simple cogs in a large heartless behemoth machine. Now? Cities are razing once-flourishing industrial sites in favor of green space and residential units that offer a live-work-and-play lifestyle. Just today in a meeting at the North Shore Neighbourhood House in North Vancouver, we talked about the new urban farm being planned in the city. Even the mayor recognizes how sprawling grassy yards can be used for urban gardens. The city again is going through a metamorphosis. It is changing from a mechanical to a more organic mentality and outlook.

Many people have simply given up on the city and moved out. Whether one views the city as organic or mechanical, it can be exhausting for some, as the density, diversity, and the pace of the city is not for everyone. Jerry was one of those. The first time I met him, I immediately knew I would like the guy. It was my first day on the job as a hiking and mountain biking guy while living in Tucson. I walked in and Jerry had a bike mechanic apron on, a pedal wrench in one hand, and a cheek full of tobacco. The first thing I learned about Jerry was that he lived in a tepee . . . a real one. As I got to know Jerry and spent time with him out on the trail, the first question on my mind was, how does a former

Marine-turned-CPA leave everything behind, buy an acre of land in the desert foothills, and build a tepee to live in? The simple answer was he got tired of the city, the city lifestyle, and the business world. He wanted a clean break and a fresh start away from the city. He preferred hiking and biking and the simplicity of a near-subsistence lifestyle. There was something serene and surreal about sitting in a high-walled canyon listening to him play a Native American wood flute.

We do not have that choice. As followers of Christ whose mission field is the city, we simply cannot abandon it regardless of how we view it, whether organically or mechanically. Developing a theological framework for understanding the city is indeed an arduous task. Sometimes it as though we're seated on a bench in solitude as we contemplate the subtleties of a brilliant work of art like the Mona Lisa. We gaze upon the city and are struck by so many features of what we see, whether it be the beauty of the architecture and built environment, the perfectly placed green spaces and public squares that make urban life enjoyable, or walking down the sidewalk in the midst of a myriad of global cultures all living in proximity with one another. On the other hand, sometimes studying the city from a theological framework is akin to studying venomous snakes. While there is so much beauty (bear with me) in the creature, we must exhibit caution and care. There are most definitely dysgenic features of the city that plague neighborhoods and communities. There's not a week that goes by without seeing fire trucks, ambulances, or local police responding to some kind of crisis in our neighborhood. There have been instances of violence and death. I have seen a dead person being wheeled out of an apartment building by an ambulance crew a block away from where we live. I once had to walk a wide radius around my normal route to get home after the police blocked off a six-block section because there was a guy on the street with a handgun. I am fully aware that cities are not all glitz and glamor. There are problematic features of the city, personal sin, and systemic evil all wrapped into one geographic setting. However, if we believe that God loves the people around us and died for them and the city, then that begins to change everything.

For me, the reason behind studying and understanding cities is multi-faceted. First of all, I am utterly intrigued. I want to know what they are, how they work, and all of the inner workings that make a city a city. Second, I live in the city. It is the subject of my attention, affection, and everyday life. Lastly, I believe that God has a heart for the world's cities. In his sovereignty, he is gathering the nations to the city. As I've mentioned numerous times already, I only have to walk outside to see this global reverse Diaspora taking place in my own neighborhood. God has a plan for the city. He longs to extend both his common and saving grace to urban (as well as suburban and rural) dwellers. I believe that God is the great author of the first city as well as mankind's urban trajectory that started back thousands of years ago in the Near East's Fertile Crescent. Civilization is marked by the city.

What is a city? While you may be able to wax eloquently about it if that question were to come up on *Jeopardy* or *Trivial Pursuit*, there is still a touch of mystery and intrigue about it. It can be a moving target. Throughout these past few chapters, we have spent considerable time poking, prodding, and exploring what a city is and what makes it great. In the next chapter, we'll continue the discussion by doing a little spelunking in history.

5

Origins

ORIGINS INTRIGUE ME. I'M not too sure where this fascination came from, but I recognize it nonetheless. It is perplexing to learn about how different things started, whether businesses like Starbucks, great civilizations like Egypt, or cities great and small, new and old. Often when I'm at the gym, whether on the treadmill or stationary bike, I'll watch the History Channel. Sometimes I feel like the oddball as the other guys around me are watching either mixed martial arts, professional wrestling, or some motorcycle show, or the ladies are watching sitcoms, home and garden shows, or afternoon talk shows. Instead, I'm caught up in a show about the life and legacy of the Roman emperor Caligula. I'm a nerd and I am interested in how things started. Origins.

As I've shared before, living without a car in Vancouver has been quite an adventure. Since I can only go as far as the transit system will take me, today I did something new. I ventured as far as I could on the transit bus to Horseshoe Bay in West Vancouver. Known for its horseshoe-shaped bay in Howe Sound, it is home to one of the numerous ferry terminals that dot the region. I woke up early, slogged down to the Edmonds Skytrain Station in the rain, rode a packed and humid Skytrain downtown, and transferred to the transit bus which brought me here. The trip, including transfers, was only an hour and a half.

Tucked away in the corner of a Starbucks across from the ferry terminal, my views this morning are of fog-drenched mountains, a gray placid ocean hemmed in by mountains and islands, chugging ferry boats, docked sail boats, a rain-pelted sidewalk, and Bowen Island that sits in the water like a humped-back sentinel watching over the bay. In the back hallway of the Starbucks are classic old sepia-toned photos from the early years in Horseshoe Bay. There are plenty of photographs of swimmers in their head-to-toe swimsuits, sail boats, old ferries, and the amazing topography that makes up the area. Origins. Everything and everyone has one, including the city. In the same way that we cannot separate ourselves from our origins, we cannot displace a city from its origins as well.

The origins of a city have a direct bearing on day-to-day life right now. The decisions the inhabitants of a city made decades, centuries or even thousands of years ago can still have relevancy today. This could range from where the city is located, whether on a coastal peninsula like San Francisco, a plateau or mesa, along the shores of a Great Lake like Toronto or Chicago, on an island like Montreal, or on a waterway like Ottawa or St. Louis. Other factors include what period of time the city's development or expansion began taking off in rapid outward expansion. Such decisions have a direct bearing on a city's built environment which in turn impacts urban dwellers today. For example, Vancouver was laid out in a grid pattern using measuring techniques from Old Europe. "Vancouver was surveyed and platted out using the medieval English measure known as a 'chain' which is 66 feet (20m) in length."[1] Disregarding the bumps and hills of the Burrard Peninsula, these early surveyors forcibly brought about the grid pattern that shaped the city and still influences it greatly today. That is simply one case among many that author Lance Berelowitz points out as he traces Vancouver's history to show the reader how this great modern city came into being and what influenced it. In regards to a city's *site* and *situation*[2], I will spend more time on that topic in a later chapter. My point here is that a city's origins are crucial and informative. They help us to peel back the layers of the physical to begin looking at the bedrock of cultural values and assumptions that drive the city still today based upon earlier decisions.

In my previous book, *Metrospiritual*, I explored the origins of the first city that we read of in Scripture, Enoch. Found in Genesis 4, the origins and circumstances surrounding the origin of this ancient city are as murky as ever. In this chapter, my goal is to continue to look at that chapter in Genesis, poke and dig around a little more, and make some

1. Berelowitz, *Dream City*, 45.

2. "These terms are often used together by geographers. Site refers to the advantages or disadvantages of a specific location for certain kinds of activities. Situation refers to the advantages or disadvantages of a site in relation to other locations and activities." http://publications.newberry.org/k12maps/glossary/index.html.

observations. My desire is not to repeat what I wrote in *Metrospiritual* but to add on to what I had already written. So why write on Enoch and Genesis 4 again?

There are several different guiding influences that are forming my decision to revisit this ancient city. The first stems from art class in high school. One of the class exercises that I remember had to do with detail. At times we'd take a still object and draw it putting in as many details as we could. It forced us to study the same object for long periods of time, looking for the effects of lighting, its texture, the variance in colors and shades, and so much more. Early on we'd simply draw the object quickly, but we discovered that we ended up missing so much. It was by careful examination and attention to detail that more and more of the object's secrets were revealed. There were many "a-ha" moments as we saw new perspectives, cued in on unnoticed details. It was almost as if the longer we observed and studied, the more layers we were able to peel back. It is the same with cities in general and Enoch in particular.

The story of the origin of Enoch, although but a fleeting mention in Genesis, has become a subject of further study and theological exploration for me. Since my initial writing on it, I've spent considerably more time reading and rereading the story, taking in what others observed and written about the city, as well as teaching it to three different seminary classes in Vancouver and San Francisco. In each of these classes, we'd take time to simply ask a lot of questions and explore. Every time new insights were revealed and we learned to ask a new set of questions.

The second guiding influence leading me to take a second look into the story of Enoch was my first hermeneutics class back in college. Sitting in class was like going on an archaeological journey as we dug and mined for treasures in Scripture. Like an explorer's guide, the professor would lead us from the world of theological speculation into the realm of practical application. One of the practices we did in learning how to interpret Scripture was akin to what I learned in art class: observation. We would be assigned a passage of Scripture, and without consulting any commentary or outside help, we'd dwell on the passage. Attention was given to reading it over and over again. Then repeat. Once we got into the flow of the passage, we'd begin writing down the observations that jumped out at us. Again, we'd repeat this process over and over again. It reminded me of high school art class and staring at the same still object, peeling back the layers to uncover what is easily missed without extensive study. It was the same with the various passages of Scripture we'd study for class. We would make fifty observations, but then turn around and come up with fifty more. At first this was incredibly difficult, but as time went on we learned to see things that we missed if we read it only with a cursory glance.

Taken together, these two stories and their ensuing practices are for me the overarching motivators for taking another look at Genesis 4 and the origins of the city of Enoch. Since my first foray into the story of Enoch, I've come to see the divergence of thought, speculation, and interpretation that surrounds the story. Some writers and theologians decry this first city, focusing on God's great displeasure at the events that preceded its formation. Others argue with equal passion that in fact Enoch is a gift from God and stands as a testament of his bountiful grace and love for humanity. Which is it? It can't be both. If Enoch was a still object under the close scrutiny of art students, pencils in hand, then what are they seeing? Does their positioning on one side of the table reveal something that the students on the other side are missing? Maybe the ceiling light fixture is angled in such a way as to cast different shadows which affect the observed texture. Maybe the sunlight beaming in from the window is also influencing what the students are observing. Or possibly, some of the students don't have much affection or appreciation for the studied object to begin with. Just like the potted plant on the table reminds them of summers of boredom at Grandma's house, or a cow's skull reminds one student of the tragic death of his father in a farming accident, any object can earn our disdain. What might be the factors in our lives that can influence the way we approach Genesis 4 and the city of Enoch?

The details are as cryptic as trying to decipher cave paintings by primitive people thousands of year ago. We've read the story numerous times. Most are not aware that in the story of Cain and Abel is found an all-too-brief passing reference to the first recorded city in biblical history: "Cain knew his wife, and she conceived and bore Enoch. When he built a city, he called the name of the city after the name of his son, Enoch."[3] This is a rather straightforward account without any of the lurid details. After the post-murder drama subsided, Cain and his wife had a son, and Cain decided to build a city. This lone sentence, and the intensity of the tragedy leading up to it, is what has caused the firestorm

3. Genesis 4:17.

of theological debate in regards to Cain's relationship with God which directly ties into the construction of the first city. "Cain named his first son, as well as the city he built, *Enoch*. The name has several connotations, including, 'dedication,' 'consecration,' and 'initiation,' and Cain's choice of that name seems to represent a promise to himself of a new beginning in life."[4]

We're not privy to the details of its founding. Was it located next to a perennially flowing river in the desert that afforded a lush riparian area that made farming a year-round reality? Having trekked the mountainous desert wilderness of southern Arizona uncovering an abundance of archaeological artifacts, I can only surmise that Enoch was located in such a setting. Water was vital. A city could not survive without it. As we came across site after site of ancient desert villages, all were either along the banks of rivers, on a ridge line above them, or somewhere in close proximity. Any city regardless of size needs access to water. An ancient Near East city, even if it only had a few thousand residents, needed water.

What about the actual construction process? We're left to assume that Cain didn't do this alone. Who helped him? How many helped him? Were they outcasts like himself? What was their plan and process? Can we assume that Enoch was the first city in history or is it simply the first one recorded in the Bible? "Enoch is the first city mentioned in the Bible, but it may not be the world's first city."[5] We do know that there were a lot more people in the region than Adam, Eve, and Cain. Cain feared for his life, that others would take revenge on him for killing Abel. Who were these others and how many were there? Where did Cain find his wife? Did he build his city based on what he had seen of other cities in the region, or did God himself supply the blueprint? Did his fear prompt him to build a wall first? On all these questions and more, we can only speculate. However, once we begin understanding such things as the climate, basic topography, and how ancient cities were developed, we can at least begin piecing together some of the fragments of the story. However, that is for the next chapter.

Seemingly the controversy surrounding the story of Cain and Abel and the construction of Enoch revolve around motive. Are a few cryptic passages in Genesis enough to warrant a definitive conclusion as to

4. Davis, *Paradise to Prison*, 102.

5. Ibid.

what was really going on in Cain's mind and his motivations for building Enoch? "The evolution of the city embodies the story of humanity as it rose from primitive origins to impose itself on the world. It also represents, as the French theologian Jacques Ellul once noted, man's fall from natural grace and the subsequent attempt to create a new, workable order."[6]

As I've interacted with a number of people in regards to Genesis 4, many have extensively quoted Ellul in his analysis of this passage in *The Meaning of the City*. Like many who have written about the account of Cain, Abel, and the creation of the city of Enoch, there is a clear line drawn in the ancient sand. While teaching a course on the theology of the city, when we came to this passage of Scripture, I wanted to ensure that I attempted to lay out both sides of the argument. Not that I was necessarily even fair in giving adequate unbiased attention to both sides, because I too have a stance, but it was and is helpful to at least take a look. I will attempt to do that now.

After Cain murdered Abel, God told him, "And now you are cursed from the ground, which has opened its mouth to receive your brother's blood from your hand. When you work the ground, it shall no longer yield to you its strength. You shall be a fugitive and a wanderer on the earth."[7] Immediately Cain is driven from the ground in which he earned his livelihood and sent packing. He transitioned from being rooted in one place as a farmer to being a nomad literally, figuratively, and even spiritually. This is where the Genesis account gets even more mysterious and murky because of what Cain says next: "Cain said to the LORD, 'My punishment is greater than I can bear. Behold, you have driven me today away from the ground, and from your face I shall be hidden. I shall be a fugitive and a wanderer on the earth, and whoever finds me will kill me.'"[8] Wait, if it was only Adam, Eve, Cain and Abel (now minus Abel), then who was Cain worrying about? His Mom and Dad? There must've been others. More children from Adam and Eve who weren't recorded in Scripture? They lived for a long time, so we can assume that they had many children. Some speculations I've heard over the years state that since this was the beginning of mankind, the gene pool was somewhat pure which is why the question of siblings marrying one another did

6. Kotkin, *The City*, xv.
7. Genesis 4:11–12.
8. Genesis 4:13–14.

not carry the same repercussions as today, however, that is for another discussion for Bible college or seminary students to have over pizza at 2:00 AM.

Cain was in a panic and feared for his life. Now that he was to become nomadic, I'm sure he envisioned making his way through one of the many canyons of the ancient Near East. The further Cain wanders into the canyon, the steeper the rocky walls become. The shadows thicken and grow as the canyon walls narrow. Large boulders litter the canyon floor, making it the perfect environment for an ambush. It's possible Cain played out in his mind how the events just might unfold following his murder of Abel. Maybe it was all of their siblings . . . hundreds or even thousands who would hear of Cain's heinous act and take justice into their own hands. This is what Cain feared. This is the scenario that he laid out before the Lord. God responded: "Then the LORD said to him, 'Not so! If anyone kills Cain, vengeance shall be taken on him sevenfold.' And the LORD put a mark on Cain, lest any who found him should attack him. Then Cain went away from the presence of the LORD and settled in the land of Nod, east of Eden."[9] God promises Cain safety and security and went as far as placing some kind of mark on him. (A sort of tattoo, perhaps?) Then the story jumps to Cain and his wife having a baby and oh by the way, Cain is building a city.

How did that happen? Who knows? We're simply not privy to all of the details of this ancient account. We're given snapshots of a story that unfolded through the course of at least a year as we factor in the murder, the reaction, the dialogue between Cain and God, Cain and his wife having sex, Cain's wife becoming pregnant, nine months of pregnancy, birth, and the building of a city. Building a city is much more than pitching a tent, too. "Cain's impulse toward city life seems to come directly out of a broken relationship with the land, his family, and his God. The city functions as a surrogate for these primary relationships, providing an alternate form of protection and provision for the banished human."[10]

Thousands of years after the fact and many cultures removed, it is a bit presumptuous for us to try to put ourselves in Cain's sandals—assuming he wore sandals—and figure out why he might have thought and acted as he did. That said, Ellul nonetheless contends, "Cain is completely dissatisfied with the security granted to him by God, and so he

9. Genesis 4:15–16.

10. Jacobsen, *Sidewalks in the Kingdom*, 37.

searches out his own security."[11] Ellul makes the case that what happened after the murder of Abel was then tainted by sin. Cain was simply disregarding what God said. God promised Cain security and Cain didn't fully trust God. Not only that, but everything he did following that was a continued act of rebellion. God told Cain not to worry . . . Cain did worry. God told Cain that he would be a fugitive and a wanderer . . . Cain builds a city and stays in one place. "Cain, driven from his fields, makes a city: the first murderer becomes the first city builder."[12] Eric Jacobsen expands this thought when he writes, "The Lord seeks to comfort Cain by providing a mark of protection that will warn off those who would seek to harm him. But Cain, apparently unsatisfied with this degree of protection, decides to take matters into his own hands."[13]

Is it really that simple? Remember the earlier story and analogy of students crowded around a table in an art room drawing a still object. Every vantage point and perspective is crucial so that key insights can be taken in and noted. So many factors and influences inform our perspective. Even when it comes to looking at our modern city, which set of lenses—assumptions and biases—are we starting with? If our vantage point in regards to the city is negative and even hostile, then it can be reasonably deduced that that perspective may taint and color our view of the story of cities in Scripture. On the other hand, if the way we view cities today and in history is truly positive and hopeful, that too will color the way we read the same stories. Ellul goes on to state, "Cain sought security not so much from God, whom he was trying to escape, as from the world, hostile since Abel's murder. The world was perhaps difficult after Adam's fall, but it was not yet marked by murder. Now it is. The city is the direct consequence of Cain's murderous act and of his refusal to accept God's protection.[14] That last statement is crucial in understanding Ellul's argument and stance. He makes the case that the first city was conceived in sin, which presumably made sin part of the DNA of every city since then. Is this the reason why our cities breed so much evil, such as gross poverty, slum-like conditions, murder, rape, and the like? Are we simply living out the affects of Cain's willful rebellious decision to build a city? Is Ellul claiming, then, that God created us to be agrar-

11. Ellul, *The Meaning of the City*, 4.

12. Ibid., xv.

13. *Sidewalks in the Kingdom*, 37.

14. *The Meaning of the City*, 5.

ian and that any pooling together of resources and collaborative human effort to build cities is disobedience? Is that the point of Genesis 4 and the building of the Tower of Babel in Genesis 11? Is the very essence of a city and urban life therefore an affront to God's plan for us? These are questions that must be answered, because the answers will also directly impact our role in and view of cities today. Ellul argues:

> The city opposed to Eden. It is certainly not unaware that Cain gave this name to his creation. Now he also is going to make the world over again. This unsatisfying world, this world from which perfection is excluded, where Cain introduced all possible pain, Cain is now going to reconstruct. In fact, the world should not be "reconstructed," but "construct." For in Cain's eyes it is not a beginning again, but a beginning. God's creation is seen as nothing. God did nothing, and in no case did he finish anything. Now a start is made, and it is no longer God beginning, but man. And thus, Cain, with everything he does, digs a little deeper the abyss between himself and God.[15]

But there is hope. Not everyone views the account in Genesis 4 with such dismay. I have to admit that the first time I read Ellul's understanding of this ancient story, I was ready to move out of the city, grow dreadlocks, wear hemp clothing, and live in a neo-hippie commune in the woods. As I circled back around the story, again and again, as I did in art class or in my freshman theology class, I began to see something different. Instead of seeing cities as cursed, I started seeing them as actually gifts. Conn and Ortiz argue that, "God gave the cities to his people as a covenant gift. They were signs of God's grace in the present, their walls signs of God's security for the future."[16] Admittedly, they also state, "Cain had built his city for self-protection from vengeance. In the cities of refuge to be set apart by God, that purpose was retained."[17] That would seem to correspond to some degree with Ellul, and yet they still hold out hope for the city, "Despite sin's radical distortion of God's urban purposes, the city remains a mark of grace as well as rebellion, a mark of preserving, conserving grace shared with all under the shadow of the common curse. Urban life, though fallen, is still more than merely live-

---

15. Ibid., 6.

16. Conn and Ortiz, *Urban Ministry*, 111.

17. Ibid., 88.

able. Even Cain, skeptical of a divine response to retaliation, acknowledges the shelter that the city offers for his posterity.[18]

The challenge comes in that what we read is hardly the whole story. Our assumptions, theological lenses, experiences and backgrounds shape the details which were left out. Our minds and eyes are intuitive that way. When I was a youth pastor, we used to play a game that involved guessing which logos belonged to which famous brands, ranging from Pepsi to Ford to sports teams. What was shown to the students was a small sliver of the logo, but with ease their minds could fill in the rest of the picture. How much are we filling in in the story of Genesis 4? A low or negative view of the city would lead one to more negative views of the story, while a positive or redemptive view may just have the opposite effect. The point of contention are Cain's motives. Did he doubt God's promise for safety, which led him to build a presumably walled city with help from other like-minded people? Something did change after Cain's conversation with God. Immediately after they talked, Cain went east to the land of Nod and settled there. Are we to assume the punishment was reduced some time after that conversation? How often have we as parents instituted some kind of punishment or discipline for our children when they've done something warranting us to take action, and yet upon further conversation, perhaps after the child has shown remorse and even repented, we've lessened our initial discipline? All we can see in the story of Cain was that whereas he was told he'd be a fugitive and wanderer, immediately following his conversation with God he moves out and settles down east of Eden.

Did Cain wander? If so, then perhaps not for long. Did he instead settle down? Eventually, yes. Are we to conclude the settling down and the ensuing construction of Enoch were acts of rebellion? What we don't find in the story is God re-entering the scene to condemn Cain's actions of settling and building. Later on in Genesis 11, we see God's direct intervention against the people who set out to build not only a tower but a city in direct defiance of God. They rebelled and God stepped in to scatter them. Yet when Cain built a city, it appears that God did nothing to stop him from building Enoch, let alone destroy it after it was built. Obviously, this is an argument from silence. But again, all we have to go on are a few cryptic sentences that span many months and possibly years.

18. Ibid., 87.

Ellul makes a strong case to say that cities originated as a result of rebellion and disobedience. That could indeed be a possible reality. But even if it were so, we also know that God ends up redeeming cities as a whole and that our future eternal destinies lie in the city. This all ties back into origins. The way something starts off is vital to our understanding. Bakke Graduate University professor Dr. Ron Boyce writes, "The manner in which something begins provides important clues as to its purpose, nature and future development. Nowhere is this more apparent than in the genesis of cities. If we were to know the reasons for their origin, we would be better able to understand their present characteristics. Yet their origin is an enigma—writing and civilization begin with them."[19] The account of the first city recorded in biblical history yields more questions than answers, but like the title of the book in which it is found, Genesis, it is only the beginning. Today we sit with thousands of years of urban development in our rear-view mirror. We're afforded the luxury of tracing its evolution. As with uncovering the origins of anything, there are usually multiple sources on the subject. Genesis is one such source. In the next chapter, we'll continue to look at the origins of the city, but from extra-biblical materials.

19. Boyce, "The Nature of Cities."

6

The Ancient World

MY FAMILY AND I have had the privilege to live in a number of places that were hotbeds for film-making, ranging from southern Arizona to northern California, and now here in Vancouver, B.C. It is almost to the point where it was and is commonplace for movie or television show productions to be happening all around us as while our lives continue on with much less pop, sizzle, and drama. My wife Katie has run into Jack Black on several occasions while working at a coffee shop in downtown Vancouver. I've hiked with numerous celebrities in the desert. Here in Burnaby, close to my local Starbucks where I regularly hang out, is the production set for the television series *Smallville*. Once in a while a nondescript white bus will pull up to the curb in front of the coffee shop and out of it will emerge a ragtag group of people. I have to be honest and admit that the first time I saw them pile out of the bus, I thought it was a group of residents from a local halfway drug rehab house. You have to understand that about sixty plus percent of my neighbourhood is made up of visible minorities, with the vast majority being immigrants. When a bus pulls up with fifteen white people getting off, they stand out, especially as they look a touch dishevelled from having come straight off the production set.

Since we've moved to Vancouver, there have been quite a few times while watching a movie as a family someone will blurt out, "Hey! That's Vancouver! That's at SFU (Simon Fraser University)," just like we saw in the movie *The Day the Earth Stood Still*. What's even funnier is when a movie is supposed to be set somewhere like New York or Washington D.C., but we know where it was actually filmed. That sense of identifying with the real story behind the scenes is intriguing, whether having hiked in the Santa Rita mountains behind the ranch house in John Wayne's

McLintock or trekked through the lush forest where *Jurassic Park* was filmed and so on. It is almost as if there is a story behind the story.

And just as a movie is often set in a place far removed from where it claims to be, today's cities can likewise trace their origins to a context and culture far removed from that of our own. In most cases—but not all—we're simply left with a more "polished production" that may only faintly resemble a city's past origins and prior history. The rhythms of the city of Vancouver were set in motion long before we ever arrived here.

One of the best decisions I made in my doctoral studies was to take a course called *The Nature of Cities* taught by Dr. Ron Boyce. I studied how cities developed, what influenced their built environment, the competition between cities such as Chicago and St. Louis, and how to better understand my own city. I was thrust into a world where I had spent little time up to that point. Most ministry-related training and education focuses on the disciplines of theology, anthropology, and sociology. The paths of understanding people, human behaviors, demographics, and so on are well-travelled, but we fail to fully comprehend how the city influences these very people. This crash course in urban geography motivated and pushed me in a direction that I hadn't previously realized was there. Instead of beginning with people, I learned to begin instead with the city, its built environment, economic realities, and the various other factors that shape and define the people who live there. I readily admit that much of Dr. Boyce's writings, conversations, and ideas permeate this book, especially this chapter, as they are inseparable from who I am now.

In the last chapter, we looked at the origins of the first recorded city in biblical history, Enoch. Now we'll transition and expand the scope of our archaeological spelunking to include *extra-biblical* material. While Genesis indeed contains one of the oldest accounts of the history of cities, there are other sources as well. How do these various sources stack up against one another? Do they play a complementary role to the story of cities found in Scripture? How and why did cities emerge in the first place? Do a few cryptic sentences about the founding of Enoch tell us all that we need to know about the origins of cities? Were cities the direct result of divine intention, man's rebellion, or the natural progression of advancing humanity? In his paper and class notes, "The Nature of Cities," Boyce writes, "The reason for the rise of the first cities is a matter of dispute. Some scholars argue that the first cities evolved simply as the result of advancements in agriculture; others think that the birth of cities was a world-shaping invention."[1]

There are a number of theories that try to explain the origins of the cities and civilizations of the Ancient Near East. They range from simply a natural progression and development to outlandish notions of some connection to an advanced alien race from another planet. For our present purposes, we'll stay out of Area 51 or Roswell, New Mexico. Instead, the three theories we'll look at concerning the origins of cities are: natural development, human invention, and divine intention.

The idea of cities forming as part of a natural progression or development seems to be on par with humanity as a whole. We develop, progress, change and adapt. It has been this way since the beginning:

> Humanity is not some static, unchanging stationary group of people spread out across the globe. Instead, humanity is a dynamic migratory people that move and shift daily. A brief look at human history finds that people are continuously migrating, adapting, and learning. Much of this was done throughout history with varying degrees of contact from one people group to another, and one culture to another. Fast forward to today in the twenty-first century and this global phenomenon of intersecting with other cultures and the shifting migrations of people is at a rapid, frantic pace unparalleled in all of human history.[2]

Not only are we changing and adapting, but so is our utilization of technology. As a child, I remember having a Commodore 64 computer with a massive floppy disk drive that seemed to take up half the desk as we played simple computer games. Computers today can do infinitely more, while taking up just a tiny fraction of the space. Natural development and progression are part of who we are. The argument that cities developed naturally is that villages transitioned seamlessly into cities. As these villages grew, became more complex, and densified, hierarchical structures solidified, technology advanced, and cities emerged as a natural by-product.

"Scholars reasoned that cities rather naturally evolved in response to advancements in the domestication of plants and animals. The argument was that there first had to be a reliable and perennial surplus of

---

1. Boyce, "The Nature of Cities."
2. Benesh, *Metrospiritual*, 1.

food—a staple that could be stored for some time--before a city could exist."[3] Boyce goes on to list several other factors that had to be in place for cities to have developed: a favorable ecology base, advancement in agricultural technology to support a burgeoning population, and a complex social organization.[4] As we'll soon see, each of these points of the origin of cities contain elements of cohesion. Certainly, for cities to exist, ranging from an ancient city on the Mesopotamian flood plains to the dense high-tech city of Tokyo, these factors needed to be present. Cities got their starts in places that were ecologically favorable, whether along a river bank, a coastal setting at the mouth of a river, or in a region with arable land. The same is true for today.

One of the points of contention with this theory is the location of villages versus cities. Villages were small and tended to be much more informal. Their small footprint afforded them the opportunity to be located in areas that are not conducive for cities to flourish. Villages can be found on rocky ridges, in a mountain pass, or in the confines of a narrow canyon. Cities need more than that. If one were to study the location of the cities in one's own region, what would it reveal? In my region, the three largest cities up and down the coast would be Vancouver, Seattle, and Portland. Each is located in favorable places that make expanded city life possible, whether along a river, on the coast, or in a protected bay or sound. On the other hand, we can think of innumerable small towns, or "villages," that are located in less strategic areas that do not allow for expansion and urban growth, such as Whistler, BC; Newhalem, Washington; or Lukarilla, Oregon. All are out-of-the-way, isolated towns or unincorporated villages in the mountains.

Were ancient cities simply overgrown villages? I have my doubts. As I alluded to earlier, a major problem with this argument involves location. The first cities arose in an entirely different physical environment than ancient villages. They were limited to exotic river valleys. Remember, water was and is key. Secondly, archaeologists have not found the remains of early villages underneath these ancient cities.[5] It was as if these cities suddenly appeared out of nowhere.

That idea leads into the second theory of the origin of ancient cities, that they were actually an invention, created from scratch. Is that what

3. "The Nature of Cities."
4. Ibid.
5. Ibid.

we find in the story of Cain and his construction of Enoch? Thumbing through the pages of Genesis, we get the impression that Enoch is a new construction project. We certainly do not have the specifics of the city. For example, which bend of what river was it located on? How large was its built environment? What was its original population? What kind of agricultural base did it have? Whatever circumstances revolved around Enoch, it does seem to have appeared suddenly as with other cities in the ancient Near East:

> The first cities, for which we have solid archaeological and historical evidence, began about 3,500 to 4,000 B.C.E. Ancient cities seem to have appeared on the horizon of history suddenly. Evidence suggests that the first city was an exploitive invention; one which provided security for its inhabitants by dominating the nearby rural population. Such domination likely was achieved by force and reinforced by religion. Religion was such an important element of all ancient cities that it dominated everyday affairs. However, while cities no doubt provided many important functions, as they do today, their primary contributions in ancient times—if that's what they may be called—are in technology, commercialism, and war.[6]

Control seems to be the operative word; control of the environment around the city as well as the citizens within. This idea does not bode well for Cain and his new city Enoch. Was his city exploitive as well? Or did it stand in stark contrast to the other regional cities of his time? Was Enoch a theocratic city marked by grace and living under the guidance of God? We can only surmise. In cities today, a strong sense of control or orderliness must be present and prevalent for them to function. Where there is lawlessness and corruption, the city, its built environment and its inhabitants suffer. "Precisely because so many of the world's problems now arise from the poor design, weak governance, and mismanagement of cities, it is imperative that we learn how to transform our cities into centers of the world's solution."[7] The city as human invention sought to create a sense of advantage, whether through collaboration, resource-sharing, control over agricultural lands, or the slotting of people into different strata for the functioning of urban life. In villages, government

6. Ibid.
7. Brugmann, *Welcome to the Urban Revolution*, 201.

was shared and informal, whereas in cities, we find the emergence of a ruling class.

This idea of control is not necessarily a bad concept, although the term itself conjures up a whole litany of abuses and other atrocities. Control means "to exercise restraint or direction over; to hold in check, curb."[8] Cities, at least healthy ones, do offer a sense of stability and civility as restraint is exercised through laws and policing, and a course of direction is set, presumably for the betterment of its inhabitants, by the leaders. We can all pinpoint where we see this beautifully taking place as well as where it is grossly neglected. Control can also mean "dominate."[9] We see the blatant effects of racism and prejudice in American cities, in particular, those which held African-Americans captive in blighted urban neighbourhoods. "Confronted with high costs and institutionalized neglect, the black districts deteriorated over a mater of decades. Their city was never upgraded or renewed, and its asset value declined, creating a structural impoverishment that still dogs American society."[10] The government leaders, who were supposed to leverage control for the betterment of the city's inhabitants, regardless of ethnicity, failed in the most basic of areas, namely, extending dignity to all and creating equal footing. "Political bosses, business interests, and urban planners fought black progress with clearances of black slum districts and forced relocations, financed through federal programs for public housing and highway construction. These clearances destroyed the equity, local markets, and social ecology of the black community. The displaced families used their new rights to move into other ethnic neighborhoods; some were relocated to new public housing, which quickly transformed into high-rise slums. White police forces remained a constant source of harassment."[11]

Control, while a basic necessity of urban life, whether in its ancient origins or today, must be exercised with fear and trembling. As those of us who are followers of Jesus, we especially have the privilege and responsibility to leverage it for the betterment of the city, particularly the marginalized. Robert Linthicum, in his book *Transforming Power*, makes the case that "in order to accomplish change, we must learn how to use

8. Dictionary.com, LLC, "Control."

9. Ibid.

10. *Welcome to the Urban Revolution*, 63.

11. Ibid., 64.

power in a Christian manner—relationally, not unilaterally—because relational power is of the essence of the gospel."[12] Linthicum argues that it is the church's responsibility to do more than simply gather for worship. We're called to care for those who are in need as well as confront the systemic evil that holds many people in the bondage of helplessness as control is abused. "We are to be winning people to Christ, confronting political systems, transforming economic systems and converting religious (or values-creating) systems. Paul is not suggesting that our involvement in public life is optional or tangential to the purpose, work and life of the church. He is declaring that involvement in public life is what the church is to be about."[13]

The last consideration for the origin of cities is that they are the result of divine intention. Could it be that cities were part of God's blueprint for humanity from the very beginning, even from the Garden of Eden? Genesis 1:28 has been referred to as the cultural mandate: "And God blessed them. And God said to them, 'Be fruitful and multiply and fill the earth and subdue it and have dominion over the fish of the sea and over the birds of the heavens and over every living thing that moves on the earth.'" Again, that theme of control (or dominion) appears. Conn and Ortiz explain that this mandate to be fruitful and multiply, subdue, and have dominion over creation necessitated the creation of cities. "God calls Adam and Eve and their future descendents to rule the earth and subdue it (Gen. 1:28). This calling has been aptly termed the cultural mandate . . . But it could just as easily be called an urban mandate. It will be accomplished through more than farming or husbandry; the founding of the first city will be one of the first achievements of this enduring mandate to expand the borders of the garden (Gen. 4:17). The future of humankind outside the garden was destined to play out in cities."[14] It is my contention that the idea behind the creation of cities is actually found in God himself. Mankind was not destined to simply be agrarian and that the fall in Genesis 3 was not the reason for our process of urbanization. While we don't have the luxury to know how things would have transpired if Genesis 3 never occurred, but we can at least consider for a moment, based upon the trajectory of mankind from Genesis to Revelation, what we were intended for.

12. Linthicum, *Transforming Power*, 20.
13. Ibid., 117.
14. Conn and Ortiz, *Urban Ministry*, 87.

Remember cassette tapes from yesteryear before the compact disc came on to the scene? One of the frustrations was when the stereo "ate" the tape. We'd be sitting on the couch with our friends listening to Def Leppard when all of a sudden the sounds coming out of the speakers became garbled and distorted. Immediately we'd pull the cassette out only to find the tape all over the place as it came unspooled. We would immediately grab a pencil, stick it in one of the holes of the cassette and rewind it until the tape was taut. The goal was to get the tape back into the cassette, since it was never meant to be outside of it. I've heard numerous lectures and sermons which declared that humanity's greatest longing is to get back to the Garden, because we were never meant to live outside of it. However, if our future destinies reside back in the Garden, why then is our final heavenly destination a mega-city? Sure, it includes elements of a new Garden, but eternity is about the city.

We circle back around to what Conn and Ortiz write: "The future of humankind outside the garden was destined to play out in cities."[15] Does the "sudden" appearance of cities in ancient Mesopotamia validate the notion of divine intention? If suddenly cities appeared whereas previously there were only villages, what does that say? What does the origin of cities thus far teach us about God's plan for humanity? How does archaeological research and theory support or detract from the story found in Scripture?

Could the answer be somewhere in a combination of all three? There were certainly human and technological advancements taking place in this region which made urban life possible. Along with that came some kind of premeditated decision to make a bold transition from village to city. Lastly, could it have been plausible that God was the One above it all prompting, nudging, and orchestrating the whole development for his grand temporal and eternal purposes? All we have is the evidence at hand, whether from ancient texts and archaeological findings, as well as our questions. Now that we've spent time exploring the origins of the ancient city, we'll continue our journey through the Old Testament to see whether this idea of divine intention plays out even more. Does God offer a blueprint or template for urban living? If the destiny of humanity was and is to be an urban people, then it would be helpful to explore how this idea percolated throughout the pages of ancient biblical history.

15. Ibid.

7

God's Template for Urban Living

L AST WEEK, WE GATHERED with several others from Southside Church here in Edmonds to pray for our neighborhood. It was a beautiful time to pray with others who all live just blocks from one another about the community that we all not only live in, but also love. In the middle of our time of prayer, someone mentioned Rosie and cried out to the Lord on her behalf. Everyone in the group knows who Rosie is and have had numerous conversations, contacts, and experiences with her. You see, Rosie is one of the homeless people in our community. At times I see her sitting on one of the benches in Highgate Village with several others talking loudly, smoking, and drinking booze out of a brown paper bag. Other times I watch her arguing with her friends, yelling at them a block away. A few weeks ago there was an altercation between Rosie and one of the managers at the McDonald's who had to ask Rosie to leave the premises. I've watched her attempt to steal the speedometer off my mountain bike. The list goes on. What was sobering and yet beautiful was that this group of leaders would intercede on behalf of Rosie. I had to fight back tears. It was one of the richest times of prayer I've ever experienced.

Our neighborhood is full of colorful characters. To me, they add spice and flavor to our community and give it life and flare. As I've shared before, most mornings I trek over to our neighborhood Starbucks to spend time reading, journaling, writing, and so forth. Everyday I end up talking with one of the locals who's a wheelchair-bound older gentleman. Riding his electric wheelchair into Starbucks, he'll often come over to chat with me. Most of the time he's scolding me for not having a King James Bible and how he's a prophet. He explains how I need to sit under his teaching and learn from him as well as watch all of his videos on his website about his various conspiracy theories. At times when I lose my patience, I'll attempt to stir the pot and enter into a friendly little debate with him. In a huff he'll become more animated and tell me how I don't know anything and I'm ignorant and prideful. We'll carry on in conversation before he wheels his chair around and parks outside where he sits every morning. Every time I see him, I'm reminded of God's love and care for him. I know he lives almost a subsistence lifestyle in one of the nearby low-income seniors' towers. Though I fail, I try to emulate love and patience, because somehow it has been stuck in my mind that "Truly, I say to you, as you did it to one of the least of these my brothers, you did it to me."[1]

I'm convinced that if one were to read the entirety of Scripture in one sitting, one theme that would not or could not be missed is God's simple and unadulterated love, concern, and preferential treatment for the poor, the widow, the orphan, the foreigner, and the marginalized. Often it is a direct challenge to a culture that marginalizes the have-nots while we obsess on self and accumulating stuff. "We are formed by the soil we grow in, and most of us grow primarily in the soil of a materialistic culture."[2] But that's only the tip of the iceberg. The more time I spend reading Scripture with a more urban-centric set of theological lenses,[3] other themes become more pronounced and even dominate the biblical landscape of ancient history. In the last two chapters, we looked at the origins of cities both within the pages of the Bible as well as outside of it. This chapter is the next step in the developmental process. If God was the author of cities, does he then offer us a way to live within them? Is there some sort of blueprint or template that we can find scattered across the pages of the ancient Hebrew Scriptures (Old Testament) that gives us a framework for living in cities in the here, the now, and the future? This opens the door for many like-minded questions that seek to poke and prod at the same idea. Does God have an urban agenda? Has he set out a pattern or paradigm for how humanity is to live in the city? Does God have anything to say in regards to life in the city? What would a city look like if people lived the way God has intended?

Bakke Graduate University President, Dr. Brad Smith, in his book *City Signals: Principles and Practices for Ministering in Today's Global*

---

1. Matthew 25:40.

2. Hjalmarson and Toderash, *Fresh and Refresh*, 17–18.

3. This is what I called *metrospiritual* and attempted to begin fleshing out at the end of my last book.

Communities, writes, "We are made by God to be city dwellers and we will have that blessing for eternity."[4] As I have argued, building on what numerous other scholars, researchers, and theologians have written, God's trajectory for mankind from the beginning was and is for us to be city-dwellers. From the cities along the banks of exotic streams in the Ancient Near East to the mega-cities of today, this trajectory continues at a mind-boggling pace. "Cities are growing at an unprecedented rate. Cities have become the catch basins of migrating humanity."[5] While it can be purported that God's greatest creation is indeed humanity, in return, "Humankind's greatest creation has always been its cities."[6] That progression started in the beginning chapters of Genesis and that theme can be traced throughout the rest of Scripture. While our eternal destiny has a distinct urban ring to it, this urban reality begins now. God's plan was more than collecting us in one place (the city) like a giant cage for containment and the better to keep an eye on us, but rather to model what life under Yahweh's love, care, and guidance is about. "Yahweh called his people to a new model for urban life. Israel was to be the exhibition place for God's redemptive grace in the city and the empires that formed around God's people in history. At the heart of the model was a new theological vision, a covenant relationship between thesuzerain God and his servant community. At the core of that vision was a concept of divine kingship new to the ancient world, and to demonstrate it, a new sociopolitical organization."[7]

In order to explore and see what God had intended for humanity in terms of the city, it would be helpful to take a journey back into the early years of the formation of Israel. God calls Abram out of a city to form a new nation that would be God's channel of love and blessing to the nations. "Now the LORD said to Abram, 'Go from your country and your kindred and your father's house to the land that I will show you. And I will make of you a great nation, and I will bless you and make your name great, so that you will be a blessing. I will bless those who bless you, and him who dishonors you I will curse, and in you all the families of the earth shall be blessed.'"[8] God, through Abram (later Abraham),

4. Smith, *City Signals*, 15.

5. Bakke and Sharpe, *Street Signs*, 81.

6. Kotkin, *The City*, xx.

7. Conn and Ortiz, *Urban Ministry*, 95.

8. Genesis 12:1–3.

forms this new nation. Years later it became a subjugated people under the terrifying and brutal reign of Pharaoh. God's chosen people experienced intense pain and suffering as their children were thrown into the Nile. They cried out to the Lord. "During those many days the king of Egypt died, and the people of Israel groaned because of their slavery and cried out for help. Their cry for rescue from slavery came up to God. And God heard their groaning, and God remembered his covenant with Abraham, with Isaac, and with Jacob. God saw the people of Israel—and God knew."[9] Now numbering in the millions, God via Moses leads them out of slavery and captivity in Egypt to this new promised land that he is giving them for an inheritance. They are to take the land and inhabit the cities that were already there. "And when the LORD your God brings you into the land that he swore to your fathers, to Abraham, to Isaac, and to Jacob, to give you—with great and good cities that you did not build."[10] God frees his people, and after wandering in the desert for forty years, they end up in cities. This is a journey that is not uncommon to many in today's global cities. "Nothing matches the sheer numbers, momentum, and universality of the Great Migration to cities that began in eighteenth-century Europe and accelerated exponentially into a global phenomenon in the twentieth century."[11]

In the process of this rural-to-urban migration of God's people, he gives them the Law. Far beyond simply the Ten Commandments, the Mosaic Law encompassed so much more. While we know that it served as a tutor or teacher that would ultimately lead us to faith in Christ, the Law also spelled out the way in which God's people were to live in covenantal relationship with him. The Law served a dual purpose; to show this new nation how this covenant relationship was to be lived out (in an urban context) as well as to demonstrate their need for redemption and a Savior. "So then, the law was our guardian[12] until Christ came, in order that we might be justified by faith."[13] But the context, the place where the Law was to be lived out by God's covenant people, Israel, is also critically important: it was in the urban centers of the new Promised Land. "Land is the fourth most frequent occurring noun in the Old Testament,

9. Exodus 2:23–25.
10. Deuteronomy 6:10.
11. Brugmann, *Welcome to the Urban Revolution*, 39.
12. In the NASB the word "tutor" is used instead.
13. Galatians 3:24.

a more dominant theme than even covenant."[14] Indeed, place was and is crucial. Whether it be the ancient Israelites or us today, we're all rooted in a context. It forms and shapes our lives as we live out our (new) covenant relationship with God today.

We read of the intricacies of the Law in Leviticus. Later on, we find something like an edited version in Deuteronomy, the fifth book of the Torah.[15] But more than simply a recap of the Law in an abridged form, Deuteronomy is more like teachings or messages given by Moses to prepare Israel for entrance into the Promised Land. "Though Deuteronomy follows the vassal treaty form, in general it is more sermonic in nature. Moses was preaching the Law to impress God's Word on their hearts. His goal was to get the people to renew the covenant made at Sinai, that is, to make a fresh commitment to the Lord. Only by unreservedly committing themselves to the Lord could the people hope to enter the Promised Land, conquer its inhabitants, and then live in prosperity and peace."[16] It had been decades since the Law was given and an entire generation has come and gone. The new generation had to be instructed as plans were made for entry into the new land. After forty years of wandering in the desert, it was time for this people to transition from rural to urban. In Deuteronomy, Moses instructs this emerging generation about what it means to live as a covenantal people in the land and in new cities. What we find across the pages of Moses' writings is rather intriguing. The locus of living out the Law was to be in the cities, which offers us a glimpse into the notion of a template or blueprint for urban life that we can learn from. Obviously today we're under grace and not the Law,[17] but there are lessons we can learn as God set apart his people and instructed them how to live. My goal here is to take a cursory look at Deuteronomy and glean some principles that may prove beneficial as we seek a guide (a tutor?) to help us know how to live in the city.

One of the first details of Deuteronomy that jumps out to me is, again, the purpose of the Law. Moses speaks (and pens) the words, "And now, O Israel, listen to the statutes and the rules that I am teaching you,

14. Hjalmarson, *An Emerging Dictionary for the Gospel and Culture*, 41.

15. Or Pentateuch.

16. Walvoord and Zuck, *The Bible Knowledge Commentary: Old Testament*, 260.

17. For further reading, Galatians 2:15–16 explains that we are not justified by the law, but instead through faith in Jesus Christ.

and do them, that you may live."[18] Moses explains that God's word to them—his rules, statutes, or laws—are for their benefit, that following them is life. Not only that, but they are a demonstration of God's blessing on Israel. Following God in obedience will prove to the nations what it means to live under God's loving sovereign care. "Keep them and do them, for that will be your wisdom and your understanding in the sight of the peoples, who, when they hear all these statutes, will say, 'Surely this great nation is a wise and understanding people.'"[19] If others would call Israel a wise and understanding people, then what would those marked differences be? What in God's Law would set them apart and how or why would that be a radical break from other peoples and urban centers of the day?

One peculiar concept that we find in chapter 4 of Deuteronomy is the cities of refuge. "Then Moses set apart three cities in the east beyond the Jordan, that the manslayer might flee there, anyone who kills his neighbor unintentionally, without being at enmity with him in time past; he may flee to one of these cities and save his life."[20] In chapter 19, the importance of these cities becomes even more pronounced. The ESV reads, "*You shall measure the distances* and divide into three parts the area of the land that the LORD your God gives you as a possession, so that any manslayer can flee to them."[21] The same passage in the NASB starts off, "*You shall prepare the roads for yourself.*"[22] (Italics added.) These cities of refuge were central to the judicial system of the day. We read that equity in justice was so important that they were specifically told to actually build roads to them. That observation alone communicates not only the value of these cities and the concept of refuge, but also that God is an impartial and just God. His people were to be set apart from the other nations in their treatment of one another.

This "setting apart" is a theme that is found throughout the book of Deuteronomy as God calls his people to a new standard and a new way of living. I contend that this new way of living has an urban scope to it. This nation is given this message (or reminder) from God through Moses at the point of them entering the Promised Land to inhabit the

18. Deuteronomy 4:1.

19. Deuteronomy 4:6.

20. Deuteronomy 4:41–42.

21. Deuteronomy 19:3.

22. Ibid.

various urban centers within. As a result, laws and commandments that we are quite familiar to them all of a sudden have a different tenor or framework about them. For example, the Ten Commandments make even more sense in the context of a city. Let's take a look at a few of these. "You shall not murder"[23] is one of the hallmarks of civility and secure urban centers. Where this is neglected, the social fabric of the city erodes and deep-seated fear and insecurity creep in. This is not what a healthy city is meant to look like. The same can be said of some of the other commandments, "And you shall not commit adultery. And you shall not steal. And you shall not bear false witness against your neighbor. And you shall not covet your neighbor's wife. And you shall not desire your neighbor's house, his field, or his male servant, or his female servant, his ox, or his donkey, or anything that is your neighbor's."[24] Adherence to each of these laws, statutes, principles, and commandments ensures that urban life (as well as rural) is marked by safety under God's care. More than simply creating a set of arbitrary rules and regulations, there is an obvious practical benefit to listening to and following God.

Another theme that jumps out from the pages of Deuteronomy is God's preferential care and treatment of the marginalized. As I was perusing through the entire book, I couldn't help but notice this reality. It's all in the lenses. I've read through this book and the Bible many times over the years but have missed out on some core truths that were there all along. My prevailing lens (cultural, ethnic, theological, etc.) blinded me from seeing obvious truths and principles not just in the pages of the Old Testament, but also in the New Testament, whether in Jesus' words and works, the activities of the early church, or in the various epistles. It was there. My lenses were smudged. "Thankfully, God is not Euro- or US-centric."[25]

Throughout Deuteronomy, there are many instances where people are called to care for the fatherless, the widow, and the foreigner. This care was to be tangible and practical. Besides, when they extended this kind of care, particularly to the foreigner, it was a reminder that they too had been foreigners in Egypt. "He executes justice for the fatherless and the widow, and loves the sojourner,[26] giving him food and clothing. Love

23. Deuteronomy 5:17.

24. Deuteronomy 5:18–21.

25. Edwards, *An Agenda for* Change, 10.

26. Other translations instead use the word "foreigner" or "alien."

the sojourner, therefore, for you were sojourners in the land of Egypt."[27] Is this not the litmus test of what makes a city great? That the needy residing within are cared for? Can a city be truly great and neglect this admonition? Obviously our cities of today are not under the rule of God on the micro level. But in a real sense, aren't we under his rule on the macro level as we hold to the notion of God's sovereign reign? As followers of Jesus, should we not take these principles and statutes and seek to incarnate them in our cities? This is all near and dear to the heart of God and has been from the beginning of urban life. "Poverty and oppression were also enemies to overcome in the mission of this new community. The stated reality that there would always be poor people in the land only underlined Israel's calling to be 'openhanded toward your brothers and toward the poor and needy' (Deut. 15:11). Faithfulness to the jubilee Sabbath system instituted by God to obviate debt and guarantee land security (Lev. 23:10–11; 25:1–55; Deut 15:2–18) would offer a different alternative: 'there should be no poor among you' (Deut 15:4)."[28]

In many of our cities, we can find where this kind of care is extended, but also where it is grossly neglected in favor of expanding economies and prevailing markets. For many, Vancouver, despite all of its beauty, whether in the built environment or surrounding wilderness, is largely unaffordable. Many live lives of quiet desperation in a postcard-worthy city that they could never afford to buy a home in. "Thousands and thousands of people jammed into faceless little boxes, trying to pay off exorbitant mortgages is not much of a city."[29] Can a city be truly great with these dynamics of rampant materialism in place? The fatherless, the widow, and the foreigner are on the heart of God. I am confronted with this everyday as we interact with the global village that has not only gathered in our city, but even in our neighborhood. Will I also pursue that which God cares about?

The challenge comes in our application of these principles for today. Are they simply reserved for the Old Testament and were superseded along with the Law? On the contrary, in the New Testament, we see Jesus embodying all of these principles, statutes, and laws: "Do not think that I have come to abolish the Law or the Prophets; I have not come to abolish

---

27. Deuteronomy 10:18–19.

28. *Urban Ministry*, 99–100.

29. Hern, *Common Ground in a Liquid City*, 54.

them but to fulfill them."[30] Fast forward to the book of James and this theme again emerges: "Religion that is pure and undefiled before God, the Father, is this: to visit orphans and widows in their affliction, and to keep oneself unstained from the world."[31] Throughout church history, we've seen the continuation of care for the widow, the fatherless, and the foreigner. The question for us today is whether or not we ourselves are embodying it. "Although two-thirds of the world's human beings live in poverty or hover close to it, only a small fraction of Christian workers actually go to live and work among them."[32] Does this absence of care apply to your church?

Another law or statute in Deuteronomy that causes consternation today is tithes and offerings. Like good theologians, we've been selective in our choice and application of texts. We have proof-texted them at length to fit our agendas. We in the Western church have been taught that the tithe pays for our church's staff, facilities and ongoing programs. In and of itself, there's nothing wrong with that. No conspiracy theories here. We can agree that Paul, who, in his letters to the new churches across the Roman Empire, makes the case for paying some leaders a wage for occupational ministry.[33] We also see in Paul's letters tithes and offerings going to help care for the needs of believers in other churches which had fallen on hard times.[34] However, we've adopted a Temple mindset in regards to our tithe and offerings. We often quote Malachi 3:10 ("Bring the full tithe into the storehouse, that there may be food in my house") from our pulpits, most often to correct a downturn in giving or to buttresses a capital giving campaign. The pastor admonishes his flock to give so that the ministry of the church can continue. But that's not the picture we find in Deuteronomy. "At the end of every three years, you shall bring out all the tithe of your produce in the same year and lay it up within your towns. And the Levite, because he has no portion or inheritance with you, and the sojourner, the fatherless, and the widow, who are within your towns, shall come and eat and be filled, that the LORD your God may bless you in all the work of your hands that you do."[35]

30. Matthew 5:17.
31. James 1:27.
32. Hayes, *Sub-merge*, 18.
33. 1 Timothy 5:17–18.
34. 1 Corinthians 16:1–4.
35. Deuteronomy 14:28–29.

So what was the point in collecting the tithes and bringing them to the storehouses? To ensure that no one among them was in need. God is very clear. In his economy, everyone is to be cared for. Again, can a city be great where this is neglected? What is interesting is that alongside non-profits (such as rescue missions and food banks) established by ministries and churches are innumerable other entities doing the same thing. This could be government-led on a national level, or spearheaded by the city on a more regional scale, or instituted by schools, non-religious non-profits, and businesses on the neighborhood level. While the church today may or may not be leading the charge, one thing seems to be clear, namely that God still has a heart for the marginalized, and is caring for them . . . with or without the church. This is not an indictment on the church as much as it is an admission that God will care for these people by whatever means necessary. As one thumbs through the pages of Deuteronomy, there are many instances where the marginalized are elevated:

1. But there will be no poor among you[36]

2. If among you, one of your brothers should become poor, in any of your towns within your land that the LORD your God is giving you, you shall not harden your heart or shut your hand against your poor brother, but you shall open your hand to him and lend him sufficient for his need, whatever it may be.[37]

3. You shall give to him[38] freely, and your heart shall not be grudging when you give to him.[39]

4. For there will never cease to be poor in the land. Therefore I command you, "You shall open wide your hand to your brother, to the needy and to the poor, in your land."[40]

5. You shall not pervert the justice due to the sojourner or to the fatherless, or take a widow's garment in pledge.[41]

---

36. Deuteronomy 15:4.
37. Deuteronomy 15:7–8.
38. A poor brother.
39. Deuteronomy 15:10.
40. Deuteronomy 15:11.
41. Deuteronomy 24:17.

6. When you have finished paying all the tithe of your produce in the third year, which is the year of tithing, giving it to the Levite, the sojourner, the fatherless, and the widow, so that they may eat within your towns and be filled.[42]

7. "Cursed be anyone who misleads a blind man on the road." And all the people shall say, "Amen." "Cursed be anyone who perverts the justice due to the sojourner, the fatherless, and the widow." And all the people shall say, "Amen."[43]

My intention here is not to berate the church, but instead to humbly question where our focus has been. In regards to church planting, as I explored in *Metrospiritual*, why are most churches being planted in either the suburbs or in trendy urban neighborhoods and districts?[44] Why are we making long detours around the parts of the city that house the burgeoning populations of the fatherless, the widow, the foreigner, and marginalized? In the same way, can churches be considered great where there is similar neglect? Cities and churches can display all of the outer trappings of success but still be lacking in the sight of God when it comes to the marginalized. "Based on most current data, churches in America today spend less than 1 percent of their annual budget on the needs of the poor and hungry of our nation and world."[45]

There are two more themes I need to highlight as I wrap up this chapter. The first is that these ancient cities under God's Law were to be marked as places where justice is embodied and embraced. "Israel's identity was established by the doing of justice, righteousness and love to the cosmic God and to the Israelites' neighbors."[46] There are numerous ways in which we find this taking place throughout Deuteronomy. In some cases, the severity of this application seems brutal and primitive compared to our modern Western societies as we read, for example, "So you shall purge the evil from your midst."[47] In other instances what we find is almost intoxicating to think about as we long for our culture

42. Deuteronomy 26:12.

43. Deuteronomy 27:18–19.

44. As I explained in *Metrospiritual*, we still need more new churches in these places and not less. I am simply advocating for more church planting to take place in these neglected environments.

45. Dorrell, *Trolls and Truth*, 49.

46. *Urban Ministry*, 99.

47. Deuteronomy 13:5; 17:7.

today to adopt some of these laws and statutes. For example: "At the end of every seven years you shall grant a release."[48] Other translations say, "At the end of every seven years you must cancel debts." How many of us long to see this next law be in effect today? Instead, many are subjugated under the growing debt that envelopes them. This form of strangulation holds many down, especially the fatherless and the widow. Many go into debt simply to survive. Surely something must change.

The last theme that I will address is in regards to equality in worship. When the people in the ancient cities of Israel gathered for worship, it was clearly on a level playing field. "And you shall rejoice before the LORD your God, you and your son and your daughter, your male servant and your female servant, the Levite who is within your towns, the sojourner, the fatherless, and the widow who are among you, at the place that the LORD your God will choose, to make his name dwell there."[49] This is a beautiful expression of God's people coming before him in worship regardless of occupation, social standing, socio-economic status, ethnicity, gender, and so on. Sometimes in our push for homogeneous churches or church planting along with the market-driven concepts of focus groups, we miss out on the counter-cultural nature of the gospel. "There is neither Jew nor Greek, there is neither slave nor free, there is no male and female, for you are all one in Christ Jesus."[50] What can be more beautiful than a worshipping community made up of various ethnicities and a wide divergence of socio-economic standings?

Space does not permit this chapter to be exhaustive in scope. There are innumerable commentaries and resources that delve deeper into the story and teachings of Deuteronomy. With that said, I believe that the context of Deuteronomy is crucial, because it paints a backdrop that is most definitely urban in hue. With an urban or *metrospiritual* lens, all of a sudden the teachings throughout the book make even more sense. As stated at the outset, they are more than simply a list of rules. Israel's adherence to these statutes was a testimony to the surrounding nations of what it means to live under the Lordship of Yahweh.[51] Whether it was preferential treatment for the marginalized, justice, equity, or equality in worship, Deuteronomy offers the modern reader a working template

48. Deuteronomy 15:1.

49. Deuteronomy 16:11.

50. Galatians 3:28.

51. Deuteronomy 4:6.

for how followers of Jesus are to dwell in the city. Certainly there needs to be a thorough examination of the book to filter out cultural nuances that were time-specific,[52] but overall, there is much in Deuteronomy for us today who live in the city, who value it, and who believe that God has made us to be urbanites. In the next chapter we'll continue to explore ancient writings in the Old Testament as we seek to develop a theological framework for understanding the city as well as living in it.

52. For example, the stoning of rebellious children.

8

Renewing the City

A S WE SAT ACROSS from her at the kitchen table in her humble apartment, we could read the concern on her face. The lines deepened around her eyes as she spoke of her son. Having immigrated (more like fled) to Canada a few years ago from Asia, life for her has been challenging on many fronts. Despite having advanced degrees in art and design, the only kind of job she could find is working the front cash register at Tim Horton's. She is facing the sobering reality that many visible minorities struggle with who've immigrated to Canada in hopes of a better life. "Recent census data show the so-called visible minorities in Canada are 20 percent more likely to have a university degree than white Canadians, but that immigrant underemployment rates are two to three times higher. Recent immigrants with degrees made less than half the salary of their Canadian-born counterparts. The average income of an immigrant with a university degree in 2005 was $24,636—in Toronto more than half of this would be needed just to rent an apartment. The gap between the educated immigrant and Canadian-born citizens has been widening for more than a decade."[1]

After a simple meal of fish and rice, in hushed tones she began asking us for help with her son. One of the reasons for moving to Canada was to get away from her abusive husband. Now she is left without means to raise a teenage boy on her own in a city and nation far from her own. Whereas in her home country, where she had servants, now she lives in an apartment with other immigrants and refugees trying to get a foot up in their new city and home. She grew up Muslim, still adheres to some of the teachings of the Koran, but now considers herself generally spiritual. Having experienced from childhood wars fuelled by religion ravage her

1. Brugmann, *Welcome to the Urban Revolution*, 173.

country, she's fearful that religion divides. But that did not stop her, as our boys played in the other room, from reaching out to us for help.

Fearful that she's losing connection with her son—who's become almost like a fourth son to us—she asked me in particular to see if I could connect with him on a deeper level. She was asking me to become more of a father-figure for her son, since it seems he looks up to me and likes me. In the course of the conversation that night, my wife Katie was able once again to talk to her about sin and grace and the need for redemption and a new heart.

In his short yet powerful book *An Agenda for Change: A Global Call for Spiritual and Social Transformation*, Joel Edwards makes this bold statement: "Transformation is the inevitable result of incarnation."[2] He posits that no one who has had meaningful contact with Jesus can ever be the same. He or she is transformed. Yet transformation did not end there; its "impact was not just limited to individuals. Society itself was changed."[3] The concept of transformation is far beyond simply doing good works to earn the goodwill of others. In fact, it is at the core of what God has been doing throughout history. "Transformation then is not an added extra which we elect into. It is the sum total of what God is doing in the world and what he invites us to join in with. Historically, evangelicalism is unrecognisable without it."[4]

We talk at length about transformation and renewal, but most often we understand it solely on the personal level. In our individualistic Western cultural milieu, these concepts find root in our own lives as we focus on *personal* renewal, *personal* revival, and our *personal* quiet times. It is all about our own *personal* walk with Jesus, since we individually received him to be our Lord and Savior. But there is also a corporate dimension to spiritual transformation. Paul writes: "I appeal to you, therefore, brothers, by the mercies of God, to present your bodies as a living sacrifice, holy and acceptable to God, which is your spiritual worship. Do not be conformed to this world, but be transformed by the renewal of your mind, that by testing you may discern what is the will of God, what is good and acceptable and perfect."[5] Church renewal is usually seen as nothing more than a longed-for remedy for a plateaued

2. Edwards, *An Agenda for Change*, 97.

3. Ibid.

4. Ibid., 101.

5. Romans 12:1–2.

or declining church. In those cases, "renewal" becomes synonymous with the goal of a healthy, growing church—when in reality this is only the foundation upon which genuine social renewal can take place. "As God's incarnation in the twenty-first century, the church is called to have the same transformational impact; life by life and culture by culture. We are called to model a better way more than we are called to criticise the existing one. We are called to be the solution we want to see in the midst of moral and social fragmentation of western societies. We are called to measure our effectiveness not by the size of our churches but by their impact on our communities and the radical discipleship of their members."[6]

In their book *To Transform a City,* authors Eric Swanson and Sam Williams explain that fundamentally, transformation begins on the small scale of the personal but then mushrooms into the life of the church and then the life of the city. The transition goes something like this: individual transformation, church transformation, and then community transformation.[7] They go on to write:

> Community transformation begins with and is led by people who themselves are being transformed. We should never underestimate how important an individual believer with a changed heart can be and how much impact he or she can have upon the world. Jeremiah 5:1 reminds us that it takes only one person to affect the outcome of a city. The highest level of transformation (that with the most measurable change) occurs at the lowest and most basic level – that of the individual follower of Christ. This individual transformation occurs when a person comes to know Jesus Christ in a personal way and begins to live under his Lordship.[8]

What does it mean for our cities to be renewed or transformed? I believe the answer to that would vary depending on one's occupation, discipline, or framework of thinking. As I explained in an earlier chapter, we in the church most often view city renewal in terms of the proliferation of new Christians and new churches. On the other hand, when we step back from a strictly church-centred way of thinking, then all of a sudden city renewal takes on a much wider scope and framework. When we narrow our conversation to simply about us (the church), then we

---

6. *An Agenda for Change*, 98.

7. Swanson and Williams, *To Transform a City*, 45.

8. Ibid.

miss out on the larger conversation taking place in the culture and what God may just be up to on this larger stage. "In the intern___ ___ Scripture, church, and culture, our predispositior ___ foremost in terms of church questions—Scripture ___ come secondary to and a function of the church eff.......ness questions. Like a frustrating computer program, we keep returning to the preset position, assuming it's the correct place to be."[9] Taking the conversation outside of the church and into the culture widens the parameters of transformation and the persons involved. Pastors, church planters, and religious leaders do not have exclusive rights to being catalysts for transformation. There are many others who are involved and in different capacities. For an architect or developer, it could mean reclaiming a decayed urban neighborhood, preserving the historic buildings, and creating new walkable mixed-use developments thus strengthening the local economy. For transportation planners, it could mean a more robust and thorough transit system which gets more vehicles off the road, more people onto public transit, and less carbon emission. For educators, it could mean academically excellent schools, better support networks for students and families, and more parental involvement. For urban planners, it could mean creating a regional development plan for densification to curb outward sprawl which in turn would preserve agricultural lands in outlying areas and creating a more sustainable city. What is city renewal? What if the answer, like on a multiple-choice test, was simply *all the above*?

Since we're still trekking through the pages of biblical and historical antiquity, are there any accounts, stories, and principles that we can uncover to offer guidance on city renewal for us today? At first glance, the exploration of stories that took place in relatively small cities in the Ancient Near East may seem incapable of providing transferrable principles that can work in any city today, whether it be a world-class global city, to a two-thirds world city ringed by squatter communities, to everything in between. On the contrary, this is what we discover in the story of Nehemiah. Most often, students of this book have dug deep and extracted from it valuable principles of leadership, organization development, and project management. But there is so much more to the story than that. Indeed, the story of Nehemiah straddles the tension in city renewal between the spiritual and the physical.

9. Roxburgh, *Missional*, 48.

What is the book of Nehemiah really about? A how-to guide for project management? An easy-reader guide for visionary leadership? Robert Lupton, in his book *Renewing the City: Reflections on Community Development and Urban Renewal,* makes this observation about the trajectory of the book of Nehemiah: "It is the firsthand account of a high-level government official who takes a leave of absence, secures a government grant, organizes the largest volunteer missions project in biblical history, transforms a dangerous ghetto into a secure city, then repopulates it by inducing suburbanites to move in."[10] Lupton's book has been very influential and formative in helping me see Nehemiah as a template for community development and urban renewal.

This brings us back to some of the ideas, conversations, and questions posed previously in this chapter. What role does the church play in renewing the city? Is it simply populating heaven or is it also enacting social justice? The story of Nehemiah shows us the importance of both. I assert that under the banner of transformation or renewal, we find a reversal of the totality of original sin. Most often when we talk about the fall as recorded in Genesis 3, we limit its consequence to being exclusively man's relationship with God. Yes, that relationship had been broken. However, there was more that was broken. The fall was in fact three-dimensional: it involved a broken relationship with God (spiritual), a broken relationship with one another (social), and a broken relationship with creation (physical). On the flip side, what is the good news of the Kingdom of God? What were the dimensions or parameters of Christ's sacrificial death on the cross? In a word, everything that had been broken in the fall. "Every aspect of God's original design is marred, broken, and flawed. But here is the news that is the basis of the good news: everything that was lost in the fall was redeemed at the cross and one day will be totally restored. The redemption of the cross goes far beyond simply bringing us to heaven. In light of this, the gospel we share should address not only the spiritual consequences of our sins and rebellion but also the social and economic consequences."[11]

When it comes to renewing the city, Nehemiah offers us a template where these different dimensions are held up and equally pursued. We just might be surprised what we find hidden in the pages of this ancient book about a city in need of more than a facelift. Nehemiah led the

10. Lupton, *Renewing the City,* 9.
11. *To Transform a City,* 135.

efforts for city-wide community transformation. Here is how I define community transformation, "Community Transformation is the process where the church, motivated by the pervasive reality of the Kingdom of God, partners with the neighbourhood, city, businesses, schools, and non-profits to bring about healing, restoration, and wholeness in the emotional, spiritual, physical, social, and economic spheres of life." Keep that definition in mind as we now dive into Nehemiah and extract some principles.

The story of Nehemiah shows us the importance of addressing the spiritual as well as the physical. We see almost a dichotomy in the efforts of Ezra and Nehemiah and how they went about their respective roles involving Jerusalem. Ezra focused on the spiritual while Nehemiah focused on the physical. Ezra brought about spiritual revival on a certain level, but the city itself was still laid waste and vulnerable. Nehemiah rebuilt the city walls and not only secured the safety of the city, but he also buttressed its economic outlook. From this, we can fashion two summary equations:

- Beautiful city + no temple (love for God) = empty shell
- Revitalized temple (spiritual renewal) + unsafe or unhealthy city = vulnerable city

The first equation harkens back to a question posed at the outset of this book: what makes a city great? Can a city be truly great but lack a spiritual fervency and love for God? Does it simply become like a beautiful yet empty facade or shell that is amazing and beautiful on the outside but dead on the inside? Also, is the reverse just as bad? If all we have is spiritual renewal or revival but fail to let it penetrate the social and physical dimensions of life and the city, then we still end up with a vulnerable city. This reeks of neo-Gnosticism where too often as followers of Jesus, we can become so preoccupied with the spiritual that we fail to consider the physical. The reality is that we cannot separate the two.

As I thumb through the pages of Nehemiah, I've found numerous community transformation principles. This is far from an exhaustive list and may differ from others, but to me they highlight the parameters of renewing the city:

First, *there was a communal (shared) responsibility for the city and the sins within.* "Let your ear be attentive and your eyes open, to hear the prayer of your servant that I now pray before you day and night for the people of Israel your servants, confessing the sins of the people of Israel, which we have sinned against you. Even I and my father's house have sinned. We have acted very corruptly against you and have not kept the commandments, the statutes, and the rules that you commanded your servant Moses."[12] As soon as Nehemiah gets word of the deplorable state of Jerusalem, he immediately cries out to the Lord. Having grown up in exile beyond the boundaries of Israel and being generations removed from the original captivity, Nehemiah's response is intriguing. When he cries out to the Lord, he takes ownership of the sins of Israel . . . even though he wasn't even alive when they occurred! He played no role in the circumstances that led to captivity and exile. However, he shouldered Israel's sins and brought them before the Lord.

What if we adopted that posture in our cities? Recently I was listening to a podcast of Dr. John Perkins, the founder of the Christian Community Development Association[13] on the very subject of taking responsibility for our past sins. Whether it was the mistreatment of African-Americans, Native Americans / First Nations, or various other ethnic immigrant groups, we still share a responsibility to take corrective measures. What would happen if more people living in the city adopted the posture of Nehemiah in his humility and brokenness before the Lord? Too often when we look at our cities, we say, "It is not *our* problem." We try to absolve ourselves of taking responsibility and action. Income inequality and lack of affordable housing continue to plague Vancouver. We can throw our hands up in the air and claim that it's not our fault or responsibility; it's simply the impact of global market forces. But we can't. I see too many people, my family included, living under the enormous weight of unaffordable housing. It elevates stress and anxiety, and can lead to desperation. My city's flaws and sins are on me. It's the same for all of us. Will we cry out to the Lord on the behalf of our cities and shoulder the weight of responsibility for them? If we did, how might that reorient the fabric of church life and our role in the city?

Building off the first principle is the second, *the positions of influence we find ourselves in are the ways that each of us can leverage renewal.* At the end of the first chapter of Nehemiah, an odd sentence stands out:

12. Nehemiah 1:6–7.
13. www.ccda.org.

"Now I was cupbearer to the king."[14] After Nehemiah's prayer, we see this seemingly insignificant admission that he was a government employee. And yet this makes the unfolding story even more remarkable. He wasn't a religious or spiritual leader . . . a priest, a pastor, a bishop or anything like that. He worked for *the man*. However, as we read in the first six verses of chapter 2, he used his unique role and position to leverage the power, influence and affluence of a despot for the benefit of his city, Jerusalem.

What role are you in? What positions of influence do you find yourself in? While you may not be a spiritual rock star, there is most certainly a role for you to play, a powerful and influential one at that, in the role of community development and urban renewal. I am constantly humbled and amazed by the stories I hear from around the world of normal everyday *non-clergy* types who sacrifice much for the sake of their city. When it comes to our involvement in community transformation, one can argue that we need both types of leaders found in the book of Nehemiah—the Ezra-types (religious leaders) and the Nehemiah-types (non-religious leaders, government or business sector leaders). How can you leverage your position for God's plan and purposes to make your city a better place?

The third principle is one that I've really been mulling over lately and have seen firsthand. *Funding for community transformation will come from outside the church.* "And I said to the king, 'If it pleases the king, let letters be given me to the governors of the province Beyond the River, that they may let me pass through until I come to Judah, and a letter to Asaph, the keeper of the king's forest, that he may give me timber to make beams for the gates of the fortress of the temple, and for the wall of the city, and for the house that I shall occupy.' And the king granted me what I asked, for the good hand of my God was upon me."[15] Admittedly, I'm a rookie when it comes to involvement in community transformation endeavors. I feel as if I'm like a toddler learning to walk as I stumble about learning things on the fly. One of the truths that I've come to realize is that all of the resources we need for community development, transformation, and urban renewal are already available. Not only that, but they're not necessarily even found within the church. It could very well be that "non-Christian" entities, organizations, busi-

14. Nehemiah 1:11.
15. Nehemiah 2:7–9.

nesses, and non-profits will fund our efforts. This is exactly what we find in the opening chapters of Nehemiah.

Who funded Jerusalem's massive gentrification project? Nehemiah secured a government grant from a pagan king to rebuild God's city. Amazing! The resources that we need to see our cities renewed and redeveloped are right there in front of us. When we first began gathering supplies for urthTREK's[16] after-school longboarding club, we initially turned to the church and those who were supporting our church-planting efforts. Sure enough, we received a few small donations which were indeed a huge blessing. That allowed us to get started by purchasing eleven longboard decks for an incredibly discounted price. We were elated! However, we still needed to purchase the rest of what we needed; wheels, bearings, trucks, grip tape, helmets, slide gloves, kneepads—and all of a sudden I was overwhelmed and thousands of dollars short. Katie and I began buying supplies out of pocket slowly but surely. Several months later, we had only two complete longboards with nine more to go. I was discouraged. I petitioned churches again both locally in our network here and in the States, but we weren't getting any more funds. Out of frustration, I began looking for alternatives and then the light went on . . .

I decided to begin contacting various longboard manufacturers directly. I explained to them our desire to start an after-school long-boarding club for students from lower-income families, immigrants, and refugees. I fired off a volley of emails hoping for the best and not expecting anything in return. Immediately I received a phone call from one of the owners of a company here in Vancouver. He took the time to check out our website, our Facebook page, and even figure out who I was. When he called, he knew not only what we were about but who also I was as a person and that I was a church planter; he knew about my education and that I had just written a book. As he said that, I thought for sure we were toast, because I attempt to keep urthTREK somewhat separate from our church-planting efforts. It's not that I'm doing a bait-and-switch or anything like that. I'm motivated to do urthTREK because of the Kingdom of God. Anyway, the owner told me that he had three complete longboards to give to us. These were top-end boards. Later, through a donation, we bought another complete board from them for a greatly discounted price. Our longboard fleet was growing! Since then,

16. www.urthtrek.ca.

another company has supplied us with free helmets. And another long-boarding company in Edmonton will soon be sending us more boards and slide gloves. Now sitting in my living room are several thousand dollars' worth of longboarding equipment that would have taken us years to purchase at the rate we were going. Our experience verified Nehemiah's principle. The funding is out there. If we ask, we will receive.

Fourth, *before engagement in community transformation begins, there needs to be an assessment taken to determine the needs, ailments, and brokenness of the city.* Soon after arriving in Jerusalem, Nehemiah took a select few with him late one night to tour the city and assess the damage. "And I told no one what my God had put into my heart to do for Jerusalem."[17] The city was worse than he thought. "Then I said to them, 'You see the trouble we are in, how Jerusalem lies in ruins with its gates burned.'"[18] Robert Lupton does a masterful job in *Renewing the City* of retelling the story. When I read of the account of Nehemiah sneaking around the city in the middle of the night and assessing what needs to be done, I could almost imagine the scene unfolding and even the emotions that were going through Nehemiah at the time. Remarkable.

What we see from this passage (Nehemiah 2:11–17) is that before Nehemiah jumped into the throes of this gentrification project, he was detailed in the process of determining the state of the city and its pressing needs. He did his research and made an assessment, and only then did he take action. What are the needs in your community? How do you know? How did you find out? How will you find out? How then will you let that determine the trajectory for your activities in the city? Sure, Nehemiah could have come into Jerusalem with a pre-set plan and blueprints already in hand. Instead, he took stock of the dire situation and then created a plan accordingly. There is much to learn from this story.

The next principle extracted from Nehemiah builds off the third. *Urban renewal is a collaborative endeavor across tribal lines as well as with those "outside the faith."* If community transformation is to be our aim and focus, it is imperative that we learn to network extensively with those of differing theological persuasions as well as with those who are not followers of Jesus. The key idea to keep at the forefront of our minds is that God's heart and desire for transformation is larger than the church. We're not the exclusive brokers of community transformation.

17. Nehemiah 2:12.
18. Nehemiah 2:17.

As we've seen thus far, God has a heart and passion for the widow, the fatherless, and the foreigner. He is going to move to meet their needs with the church . . . or without the church. It would appear that he does not necessarily wait around for the church to decide whether or not to get engaged. This could explain why we find so many amazing organizations and non-profits which are pioneering care and concern for the needy in their neighbourhoods. For those who seek to be involved in community transformation, it therefore becomes essential to navigate inside these circles.

Be forewarned. Not everyone shares your theological, cultural, or moral convictions. On the other hand, if the goal is to see community transformation, where are the common touch-points for collaboration? If evangelicals refuse to come to the "party," then what is that communicating about what we believe about social issues, our neighborhoods, and cities?

The sixth principle found in Nehemiah is that *we trust in God's desire to see our cities renewed*. Facing ridicule for his desire to rebuild Jerusalem's walls, Nehemiah "replied to them, 'The God of heaven will make us prosper, and we his servants will arise and build, but you have no portion or right or claim in Jerusalem.'"[19] Nehemiah's confidence was not simply in the Lord, but also in the belief that God cared deeply about the renewal of Jerusalem. Nehemiah wasn't out blazing his own trail; rather, he acted solely out of a passionate conviction that this indeed was what God wanted.

Do we believe the same? Are we rooted in the conviction that God desires even more than we do to see our cities transformed? This transformation goes far beyond reclaiming historic buildings and creating trendy urban districts for young hipsters. It is much more comprehensive than that. God desires to see justice and equity as part of the urban fabric. He desires to see the captives set free, sight restored to the blind, debtors forgiven their debts, and so much more. When we engage in these activities, we are participating with what God desires.

The seventh principle uncovered in the book of Nehemiah is the reality that *not everyone is willing to be involved in community transformation*. Sometimes the genius of a book is found not in the main points that leap off the page, but in the small and almost hidden points that can be easily overlooked. In the third chapter, there is a vivid description of

19. Nehemiah 2:20.

those involved in the construction process and which parts of the wall they were rebuilding. Name after name is listed along with their activity. Eliashib was working on the Sheep Gate, the sons of Hassenaah built the Fish Gate, Meremoth was repairing a section, and the list goes on. Then in verse 5 there is an observation that stands in stark contrast, "And next to them the Tekoites repaired, but their nobles would not stoop to serve their Lord."[20] Maybe as he was penning the words, he pressed on his pen a little harder, smearing the ink as he recalled in frustration their aloofness.

Often we're confronted with the same reality. For a variety of reasons, there are those who simply will not be involved. Maybe there is just no place in their theology or eschatology for the renewal of our cities. There will be pushback. I've had people say to me, "Sean, while I appreciate your efforts for urban renewal, it is not the most important thing you need to be doing." They have urged me to do more "spiritual activities" like baptisms, discipleship, evangelism, leadership development. As I've said many times before, if we do all these activities in a cultural vacuum, we may never see our communities transformed. What will it take to see urban renewal as part of basic discipleship? The key is found in the Great Commission.

We typically interpret Jesus' call for us to engage the world as a purely spiritual activity—as if Jesus himself was a Gnostic. However, there is a key part of Jesus' commissioning of his followers that we either overlook and misinterpret. Jesus said, "[Teach] them to observe all that I have commanded you."[21] That begs the question: What did Jesus command us to do? A quick perusal of the Gospels reveals that Jesus took up is the same themes of social justice that first emerged in the Old Testament, such as the preferential treatment of the poor, the marginalized, the orphan, foreigner, widow, sinner, and so forth. If we are to teach new disciples everything that Jesus commanded and exemplified, wouldn't community transformation then be one by-product, since we would be engaged in activities similar to what Jesus did? Keep in mind, once you begin talking about social issues, there will be those who will distance themselves from you.

The eight principle is *urban renewal ought not to simply be a government initiative or a business idea from a venture capitalist. Pastors,*

20. Nehemiah 3:5.
21. Matthew 28:20.

church planters, and other Christians who have a heart for the city should be willing to take the plunge. Again, in Nehemiah's attention to detail, we read of the peculiarity of those involved in the rebuilding process. What is interesting in the lists that he provides is that we read such things as, "Then Eliashib the high priest rose up with his brothers the priests, and they built the Sheep Gate. After him the priests, the men of the sur-rounding area, repaired. Above the Horse Gate the priests repaired, each one opposite his own house."[22] The spiritual leaders were just as much part of the rebuilding process as everyone else! There was no dichotomy between those who did "spiritual" activities while everyone else wielded a hammer or chisel. They were all part of the team that rebuilt the walls of Jerusalem. The application for today is that community transforma-tion is an activity that all should participate in equally.

Across the pages of Nehemiah, there are countless observations one could make that yield practical and relevant principles that we can mine and extract for use today. The ones I have highlighted make up just a small fraction of all the nuggets waiting to be unearthed. My goal here is not to be exhaustive, but simply to point out that the book of Nehemiah is actually very relevant and applicable for those who desire to be about community transformation. In closing this chapter, let me leave you with two more principles worthy of sober consideration.

The pursuit of seeing the Kingdom of God become a tangible reality in our neighborhoods will require pioneers who are prepared to sacrifice much. Urban renewal and community transformation is not for the weak of heart. We read in Nehemiah:

> Moreover, from the time that I was appointed to be their governor in the land of Judah, from the twentieth year to the thirty-second year of Artaxerxes the king, twelve years, neither I nor my broth-ers ate the food allowance of the governor. The former governors who were before me laid heavy burdens on the people and took from them for their daily ration forty shekels of silver. Even their servants lorded it over the people. But I did not do so because of the fear of God. I also persevered in the work on this wall, and we acquired no land, and all my servants were gathered there for the work. Moreover, there were at my table 150 men, Jews and officials, besides those who came to us from the nations that were around us. Now what was prepared at my expense for each day was one ox and six choice sheep and birds, and every ten days

22. Nehemiah 3:1, 22, 28.

all kinds of wine in abundance. Yet for all this I did not demand
the food allowance of the governor, because the service was too
heavy on this people. Remember for my good, O my God, all that
I have done for this people.[23]

Nehemiah had every right to live in affluence and luxury. Instead,
he sacrificed his privileged life for the greater good of the city. He stepped
away from his place in government service in Susa, trekked back to
Jerusalem, and in the face of overwhelming odds and circumstances, led
the people to rebuild. As governor, he did not abuse his power or even
take what was rightfully his.

How much is urban renewal or community transformation worth
to us? How much are we willing to sacrifice and lay down for the betterment of our city? Even in occupational ministry circles, most of us
are on the treadmill of upward mobility. Are we career-oriented first
and foremost? Or is the goal to see our cities renewed so paramount
that everything else takes a backseat? I'm not suggesting that we can't or
shouldn't use our skills, expertise, and education for the betterment of
the city. Quite the opposite. But what we find in the person of Nehemiah
was someone willing to step away from comfort, security (financial and
personal), and probably a largely carefree lifestyle and instead dedicate
his life to the rebuilding of Jerusalem. Are we willing to do likewise?

The last principle from Nehemiah is that *urban renewal and redevelopment brought about economic stability, a renewed spiritual vitality,
and a reinvigorated care and concern for the poor and needy.* The recon-
struction of Jerusalem was more than a construction project. Through
securing the city's walls, the local economy was stabilized, safety was
restored, and stability ensued. With these in place came a renewed passion for worship. God's goodness was recounted and extolled. So many
amazing elements and events happened simply through the reconstruc-
tion of the city walls. Should we not have this same kind of expectation
as a result of our involvement in rebuilding the city? Do we believe that
this is what God desires? As I wrote in *Metrospiritual*, "A neighborhood's
renaissance can lead to a spiritual reformation. As these old communities revitalize there is vibrancy that returns, creating a buzz, and even
momentum. Pretty soon this movement takes on a life of its own where
urban renewal is widespread as it reaches a tipping point. Could this be

---

23. Nehemiah 5:14–19.

one of the triggers that leads to a spiritual reformation, where people's hearts are open to spiritual issues?"[24]

Nehemiah, although an ancient book, has much for us to consider today as we live in and daily engage the global city. It provides the impetus and even a template to participate in the whole of urban life in both the physical and spiritual realms. They are symbiotic. We can no longer separate one from the other. We see this in Jesus; he forgave sinners and healed the sick, he taught the mysteries of God and raised the dead, and he fed the multitudes and pointed people to the reality of the Kingdom of God that was crashing in on them. Jesus, like Nehemiah, gives us not only the theology behind what we do but also a blueprint and a template.

24. Benesh, *Metrospiritual*, 48.

9

Jesus and the Ancient Urban Church

TRANSITIONING FROM NEHEMIAH TO Jesus is a huge span in relation to both time and culture. Much happened in the intervening centuries politically and in the continued development of the urban fabric of the ancient city. After Nehemiah successfully led the rebuilding of the walls of Jerusalem, the condition of Israel continued to decline as the nation again turned away from the Lord. There are large gaps in the story of biblical urban development in the prophetic, poetic and other historical books of the Old Testament that I'm purposely skipping over. Books such at *A Theology as Big as the City* by Ray Bakke or *Urban Ministry* by Harvie Conn and Manuel Ortiz do a remarkable job of walking through these eras and fleshing out a theological understanding of the development of cities. For my purposes and the trajectory of this book, I find it essential to rather quickly make the transition to Jesus and the early church for reasons that will soon be evidenced in this chapter.

The teachings and the earthly life of Jesus have been under constant scrutiny from even before his crucifixion up to the present day. In our westernized cognitive framework of reductionist thinking, we've reduced Jesus to mere sound bites, pithy statements, or a litany of how-to's. The Jesus of the early years of my Christian faith stands in stark contrast to the Jesus I see today in the global urban cities. How can that be? In the formative years of my new faith in Christ, during college, I never really considered whether Jesus was rural or urban. Obviously he is neither and both at the same time, but I only knew the rural Jesus because that was my dominant cultural and even theological lens. It seemed like whenever I read the gospels, Jesus was always in the wilderness. I envisioned him walking dusty roads in sandals and a toga as he went from small village to small village. Then after his death, resurrection, and ascension,

the church hung out in Jerusalem until they were scattered when persecution broke out. Like scattering mice when the light is turned on, many
of them fled the city and went to live elsewhere. I imagined them hiding
out in caves, forests, and in something like hippie communes. Never did
I connect the dots that in fact, first of all, Jerusalem was a decent-sized
city, and secondly, that the church actually scattered to the largest urban
centers of the day. In hindsight, the scattering seemed like a strategic
initiative as the Roman roads carried the church and the good news to
the cultural hotspots of the age, the political centers, the transportation
crossroads, the economic kingpins, and the foci of military might. The
church was birthed in the city, fled to other cities, and took root in the
city.

In this chapter, I will take a step back and look at the nature of the
urban centers of the time of Jesus as well as the urban milieu that the early
urban church found itself in. The point isn't to create an "urban Jesus"
who displaces the "rural Jesus" in our psyche and imagination, because
neither the city nor the countryside can contain God. He is ever-present
in both. However, I do believe that a corrective measure is needed to
emphasize the early church's urbanity. The locus of the story begins with
the person of Jesus himself. Is it even necessary and appropriate to argue
for or against Jesus' rural-versus-urban roots and lifestyle? If put in our
modern context, was Jesus a latte-drinking, techno-listening, urban loft-
living urbanite? Or was he a blue jeans-wearing, cheap coffee-drinking,
country music-listening, ranch-house, split level-living rural- or small-
town dweller? With so much emphasis made today on adopting Jesus'
incarnational approach to life and ministry, how much of it do we actually "go and do likewise?" Is there then a contrast in the New Testament
between an agrarian Jesus and someone like an urban apostle Paul?
"Some scholarship argues that way. Jesus' early ministry, it is argued, was
located in the Galilean countryside's small and often anonymous places.
How do we respond to this argument? Without a doubt, Jesus' transition from his public ministry to his postresurrection church generally
involved a transition from smaller population to larger ones."[1]

The story of the cities in the Ancient Near East started off along
the banks of exotic streams. Their development stemmed from necessity
and the needs of efficiency, much like cities today. "Cities form because
they concentrate goods, services, and ideas than can be exchanged in a

---

1. Conn and Ortiz, *Urban Ministry*, 120.

manner that minimizes transportation costs."[2] Over the centuries, these cities matured and multiplied. "To move from the cities of the Ancient Near East to those of Jesus' day is to take a large leap. Cities, after all, change and adapt in function as the social systems of which they are a part change. Scholarship is learning that we cannot judge the Bible's preindustrial cities by industrial city models."[3] We recall that the conditions present in this region acted as the perfect catalyst for urban development. "The alluvial basin between the Tigris and Euphrates rivers, in contemporary Iraq, proved an ideal environment for a precipitous leap to urbanism."[4] In regards to the physical size and population of these ancient cities, they would be deemed unimpressive by modern standards. "Even by the third millennium [BC], the powerful 'metropolis' of Ur may have been no more than 150 acres and accommodated roughly twenty-four thousand people."[5] However, when Jesus stepped onto the stage of history, the dynamics, size, and scope of urban life had changed radically.

By the time the first century rolled around, there was a decisive shift in population and power. For centuries the region that is now Iraq housed the largest cities in the world . . . Babylon, Ur, Uruk, Seleucia. Each century saw the urban populations of these burgeoning cities grow; twenty thousand, thirty thousand, one hundred thousand, one hundred and fifty thousand, three hundred and fifty thousand, and all of the way up to the six hundred thousand people were purported to have lived in Seleucia around 300 B.C. Then the center of power, population, and influence shifted to Europe. Rome became the new super city. When Jesus walked around the Galilean countryside, Rome's population had mushroomed to around one million inhabitants. From the second-century B.C. to the fourth-century A.D., Rome was the global super-power before the population balance shifted to east Asia. It wasn't again until the nineteenth-century, a full fifteen hundred years later, that Europe claimed the largest city in the world (London). Not only was Rome a large city but the other cities at the time of Christ and the early church were also growing. Jerusalem's population could have been as high as two hundred thousand people, Corinth and Thessalonica were similar

2. Levinson and Krizek, *Planning for Place and Plexus*, 195.

3. *Urban Ministry*, 116.

4. Kotkin, *The City*, 4.

5. Ibid.

in size, and by 100 A.D., Ephesus boasted an urban population of close to a half a million. Truly the city had made significant strides.

The world of Jesus in the first-century was hardly a story of a Messiah in rural obscurity. There were plenty of places globally where the story could have unfolded, but the Messiah for the world came to the most prominent urbanized region of the world. Ray Bakke writes of this epoch: "First-century Palestine was a far more international and politicized environment than the Sunday-school literature had communicated."[6] He adds, "Josephus tells us there were more than two hundred cities and villages in Galilee."[7] In comparison to the then "mega-cities," the "city" of Jesus' birth, Bethlehem, possibly housed a thousand inhabitants.[8] Where he grew up, Nazareth, wasn't much larger, reaching a ceiling of upwards of two thousand people.[9] Despite his small-town upbringing, after Jesus launched his public ministry, he had Jerusalem on his heart and mind. Jesus visited there (Matt. 21:10; Mark 11:11), was tempted there (Luke 4:9), lamented its fate (Matt. 23:37; Luke 13:34), wept over it (Luke 19:41), made it his ultimate destination (Luke 9:51–53), and so on. Jerusalem was the focus for what he knew he needed to do.

Many who flock to the city do so to try to fulfill their hopes and aspirations. Jesus went to the city to die for the world; today the world moves to the city in hopes of finding life. What great news! The Savior who died and was raised again in a city now is drawing billions to the city. The geography of mission has decisively shifted to the city. Was this God's plan all along in the creation of the city? Was God the great Author of the city whose origins ultimately were the result of divine intention? Could the purpose of the city then be about mission and accessibility to the good news? The good news is that not only is Jesus' death and resurrection here and available, but it's more accessible than ever before. *For God so loved the world that he drew them to the city to hear the good news.*

One of the critiques that I hear at times is whether I'm placing too much emphasis on place, and in particular, the city. That is a valid point. Most often in the drama of humanity, we narrow our focus to the actors on a stage, which in this case is people. However, every story or

6. Bakke, *A Theology as Big as the City*, 130.

7. Ibid.

8. BBC, "King Herod."

9. Wikimedia Foundation Inc, "Nazareth."

drama has a stage, a setting, or a context. It is this context that acts as the backdrop in order for mankind to live. By emphasizing the city is not making a case for some obscure point in constructing a theology; rather, it is the locus of humanity throughout the Old Testament starting in Enoch, embedded in the life of Jesus, and inseparable from the early church, as we will see. Whether we're referring to theology, textual exegesis, or cultural exegesis, context is everything. Today with over half the world's population now living in the city—it's above eighty percent in Canada and the United States—we cannot relegate place (or the city) to the obscure background. The city is the context in which the drama of humanity is being played out. More than simply a collection of concrete, glass, and steel, the city not only provides the context but also the factors influencing those who reside within. "Cities bring people, technology, ideas, and equipment together, using proximity and concentration to foster innovation and productivity."[10]

In our western worldview, we're still unsure exactly what to do with the concept of place. Sometimes it would appear that those outside of the church have a deeper appreciation of place while we're still lagging behind. A century of enduring the divisive effects of the "great reversal" of the early 1900s has left many with an under-developed theology of place. "For most of the past century, conservative churches emphasized personal salvation with virtually no expectation of corporate change. Whereas historic movements like the Great Awakening and Wesley revivalism had emphasized confrontation of both personal and systemic sin, the modern evangelical movement, couched in the hyperindividualism of the West, concentrated almost exclusively on private faith. For the majority of the 1900s, churches ignored the injustices of the culture in which they existed."[11] It is this divide which hampered the church's involvement in the city. Many simply opted out of social responsibility. "Perhaps 90 percent of the real barriers to effective city ministry today are not in the city; there are inside the church. Our leadership and our people are unprepared or unwilling to risk. We are afraid that our denominations will label us liberal and/or cut our funding."[12] It all ties into place. Worshippers of God throughout the ages understood the importance of place. Place played a key role in God's promise to Abraham

10. Staley and Moore, *Mobility First*, 40.

11. Dorrell, *Trolls & Truth*, 151.

12. Bakke and Sharpe, *Street Signs*, 122.

and his future descendents. As we explored in the previous chapter, Nehemiah was distressed over the condition of place (Jerusalem). So also in the New Testament, where we find Jesus weeping over the same city. Lastly, it is this same city—which has caused so much grief, condemnation, and distress to this very day—that will be our future home someday. Heaven is a city.

Upon exiting the Garden of Eden, humanity transitioned straight to the city which served as the backdrop of the Old Testament. It should be no surprise that the church was birthed at Pentecost in the city. Notice where Jesus told them to go. "And while staying with them he ordered them not to depart from Jerusalem, but to wait for the promise of the Father."[13] Coincidence? Jesus could have ordered them to wait by the lake, on the mountain top, or in the depth of the wilderness. Instead, he tells them to stay put in the city. When the disciples were gathered there, they asked Jesus about the nature of the Kingdom. They were still anticipating a restoration of place. In their minds, Jesus would now, post-resurrection, clear out Rome once and for all and restore Jerusalem (city) and Israel (place) to prominence. Instead Jesus expands the scope of the locus of mission. The outward trajectory of the Kingdom is not limited by ethnicity or culture. As the first generation of globe-trotting evangelists were commissioned, the risen Christ told them, "But you will receive power when the Holy Spirit has come upon you, and you will be my witnesses in Jerusalem and in all Judea and Samaria, and to the end of the earth."[14]

This all goes back to the theological questions we explored earlier in the book. Was the city simply a product of human development and progression? Or was the city the apex of creativity and innovation? Or was the city the result of divine intention? While answering this requires a degree of theological speculation, the more I explore these topics, the more I find myself leaning towards the city as the result of divine intention. Sure, God could have, or probably did, use the first two options, but like Aslan the lion in *The Horse and His Boy,* he was the one pushing the circumstances along with young Shasta. Apart from the first three chapters in Genesis, the drama of humanity played out in the city. So it is no small leap to contend that the birth of the church in the city was a strategic initiative.

13. Acts 1:4.
14. Acts 1:8.

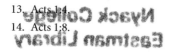

God, the ultimate strategist, set in motion the birth of the church and the rapid spread of the good news in the city. What better place in the world to fan the flames of the birth of a movement than the city! "Now there were dwelling in Jerusalem Jews, devout men from every nation under heaven."[15] People from all over the "known world" descended upon Jerusalem for Pentecost. There were representatives from three different continents (Asia, Africa, and Europe) who listened intently as Peter proclaimed the good news of Jesus and the Kingdom. This global gathering is not unlike what we find in our cities today. It is indicative of my own neighborhood. The church was birthed as a multi-cultural and multi-ethnic urban movement. As the worshippers of God from the nations that were in Jerusalem understood how Jesus fit into the equation as the promised and long-awaited Messiah, a fire was lit that has only grown and intensified over the following two thousand years. The persecution that was intended to crush the growing numbers of Jesus-followers ironically had the effect of scattering the faithful, who took the gospel to other cities. "And there arose on that day a great persecution against the church in Jerusalem, and they were all scattered throughout the regions of Judea and Samaria, except the apostles."[16] This paints the backdrop of the rest of the New Testament, especially the Pauline epistles.

What was the nature of these collected epistles? They were letters written to urban Christians spread throughout the Roman Empire who were having difficulty understanding what it meant to follow Jesus in the city. The reality of the Kingdom was crashing in all around these new believers who were later dubbed *Christians* by their mockers. The Kingdom of God, which was "the central message of Jesus,"[17] was now invading how they lived in the city. The scope of the good news was so much more counter-cultural and counter-intuitive than they could have surmised. It began breaking down ethnic, linguistic, cultural, gender, and religious walls. This in turn created new tensions. All of a sudden, these new urban-dwelling Christians had to begin struggling through what it meant to follow Jesus in the city. What exactly did that look like? Each city posed its own challenges, whether it had to do with the hostility of Jews and Gentiles or wondering what to do about men who visited temple prostitutes. Jewish Christians understood the Law

15. Acts 2:5.

16. Acts 8:1.

17. Ladd, *A Theology of the New Testament*, 55.

and the prophets and could acknowledge that Jesus was indeed the long-awaited Messiah. They were theologically and Scripturally rooted and grounded. Their struggle was now what it meant to live under grace. The Gentile Christians, on the other hand, were a different lot. Coming from a culture that worshipped all kinds of local and national gods, they were on a steep learning curve as they struggled to embrace and defend monotheism.

It can be argued, then, that Paul's letters were addressed to urban Christians who were struggling with what it meant to now follow Jesus in the city. It was—and is—messy. People had plenty of pre-conversion baggage, regardless of whether they were Jew or Gentile. Each set of baggage was unique and posed a different set of challenges. We read in the letter to the Galatians how the Jewish Christians were under pressure to slide back into Judaism and life under the Law. "Paul saw clearly that the issues raised by the subversive activities of the Judaizers had wider implications than were realized by the dominant Jewish Christian element, and the rapidity with which the Galatians had departed from the freedom of the gospel served as a goad to the apostle."[18] On the other hand, the Gentiles were an ornery group as we find, for example, in Corinth. "The Corinthian church was bound to be troubled with many problems arising from the impact of Christianity on its pagan environment."[19] I can imagine Paul, after getting word back about the condition of some of these churches, sitting down in disbelief and frustration about them "not getting it." Maybe he sighs and weeps out of desperation over their toddler-like ways as they grasp and fumble with following Jesus. Surely, the city posed a unique set of challenges. Men who were used to living loose lives under pagan gods now had to say no to their sexual impulses. Paul dealt with brawlers, drunkards, swindlers, idolaters, and so forth.[20] Rather than normally eating meat that was dedicated to the gods, now there arose division within the church about what to do.[21] As for the Jewish believers, he had to constantly remind them that they are justified by faith and not by the law.[22]

18. Guthrie, *New Testament Introduction*, 482.

19. Ibid., 433.

20. 1 Corinthians 5:9–13.

21. 1 Corinthians 8.

22. Galatians 2:15–16.

Today, we can read these letters and presume to pat ourselves on the back, because of how far we've evolved spiritually from the days of these theological Neanderthals. We have seminaries, endless volumes and tomes on theology, and of course *Veggie Tales* cartoons to teach our kids about God. However, we struggle just as much as the early church did in living out our faith in the context of the city. While we may not struggle with issues of temple prostitution, meat sacrificed to idols, or bowing down before statues of Zeus or Apollo or Athena or declaring "Caesar is Lord," we're still bombarded daily with the idols of our own age. Our idols are more "sophisticated," whether they be things like materialism, consumerism, social status, or even syncretism as we blend the good news of the Kingdom with the latest self-help guides, ladder-climbing techniques in business, or with the various religions and spiritualities housed within our cities. If Paul were alive today writing to the church in Vancouver, Chicago, Miami, Montreal, or New York, what would he say? What are our blind spots? Where have we slipped into idol worship, gross immorality, or syncretism? Now the urban nature of the books of the New Testament carry more weight once we locate them in their proper place—the city.

Paul's journeys took him to some of the leading urban centers of the day. There, he worked with the newly forming and growing Christian communities as they faced considerable obstacles. Peter also wrote to newborn churches in the Diaspora (the Jewish believers who had fled Jerusalem and Judea in the face of mounting persecution) to give them help, hope, and instruction.

In his book *Seeking the Welfare of the City: Christians as Benefactors and Citizens*, Bruce Winter makes the argument that Peter was drawing the attention of the church back to Israel's exile and creating parallels. As Israel was forced into exile under the Babylonians, so too did the followers of Jesus become an exilic people.

> Likewise in 1 Peter 1:11, the Christians are aptly called 'elect sojourners of the Dispersion'. This is a theological and not sociological description of the letter's recipients. It was an appropriate phrase for the elect pilgrim people of God in their present temporal situation. Far removed from their promised inheritance or homeland, they are assured that they will reach their promised destination preserved by the power of God. They were not to be disappointed with the nature of their inheritance as were the exiles when they returned from their Babylonian captivity (1:4–9).

They are not to retaliate, but to bless (3:9). The twin concepts 'to do good' and 'to seek peace' are picked up later in the letter (3:11) in a citation from Psalm 34:12–16, but the language is also reminiscent of the theme of Jeremiah to seek the welfare of the city and to pray for its peace (29:7). The parallels between Jeremiah 29 and 1 Peter are compelling.[23]

Many of us have been drawn to the prophet Jeremiah's words from the Lord to exiled Israel. "Thus says the LORD of hosts, the God of Israel, to all the exiles whom I have sent into exile from Jerusalem to Babylon: Build houses and live in them; plant gardens and eat their produce. Take wives and have sons and daughters; take wives for your sons, and give your daughters in marriage, that they may bear sons and daughters; multiply there, and do not decrease. But seek the welfare of the city where I have sent you into exile, and pray to the LORD on its behalf, for in its welfare you will find your welfare."[24] The early Christians were fleeing for their lives. Peter's reminder was to breathe hope into this scattered people. His appeal was not simply for them to hang on somehow until the Lord's return. Instead, he almost chides them to get involved in their cities. First Peter is about the city. "Of all the letters in the New Testament, it is 1 Peter which considers the theme of the welfare of the city in detail."[25] To the Jewish Christian, this has a ring of familiarity to it. We see Peter using words like "exiles" which may have either smarted a bit or offered hope. He then commands them to seek the welfare of the city. "Keep your conduct among the Gentiles honorable, so that when they speak against you as evildoers, they may see your good deeds and glorify God on the day of visitation."[26] Peter does a masterful job of pushing the church towards the city.

First Peter as a letter to urban Christians in the first century has a tone to it that is applicable for today's urban Christians. Winter writes:

There are three reasons given why transient Christians should be concerned for the welfare of the hostile and ungrateful city. The fundamental purpose of the elect race, the royal priesthood, the holy nation, the formerly stateless group who were now the people of God, was to declare the virtues or characteristics of the

23. Winter, *Seek the Welfare of the City*, 16.
24. Jeremiah 29:4–7.
25. *Seek the Welfare of the City*, 12.
26. 1 Peter 2:12.

notes that "Christians could be found in all parts of the empire by 200."[2] The manner in which the church spread was sporadic, not uniform, and achieved its greatest momentum as it headed towards and eventually across Europe. While much of the drama in church history found its context in the city, it would appear that there's been a recent course correction that has driven the church not to merely engage in mission in the city, but to do so as a strategic initiative. I will touch on that later in this chapter.

The early church blossomed despite times of heavy persecution. The seed of the gospel spread as Christians bore this "*missional* DNA" within them. It wasn't merely that they carried the good news as if it were a tote bag; it was who they were, their identity, a part of the genetic DNA. Alan Hirsch, in *The Forgotten Ways*, notes the spiritual genetic make-up of Christians who have the latent power of the Spirit embedded into their DNA.

> So what then is mDNA? The *m* is inserted purely to differentiate it from the biological version – it simply means *missional* DNA. So what DNA does for biological systems, mDNA does for ecclesial ones. And with this concept / metaphor I hope to explain why the presence of a simple, intrinsic, reproducible, central guiding mechanism is necessary for the reproduction and sustainability of genuine missional movements. As an organism holds together, and each cell understands its function in relation to its DNA, so the church finds its reference point in its built-in DNA. As DNA carries the genetic coding, and therefore the life, of a particular organism, so too mDNA codes Apostolic Genius (the life force that pulsated through the New Testament church in other expressions of apostolic Jesus movements throughout history.

The church experienced explosive growth across the Roman Empire despite overwhelming obstacles and difficult conditions. Hirsch lists the factors that were daily realities of the church in this era: They were an illegal religion throughout this period, they didn't have any church buildings as we know them, they didn't have the Scriptures as we know them, they had neither an institution nor the professional form of leadership normally associated with such an institution, and so forth.[3]

---

2. Ibid.
3. Ibid., 18–19.

The decisive turning point in this rapid growth can be found in Acts 16. Paul and his companions were in what is now Turkey. Barred by the Spirit of Jesus from heading north and east, they went west—and found themselves in Europe.[4] This made Europe for centuries the center of gravity for the gospel and church expansion.

But it was not the only place where the gospel was taken. Too often, as those who've taken church history courses or have read books on the subject have found, there is certainly a Euro-centric bias to this historical narrative. While this makes sense in that the bulk of the story took place in the European context alongside other time-periods such as the Dark Ages, the Renaissance, the Reformation, and the Enlightenment, it was never exclusively a European story. One of the requirements of my doctoral program was to take a course overseas. This two-week intensive course is offered in a variety of places such as China, India, the Middle East and Ethiopia. One of its goals is to explore the global church and to see what God is doing in the world, by interacting with government, non-governmental organizations and Christian leaders, and university professors. I chose to go to China.

Part of our whirlwind journey took us away from the coastal cities. We rode inland on an overnight train for ten hours to Xi'an. After a rough night, I spent the morning gazing out the window, peering through the smog-drenched countryside at the region's unique topography. As we got off the train we could already feel the distinctive nature of the city. Xi'an is an ancient city, having been the cultural and political center in China in the eleventh century BC.[5] The old part of the city is ringed by a wall, one of the best-preserved in China. In between our classroom sessions, we engaged in the local tourist activities whether it was riding bicycles around the circumference of the city wall or viewing the famous terra cotta soldiers. However, one of the most memorable experiences was visiting a Christian pagoda.

Near the pagoda was a stele, or ancient stone tablet, that had been buried for over eight centuries before being unearthed in the seventeenth century. It became known as the Nestorian Tablet—"a two-ton stone tablet standing more than nine feet tall and three feet wide, . . . inscribed with 1,900 beautiful carved Chinese characters. It was an official account of the first major Christian mission to China, an event

4. Acts 16:6–10.

5. Wikimedia Foundation Inc., "Xi'an"

that took place in A.D. 635, a short seventeen years after the start of the Tang Dynasty (A.D. 618–907), one of the most brilliant eras in China's history."[6] That event allowed the gospel to begin taking root in China under Alopen, the leader of the Nestorians (or Syro-Oriental Church). "Three years after the arrival of Alopen, the emperor issued the edict allowing the diffusion of Christianity in China and also permitted the first Syro-Oriental monastery to be built in the capital."[7]

We parked at the bottom of a hill and had a little hike to get up to the pagoda. On arriving, we were greeted by the resident Buddhist monk. The opening in the bottom level is still used as a Buddhist shrine. To access the upper levels meant climbing a rickety twenty-foot ladder the monk had found for us. It wasn't for the faint of heart. As we climbed out towards the edge of an open window, we found traces of the Nestorians who had trekked to China all the way from modern-day Iraq in the seventh century. Etched into the bricks, like ancient graffiti, was clearly Syriac script.

The Nestorian Tablet reminds us that even while Christianity was flourishing in Europe, God was still expanding his church elsewhere. While it is true that for centuries the storyline and most of its major players were located in Europe, there is today a new and very different reality as the locus of the center of gravity of the global church has shifted to Africa and Asia. "The economic, political, and cultural dynamics of the first three centuries of church history affected virtually every aspect of the nascent church's development. The Western church of the twenty-first century shares little contextual similarity with the early church."[8]

In the last half of the twentieth century, as a new Europe emerged from the ashes of the Second World War, the old world dominated by Europe ended, and a new mass movement began reshaping and impacting the global landscape. Increasingly, it is in the twenty-first century cities where this drama is being played out. Urbanization, immigration, and rapid globalization have all had a reorienting effect on our cities. And as Philip Jenkins writes in *The Next Christendom*, woven into these historic seismic shifts is religion. "Over the past five centuries, the story of Christianity has been inextricably bound up with that of Europe and European-derived civilizations overseas, above all in North America.

6. Aikman, *Jesus in Beijing*, 20.

7. Uhalley and Wi, *China and Christianity*, 13.

8. McAlpine, *Scared Space for the Missional Church*, 66.

Until recently, the overwhelming majority of Christians have lived in white nations, allowing some thinkers to speak of 'European Christian' civilization. Over the last century, however, the center of gravity in the Christian world has shifted inexorably southward, to Africa and Latin America. Today, the largest Christian communities on the planet are to be found in those regions."[9]

Here's one example of how things have changed, according to Jenkins: "In 1800, perhaps 1 percent of all Protestant Christians lived outside Europe and North America. By 1900 that number had risen to 10 percent, and this proved enough of a critical mass to support further expansion. Today, the figure stands around two-thirds of all Protestants."[10] Keep in mind that the setting in which these changes have taken place is the city. Whether it is the re-centering of Christianity, mass urbanization, globe-trotting immigration, and ever-denser globalization, it would appear that they are all related. And all are linked inextricably to the rise of the global city. Author Jeb Brugmann contends that instead of looking at the multiplicity of cities worldwide, we should begin to simply look at it as *the City*. "The media have been keen to report that 'half the world's population now live in cities,' but we are overlooking the main event: half the world *has become the City*."[11]

Without a doubt the city is the focus of mission. Over the past couple of centuries, the geography of mission has shifted. Early mission attempts focused on the coastal regions, whether in Asia, Africa, or South America. Ships delivered these pioneer missionaries, these bearers of the good news as well as European culture, to shores far from home. In being faithful to God in their era, these sacrificial saints left much behind for the sake of the gospel, even when their worldview was obscured by colonial ambitions and cultural superiority—the "white man's burden." Most of us are oblivious to our own cultural blind spots that in some ways can taint the good news, but we rejoice in God's grace and patience regardless. After the beachheads in these coastal regions were established, the second wave of mission found these missionaries venturing further inland. Many of us can recall hearing or reading riveting stories of missionaries coming in contact with indigenous peoples who had yet to be exposed to Western culture. Up to this point, most of what took

9. Jenkins, *The Next Christendom*, 1.

10. Ibid., 45.

11. Brugmann, *Welcome to the Urban Revolution*, 10.

place, while it may have included the city, was not particularly focused on cities. In our imaginations, we envision these missionaries in pith helmets wielding machetes hacking their way through thick jungles in hopes of reaching primitive villages who had yet to hear the good news. The valor and courage of these missionaries is to be commended.

The third wave in mission is one I can vividly recall learning about in college as we talked at length of unreached people groups and the 10/40 window, as the mission focus shifted to this geographic region that encompassed north Africa, the Middle East, and south Asia. This was the part of the world where the gospel was getting the least amount of traction. Like each wave before, this was indeed pioneer work as missionaries trekked into regions where Christianity was not looked upon favorably for a variety of reasons. Most of this region housed the densest populations of Muslims, Hindus, and Buddhists. While in college I served as vice-president of an on-campus missions club. Through that experience as well as simply being on campus at Grace University, I was exposed to what God was doing globally. I can still picture in my mind standing and talking with some of the older saints who embodied the second wave of mission as they told stories of taking the gospel to loin-cloth-wearing villagers deep in the jungles of Central and South America. I sat and listened to the stories of those who were first on the scene after missionary Jim Elliot was killed with four others in Ecuador in 1952. I also was exposed to those who were living in the 10/40 Window in the Middle East. I listened in amazement to their stories. But then something changed. There were seismic shifts already at hand globally that were reorienting the fabric of the world's population. As Brad Smith notes in *City Signals*, the world was moving to the city. "In the US, the urban migration over 100 years has drastically changed US society. Even more so, in places such as China, India, and Africa, people are moving from villages that have ancestral roots, beliefs, and traditions that have remained largely unchanged for several hundred years. The city turns these belief systems upside-down and opens them up for whole new ways – either for good or for bad. Never has the world been so open to new ideas and new faith."[12]

Smith goes on to trace the decisive shift of the world's population to the city. He writes, "The gateway to engaging this newly connected

12. Smith, *City Signals*, 39.

and accessible world is your own city."[13] Welcome to the fourth wave of mission. While the first three eras or waves of mission are still ongoing, the momentum has moved to the city. Instead of us going to the world, the world is coming to our cities. Bob Roberts Jr. writes in his book, *Glocalization: How Followers of Jesus Engage a Flat World*, "It's not about missions; it's about globalization. People have become global beings. The problem with the word global is that it says 'way over there.' That is incomplete. It's way over there and here at the same time. That is why it's *glocal*."[14] The church was birthed in an urban context, and now, two thousand years later, it is most decisively an urban movement. It is as if the church is rediscovering its missional thrust in places like North America and Europe, a return to the urban milieu in which it was born. Roberts further notes:

> The early church was foremost an urban movement: first from Jerusalem, then to Antioch, and eventually spreading out into the villages and other cities. To a large degree, much of missions for the past two hundred years has been in the villages and rural areas. Cities like Bangkok or Nairobi served as the center for mission agency headquarters. However, the focus of the ministry was not Nairobi or Bangkok but the villages and rural areas. That is changing today—the nationals in the church in Nairobi, Bangkok, Jakarta, Seoul, and dozens of other cities are reclaiming their cities and spurring on the spread of Christianity at a pace and in ways never seen before. This will continue in the future.[15]

This mass exodus to the city, due in part to heightened globalization, is what Brugmann calls the Great Migration. "Nothing matches the sheer numbers, momentum, and universality of the Great Migration to cities that began in eighteenth-century Europe and accelerated exponentially into a global phenomenon in the twentieth century."[16] This has most certainly reoriented the fabric of our cities, but it is also recalibrating the church. We're living in an era of ever-denser globalization. In my own neighborhood, I can worship with a first-generation Mandarin-speaking Chinese church, a first-generation Korean church, a second-generation Korean church, and an assortment of multi-ethnic and multi-cultural

13. Ibid., 41.

14. Roberts, *Glocalization*, 27.

15. Ibid., 58.

16. *Welcome to Urban Revolution*, 39.

It is now a few more days removed from these events. We've heard countless social commentators, politicians, professional athletes, and so on reflect and offer up an opinion of what went wrong. It all began to reveal, at least to me, something deeper that is at the heart of not only the modern city, but one like Vancouver. In a recent conversation with a friend who's an urban planner in a large city in the American Midwest, he mentioned how Vancouver is the poster-child for the cutting edge of urban development and transportation planning. It is truly a remarkable city. Yesterday, I was teaching a session at a two-day primer on the missional church for Forge Canada. As we were talking about the story of Nehemiah and what makes a city great, we were drawn back to the story of our own city of Vancouver. While we have so much going in regards to our built environment, as the 2010 Winter Olympics displayed for the whole world to see, what transpired here just days earlier revealed a more troubling side. Despite all of the forces that are shaping our cities, whether urbanization, globalization, immigration, gentrification, densification, and so much more, there's the ever-present reality that we desperately long for the in-breaking, felt presence of the Kingdom of God. We are students of the city, because we believe and hold onto the conviction that God loves the city and desires to see it redeemed. The fourth wave of mission is here to stay as the world floods to the city.

11

Layers of the City

As much as I love my neighborhood and the people of Edmonds Town Centre in Burnaby, I have to venture out periodically; otherwise I begin getting something akin to cabin fever . . . but in the city. By nature, I'm curious and an explorer, which is why I felt like I had hit my stride when I was simultaneously planting churches and a hiking-and-mountain-biking guide. My life revolved around exploring, discovering, learning, leading, guiding, and helping. Whether exploring new trails to hike, discovering thousand-year-old pottery shards in the desert, or helping to create ways for the new church plant to love, worship, and serve, many of these activities were like kindred spirits. Fast forward to now. Being so focused on investing relationally in our immediate city center and neighborhood sometimes leaves me with tunnel vision. I lose perspective on what else is going on throughout the city. So I make sure that at least once a week I jump on the bus, Skytrain, or my bike to venture to some other part of the city to explore and soak in the vibe of a new locale.

This morning, my Skytrain trip brought me to downtown Vancouver. It is a mid-June morning with the sun climbing higher in the sky. I step outside Waterfront Station as a cool breeze blew in off the ocean. My destination today is Gastown, the city's oldest neighborhood. Gastown's overall architecture and flavor make it an oddity for metro Vancouver. Its look and vibe are similar to Pioneer Square in Seattle. Its origins date back to 1867, the same year that Canada became a nation. A walk through Gastown is a walk through history, as it is one of the few places in this relatively new city where one can find old brick buildings, architectural richness and diversity that is not modern, and cobbled streets. Nowadays Gastown is a bastion of hipness housing a vibrant nightclub and restaurant scene. On the other hand, it is also known for its poverty and homelessness. It is a neighbourhood and district that straddles the worlds of the haves and the have-nots.

Paramount to understanding places like Gastown is to see it through multi-faceted sets of lenses. One lens alone is insufficient. What would be the best lens through which to view and understand Gastown? Sure, we could become familiarized with the historicity of the neighbourhood with its colorful characters, the fight for preservation in the 1960s against the forces of demolition for a downtown freeway, or the riot between the hippies and police in 1971. That would indeed be helpful, but it is incomplete. Another lens would focus on the architecture or built environment of Gastown. One can readily see immediate contrasts with the sleek glass and steel towers that dominate the Vancouver skyline. In Gastown, the signs of history are evident, ranging from the carved keystones, cast-metal lamp posts, and many heritage buildings. But again, that lens would be inadequate. What about the human or social or anthropological framework? Economics? Safety and security? What is needed is a set of lenses, not simply one, to not only view neighbourhoods and places like Gastown, but cities as a whole. There are numerous layers or perspectives to the city.

The challenge comes when we utilize only one lens, layer, or perspective with which to view the city. While we may be correct in what we see and uncover, we are limited by the enormity of what we're taking in and experiencing. Most of us are only trained to use one, two, or maybe three lenses, but there are more. An essential ingredient in developing a theology of the city is to label, define, and explore these various layers or perspectives. This will expand our framework for understanding the city and ultimately enlarge the ways in which we're to engage in the city, whether church planting, community transformation, and so forth. It also reveals that we're all wired differently. In other words, uncovering these layers of the city will help clarify the nature of our particular involvement in the city, as we identify its needs on the one hand, and on the other, how God has uniquely equipped us to meet at least some of those needs.

How we view the city *affects everything*. As we've seen in previous chapters, one hallmark of human history has been rural-to-urban migration. Not only are people continuing to flock to the city, but that migration is changing the very fabric of the city, from services to infrastructure to architecture and the built environment. At the same time, the city influences those who live there. "As cities densify, it means the built environment has a direct bearing on one's worldview and outlook."[1] This transformation is happening at a frenetic pace that shows no sign of slowing down, let alone reversing itself. "Urbanization and higher-density living is an irreversible path of human development."[2]

There are a few questions to ponder as we begin looking more in-depth at the layers of the city. To begin with, how do you view the city? In other words, what lens or perspective are you using? It would be helpful to recognize this from the onset. If nothing is coming to mind immediately, then try this question: what do you see when you look at the city? Do you notice the people? The built environment? Transportation? The natural topography? The economy? As a result of our divergent backgrounds, we all approach the city with an established set of lenses based upon various factors, whether cultural, geographic, or even rural versus suburban versus urban. Our personality-types also influence our view of the city. To the highly introverted, cities might feel draining and even suffocating, while extroverts thrive in dense environments. Another factor is how we view Scripture. Is our interpretive lens rural or urban? If it is rural, for example, we might dismiss the city as the source of all that is evil and corrupt in the world. Lastly, our intellectual, cultural, or lifestyle pursuits form and shape our view of the city. While I may have grown up in small-town Iowa, I was at heart an artistic person who longed for diversity, creative and stimulating environments, multi-cultural settings, and places with a proliferation of architectural variety. Although my rural lens and fear of cities initially influenced me, once I worked through that, it was no surprise to me that God had hardwired me to make my home in a city. In many ways, this calling began as God was forming me in my mother's womb. I was created for the city.

The city is a complex, multi-faceted entity that combines the organic, structural, spiritual, and the mechanical nature of the city all into one geographic setting that houses a high-density population. Cities are also made up of various layers that collectively make up the whole that can and should be studied and understood individually and collectively. I was first exposed to this framework at Bakke Graduate University. Again, I find myself crediting Dr. Ron Boyce for his influence on my life

1. Benesh, *Metrospiritual*, 158.
2. Ng, *Designing High-Density Cities*, xxxi.

and understanding of the city. These perspectives, based on notes from one of his courses are, I believe, worth repeating and sharing. They are as follows:

1. Temporal Perspective

2. Sacred Perspective

3. Security Perspective

4. Economic Perspective

5. Spatial Perspective

6. Social Perspective

7. Theological Perspective (my own addition)

These seven perspectives offer the urban practitioner the opportunity to understand the city on various levels as well as provide differing ways of cultural engagement. They also free us up to embody and proclaim the good news in ways that are true to the way God formed, wired, and shaped us.

TEMPORAL PERSPECTIVE

"Temporal" means, "enduring for a time only; temporary; transitory."[3] This perspective is about looking at the changing landscape of cities in our time as well as across history. Not only are issues of the rise and fall of cities explored on a macro level, along with other topics like urbanization, gentrification and urbanism, but the micro level is emphasized within each city in regards to its past, growth, revitalization, and other shaping influences. On the larger scale, we watch in fascination as cities like Dubai emerge seemingly out of the nowhere to become world-class cities while others like Detroit transition from economic powerhouse to a faltering economy with rampant urban decay. On a smaller scale, there are neighborhoods like Gastown that moved from vibrancy to neglect, decay, and almost destruction to preservation and then renewal. While it may seem to the casual observer that cities are stationery in terms of momentum and transformation, most are somewhere along the continuum between decay and growth or decline and renewal.

This brings us back to the phenomenon I touched on in the previous chapter known as globalization. This process in a nutshell is the

3. Dictionary.com LLC, "Temporal."

ongoing movement of the world towards one enormous global village. Communication lines are densifying and instantaneous, travel is quick, accessible, and easy, trade and commerce are integrating more thoroughly, and cultures interact and overlap with high levels of frequency. Thomas Friedman in *The World is Flat* breaks down globalization into three periods. He calls them Globalization 1.0, 2.0, and 3.0:[4]

1. Globalization 1.0—(1492–1800) Shrank the world from large to medium. Nations are globalizing. "Where does my country fit into global competition?"

2. Globalization 2.0—(1800–2000) Shrank the world from medium to small. Multinational companies were globalizing. "Where does my company fit into the global economy?"

3. Globalization 3.0—(2000-Present) Shrinks the world from small to tiny. The newfound power for individuals to collaborate and compete globally. "Where do I fit into the global competition and opportunities?"

This helps us understand the global seismic shifts taking place in our cities today. There is a massive reshuffling at hand.

History shows that cities rise and fall like the changing tide. They follow the same pattern as organisms: birth, growth, maturity, decline, decay, and even death. Many cities go through the process numerous times throughout their history as they are "reborn" over and over again. This same phenomenon also takes place on a smaller scale in neighbourhoods and districts across the city. As I wrote in *Metrospiritual*, (p. 44) "One of the interesting perspectives in the study of cities is the continual cycles they go through. In particular, the older a city is, the more numerous these cycles of birth, growth, maturation, decline, decay, and rebirth appear." This is at the heart of the idea of the temporal perspective. Seemingly nothing in the city is permanent. I see this evidenced all around me today from my vantage point in Gastown, peering out the window of a Starbucks. "History is replete with this notion of birth, decay, and rebirth. We have a panoramic view of the past hundreds and thousands of years as we take note of civilizations ebbing and flowing

---

4. Friedman, *The World is Flat*, 8–11.

like the tide. Ancient cities came and went while others have endured up until the present."[5]

SACRED PERSPECTIVE

The Sacred Perspective explores the religious and spiritual fabric of the city. In what ways is spirituality prominent in cities and even more so, how is it expressed? How does it shape the city and influence its urban denizens? This is an exploration into how religion and spirituality play a role in the city ranging from its built environment (architecture, urban planning) to the lifestyle of its inhabitants. Although I'll focus more on the topic of the built environment of the city and its theological under-pinnings in a separate chapter, here I'll highlight the topic and a few of its features.

We noted that from the beginning of urban life, cities possessed an over-arching spirituality. The degree to which this was noticeable varied from era to era. Religion was the glue that held ancient cities together. "Throughout history, cities have been citadels of religion."[6] The ques-tion at hand for our modern cities today is: is religion or spirituality the glue that still holds it together? Part of the difficulty lies in how we view our cities today versus the way the ancients viewed theirs. Religion or spirituality in the Western world is separated and compartmentalized from life's mainstream. It wasn't always that way: "The link between the city and religion in the ancient Near East was more explicit than it is in our world today. Western scholarship is used to treating religion as one isolated component of urban life - and a private, individualistic component at that. But in the ancient world and in the Bible it was, and still is, the hub connecting all the urban spokes. It is as integral tounderstanding the city then and now as it is to understanding life, self-hood and culture."[7] How then are we to view the city today from a sacred perspective? What do we see when we look through this lens? Ron Boyce writes, "Until the Twentieth Century, the configuration of cities reflected sacred relationships. Today, it would appear that the gods have fled. Until the development of the skyscraper, the cathedral or church spire was always the tallest building in a European or American

5. *Metrospiritual*, 44.

6. Boyce, "The Nature of Cities."

7. Conn and Ortiz, *Urban Ministry*, 92.

city. This has caused some to declare that skyscrapers are now the new temples—monuments to Mammon."[8]

Are our modern cities reflective then of our religious or spiritual values? What does the built environment of our cities today tell about their spiritual climate? Apart from the built environment, what else do we see in regard to the sacredness, religious climate, or spirituality of our city? Some may be predominantly secular while others have a Christian heritage. Others may be officially 99 percent Muslim and many other cities are incredibly pluralistic. The sacred perspective notes and studies this aspect of the city.

SECURITY PERSPECTIVE

This perspective looks at topics broader than simply military might and fortified walls. There are basic questions that can even be asked on the neighborhood level, such as: Am I safe? Is my neighborhood safe for me and my family? Related topics worth looking at are a city's justice system, public safety, adequate and affordable housing for the marginalized, income equality (or inequality), the overall regional stability, both politically and militarily, and more. In *The City*, Joel Kotkin wrote that security is one of the three critical factors that determine the overall health of cities. (The other two are sacredness of place and the animating role of commerce.) "Where these factors are present, urban culture flourishes. When these elements weaken, cities dissipate and eventually recede out of history."[9]

The safety of cities is crucial and important to those who live there. "Cities are places whose inhabitants are concerned with security."[10] We've seen the effects of what happens to urban dwellers when their safety is threatened. It can happen on many fronts from local neighborhoods to city-wide. This past week has brought to light numerous issues of concern for safety, whether locally, nationally, or internationally. Two days ago, my landlord's car was broken into and the stereo stolen. His car sits just feet from our door. We've also had two bikes stolen as well as our own vehicle vandalized. The conversation we had with our landlord revolved around the safety of our neighborhood. Also in our city,

8. "The Nature of Cities."

9. Kotkin, *The City*, xxi.

10. "The Nature of Cities."

as I mentioned in the last chapter, were the riots that erupted after the Vancouver Canucks failed to win the Stanley Cup. Many people told me that even though the riot took place downtown, it still made them feel insecure. And internationally, it seems like daily we receive news of cities under threat whether through war or terrorism. Safety and security are vital to the overall health of cities.

Without security, there is a breakdown in urban life. Here in North America, the phenomenon known as "White Flight" took place because people were fleeing unstable and dangerous parts of the city. This is nothing new. "When a city's ability to guarantee safety has declined, as at the end of the western Roman Empire or during the crime-infested late twentieth century, urbanites have retreated to the hinterlands or migrated to another, safer urban bastion."[11] What is evident in your city when this lens is utilized?

ECONOMIC PERSPECTIVE

In today's global economy, the city is at the forefront. Cities are in direct competition with one another to gobble up and expand new industries, woo Fortune 500 companies, expand tourism, host national or international events, attract and retain the Creative Class, and anything else to put them on the map and move up their global ranking. Boyce writes of this perspective: "The economic perspective is probably the most distinctive feature of cities. In fact, most people classify cities according to economic criteria. This perspective provides an insight into what cities do. It also provides the way in which cities are used primarily to differentiate one from another. For example, we might describe certain cities as tourist centers, political capitals, regional capitals, manufacturing centers, sacred centers, or places of great historical interest. By so doing, we are really identifying some economic attribute."[12] Cities act the same way as businesses when it comes to marketing and branding, but on a larger scale. "Time and again, I heard financiers argue that cities have to repackage themselves as commodities, that cities have to learn to market and package themselves just like every other corporation."[13] Place is important!

11. *The City*, xxii.
12. "The Nature of Cities."
13. Hern, *Common Ground in a Liquid City*, 110.

Those who devalue place in terms of economics are not looking at the larger picture. As I follow professional sports and listen to national sports radio, I often hear the argument about the importance of place. As athletes develop more negotiating power, they are either choosing to play for teams in major markets (large cities) or historic franchises which also tend to be in large, vibrant cities. The New York Yankees or Los Angeles Lakers do not have difficulty drawing talent, but places like Cleveland or Buffalo do. It is economics. The larger, more appealing cities are drawing the top athletes to them. But there's also a competition and sorting that takes place in cities at the local level in regard to who lives where. "All cities have an informal sorting process whereby residents gravitate to those places that reflect their class position. Perhaps the best symbol of this sorting process is where you live. The housing you have and where it is located reflects the inequalities that exist in a city."[14] I remember that point hitting home when I was doing research for my dissertation. I sent out surveys to church planters looking for those in gentrified neighborhoods so I can follow up with more questions. One church planter responded how his neighborhood is the result of displaced people from gentrification. They were poorer minorities who were priced out as their inner ring urban neighborhoods became desirable and expensive.

Richard Florida makes the argument in *Who's Your City?* that not only is place not dead, it is more important than ever before when it comes to economics. "Where we live is increasingly important to every facet of our lives. We owe it to ourselves to think about the relationship between place and our economic future, as well as our personal happiness, in a more systematic—if different—way."[15]

SPATIAL PERSPECTIVE

The spatial perspective explores the city's physical nature, not only its built environment, but also where the city is located (i.e., on a river, in a mountainous area, in a valley, etc.). It is observing what is most readily noticeable and how the city is designed, built, and laid out (i.e., a ring city, post-modern urbanism[16], etc.). There are two key components that

14. Hiller, *Urban Canada*, 276.

15. Florida, *Who's Your City?*, 4.

16. Michael Dear in *From Chicago to L.A.* describes an example of post-modern urbanism on page 85 as, "a city composed of multiple, differentially interconnected

we will take a look at in this perspective: the *site* and *situation* of cities. Both have more influence on urban inhabitants than initially realized. This is a case of where the physicality of the city and its environment shape the lives of those who reside within.

For our purposes, the *site* is defined as "the actual location of a settlement on the earth and is composed of the physical characteristics of the landscape specific to the area. Site factors include things like landforms (i.e., is the area protected by mountains or is there a natural harbor present?), climate, vegetation types, availability of water, soil quality, minerals, and even wildlife."[17] Such factors influenced where cities got their start and why. They also determine how a city is laid out and continues to expand. Vancouver, for example, is situated at the mouth of the Fraser River and is hemmed in by mountains, the ocean, and the U.S. border. The city offers a sheltered port for shipping, an abundance of fresh water, ample forest land and other natural resources, and a cool year-round climate. On the other hand, having lived in a desert in the American Southwest for ten years, I also have seen how *site* impacted so much of daily life. Water was channeled down from northern Arizona, the climate was hot and oppressive for eight months of the year, and the cities of Phoenix and Tucson were surrounded by small mountains which meant that expansion outwards was through the gaps in between. Even though both cities got their start in river basins, the rivers no longer flow perennially due to the water table dropping due to human use. The *site* of a city raises a lot of issues that can influence the day-to-day lives of its inhabitants.

Along with a city's *site* is its *situation*. "Situation is defined as the location of a place relative to its surroundings and other places. Factors included in an area's situation include the accessibility of the location, the extent of a place's connections with another, and how close an area may be to raw materials if they are not located specifically on the site."[18] The *site* is where a city is located; the *situation* is the relationship between the city and its region. "For example, Canada's Eastern Provinces of New Brunswick, Newfoundland and Labrador, Nova Scotia, and Prince Edward Island are some of that country's most economically downtrodden areas due in large part to their situations. These areas are

sites, arranged in a decentered, nonhierarchical fashion."

17. About.com, "Site and Situation."

18. Ibid.

isolated from the rest of Canada making manufacturing and the little agriculture possible too expensive. In addition, there are very few close natural resources (many are off the coast and due to maritime laws, the government of Canada itself controls the resources) and many of the traditional fishing economies they did have are now crashing along with the fish populations."[19]

A city's *site* and *situation* are influential factors in its role on the global stage. Cities like Los Angeles and New York City are prime locations on the west and east coasts of the United States. They are easily accessible. While Vancouver is a global city, it is also geographically isolated from the rest of Canada as it is separated by numerous mountain ranges and long distances from the next largest cities. And yet in a real way it is inter-connected with other major cities that make up the Pacific Rim. "As nations around the world continue to develop, their sites and situations will play a large role in whether or not they will be successful. And though today's ease of transportation and new technologies such as the Internet are bringing nations closer together, the physical landscape of an area as well as its location in relation to its desired market will still play a large role in whether or not such areas will grow to become the next great world city."[20]

SOCIAL PERSPECTIVE

Usually when we look at cities, we take in only what our eyes can see: the skyline, architectural variances, the transit system, parks and green spaces, and so forth. But in so doing, we can "forget that all these are shaped by human decisions."[21] It is this human factor that is driving what Jeb Brugmann calls the *Urban Revolution*: "The first thing that anyone notices on entering a city is the concentration of people and their activities. Simple as it is, this density has been little understood, and its benefits are too often squandered through the low-density development of cities today. The density of cities is their most basic advantage over any kind of settlement. Without density of settlement, most of what we learn, produce, construct, organize, consume, and provide as a service in the world would simply be too expensive. Density increases the sheer

19. Ibid.
20. Ibid.
21. "The Nature of Cities."

efficiency by which we can pursue an economic opportunity."[22] While a city's built environment, site, and situation affect and influence much, there is no denying that the human factor permeates everything else. In regards to high-density cities and neighborhods, what makes them vibrant and appealing go beyond the built environment. The built environment creates the cultural milieu where heightened interactions take place compared to their low-density counterparts. In high-density walkable neighborhoods, there's a great chance for what Eric Jacobsen calls *incidental contact*. "Incidental contact allows us to get to know people in their ordinariness and even in their pain."[23] People influence the city, but the density of cities allows us to come in constant contact with others.

The social impact of high-density cities and neighborhoods are great and varied. The social perspective reveals how people and cities interact. Here is what transpires in that interaction. First, we find that high-density contexts promote social vibrancy. "Close observation of cities such as Paris reveals that it is the densest parts of the city that have the greatest vitality."[24] Second, higher density creates environments for innovation and collaboration. "Careful design of density multiplies the number of achievable activities and interactions."[25] Third, it fosters networking and social capital. Lastly, the built environment informs, shapes, and dictates social interaction. The higher the density, the greater chance of interaction. One affects the other.

THEOLOGICAL PERSPECTIVE

In many ways, it could be argued that this last perspective overarches and transcends the others. Said another way, the theological perspective is the lens through which we view and interpret all of the other lenses, layers, or perspectives. Rather than creating a separate perspective for a theological view of the city, it is my contention that this perspective gives us the biblical basis for seeing the city, while not dominating or making the other perspectives inferior. Therefore, when we view the city from a social, spatial, or economic perspective, we do so with an understanding of the past, present and future eternal destination of cities. A question

22. *Welcome to the Urban Revolution*, 27.

23. Jacobsen, *Sidewalks in the Kingdom*, 90.

24. *Designing High-Density Cities*, 42.

25. *Welcome to the Urban Revolution*, 85.

that could be asked here is, how does the reality of the Kingdom of God affect the way we view, understand, and live in cities today as followers of Jesus?

This perspective forces us to ask questions such as: is there a theological understanding of the city's built environment? Are transportation systems thorough and equitable, giving the marginalized access to urban necessities? If not, how should the church respond? How are we to view the rise and fall of cities through a biblical lens? As cities are divided and ranked into classes (i.e., global cities) how should the theological perspective speak to that?

Understanding God's role in the city is paramount to guiding our understanding, role, outlook, and work in the city. However difficult it may be for us to discern exactly how God is moulding, shaping, and influencing cities in the overarching divine story, we believe and trust that he is active and intimately involved.

These layers or perspectives of the city help us to know how to live in the city and understand it. Taken together, they inform us on all that is taking place in the city. There is no one-size-fits-all approach to the city. Many Christians often feel boxed in when it comes to serving God in the city. What the various perspectives reveal is that there are more ways to get involved in the city beyond the very foundational elements of church planting, evangelism, and church ministry. As was noted previously in the story of Nehemiah, community transformation requires both Nehemiah-types and Ezra-types. Looking at the various layers or perspectives of cities has the potential to blow the lid off the perceived potential of what followers of Jesus can do in the city.

12

Pilgrims and Place

Tom lived in the neighborhood where we were planting a church. He was a brilliant man with a PhD and an agnostic and I was a late-20s church planter. I met him one day at the park across from where we lived. Every evening as the desert sun was setting, the park came alive with families and older couples with their dogs. After a few times of meeting and chatting with Tom at the park, we met up for coffee at Starbucks. Even though he was a good thirty years older than me, we struck up a friendship. He knew I was a church planter and interested in spiritual things. He was somewhat of a scientist who was interested in spiritual things as well, albeit of a different kind. At the time, we were both interested, for differing reasons, in Native American spirituality. I was immersing myself in the world of the desert environment as a hiking and mountain-biking guide learning what I could about local history, archaeology, the various Native American tribes, and geology. This brought me into direct contact with Native American spirituality, given my relationship with other hiking guides who were interested in it, the proliferation of tribes in our area and across the state of Arizona, as well as our new church plant that was forming a relationship with a ministry project on the Hopi Reservation in the northeast part of the state. I think Tom was simply interested because he was interested.

Being the academic that he was and with my love for books, we decided it'd be fun to meet weekly to read a book and discuss it together. His pursuits were enjoyment, exploring new ideas, and exercising his intellect, while mine was ultimately to see him come to faith in Christ. We settled on the book *God is Red: A Native View of Religion* by Vine Deloria Jr. It turned out to be a fascinating book to read and discuss. Deloria's intent was to compare and contrast Native American spirituality versus conventional mainstream American Christianity. The Protestant up-bringing of his childhood had left a bad taste in his mouth, which led him on a journey of discovery of the religion of his Native American ancestry. Needless to say, the book did not paint the church in a very positive light and based upon his examples, there was no denying its past ugliness.

For the purposes of this chapter, Deloria brought up some perti-nent points that are applicable to the idea of a theology of place. It wasn't until I read his book in 2003 that I gave this notion much consideration. I felt there was something missing in our theology, particularly as evan-gelicals, that I couldn't put my finger on. As I read *God is Red* and then took a trip to do a work project on the Hopi Reservation, I began feeling that there was a disconnect between the church and this idea of place. On the trip, I was exposed to the village of Old Oraibi, which is the old-est continuously inhabited settlement in the United States. People have been living generation after generation in that same village since before A.D. 1100. Talk about putting down roots. At that time in my life, I was merely a migrant, having moved into a suburban setting with thousands of other migrants who had little to no tie to the community or the land. Tom and my book club and the experience in Old Oraibi began pushing me to study and uncover a biblical theology of place.

In *God is Red*, I encountered a Native American view and concept of place that was in stark contrast to the suburban evangelicalism that I was most acquainted with. As I thumbed through the chapters and read, there was a striking familiarity between what Deloria described and the concept of place as found in the Old Testament: "The vast majority of Indian tribal religions, therefore, have a sacred center at a particular place, be it a river, a mountain, a plateau, valley, or other natural feature. This center enables the people to look out along the four dimensions and locate their lands, to relate all historical events within the confines of this particular land, and to accept responsibility for it. Regardless of what subsequently happens to the people, the sacred lands remain as permanent fixtures in their cultural or religious understanding.[1] Our first response may be to scoff at what Deloria is trying to communicate. However, if we remove *Indian tribal religions* and inserted *the ancient people of Israel*, then all of a sudden it does not seem so outlandish. Over and over what we find across the pages of the Old Testament is a

---

1. Deloria, *God is Red*, 67.

people rooted in context (land, place) through their relationship with the Promised Land. Also, intensely spiritual activities (encounters with God) were memorialized by the construction of an altar, a pile of rocks, or something to remember *when we met God*, so when successive generations came across this memorial, they would be reminded of the story of what God done for their forefathers in that place.

We find one such story when Israel crossed the Jordan River and entered the Promised Land. The crossing was no mere fording of a river; rather, God miraculously stopped the water flowing so the entire nation could cross on dry ground. Upon reaching the other side, God told Joshua to mark the crossing as a place of remembrance.

> When all the nation had finished passing over the Jordan, the LORD said to Joshua, "Take twelve men from the people, from each tribe a man, and command them, saying, 'Take twelve stones from here out of the midst of the Jordan, from the very place where the priests' feet stood firmly, and bring them over with you and lay them down in the place where you lodge tonight.'" Then Joshua called the twelve men from the people of Israel, whom he had appointed, a man from each tribe. And Joshua said to them, "Pass on before the ark of the LORD your God into the midst of the Jordan, and take up each of you a stone upon his shoulder, according to the number of the tribes of the people of Israel, that this may be a sign among you. When your children ask in time to come, 'What do those stones mean to you?' then you shall tell them that the waters of the Jordan were cut off before the ark of the covenant of the LORD. When it passed over the Jordan, the waters of the Jordan were cut off. So these stones shall be to the people of Israel a memorial forever."[2]

This is not too unlike what Deloria writes when he states, "Context is therefore all-important for both practice and the understanding of reality. The places where revelations were experienced were remembered and set aside as locations, through rituals and ceremonials, the people could once again communicate with the spirits."[3] In mostly preliterate societies, we find this idea of physical remembrance vital to the ongoing identity of the people. Somehow and somewhere along the way we "modern day" worshippers of God have lost our roots and connectedness to place.

2. Joshua 4:1–7.
3. *God is Red*, 67.

A theology of place gets its beginning in the Old Testament where place mattered in God's plan and for God's people. Since then, we've lost touch with place and the church has become mobile. What would happen if we become rooted in place? In a highly mobile society, the church, rooted in a neighborhood, can become a stabilizing agent of community transformation. Before we dismiss the notion of place as simply an Old Testament concept and not applicable for today, let me share with you a familiar example of the kind of tragedy that can occur when we undervalue place in the role of mission.

While I served as a church planting strategist in Tucson, Arizona, I had the privilege of working and networking with church planters and pastors across the city spanning denominational lines. My heart was for the city, the city center in particular, and the surrounding neighborhoods, which brought me to that area on a weekly basis, whether for meetings, shopping at one of the ethnic grocery stores, or simply to work out of coffee shops. One of the cultural hubs of the area is Fourth Avenue between the downtown core and the University of Arizona. It is a vibrant, funky place full of odd shops, restaurants, coffee shops, and the like. A perfect place for mission. "It can be argued the most creative new frontier was back in the central cities."[4] Just off the avenue was the old historic First Baptist Church. Back in the early part of the twentieth century, it was *the* church in the city and a mega-church before there were really very many with thousands of weekend worshippers. Fast forward to today (or when I left a few years ago), there were but a handful of elderly people left in this massive, grand, historic, and architecturally beautiful building. Authors Ray Bakke and Sam Roberts write eloquently about the story that has unfolded concerning these historic city center churches that they refer to as *Old Firsts*:

> Old Firsts have now come upon hard times. Their once thriving memberships became depleted when countless members chased the "American Dream" to the outer fringes of the suburbs. The large, magnificent edifices, so imposing in their grandeur in an earlier time, now appear forlorn as row upon row of empty pews give mute testimony to a faded glory. The few loyal worshipers who do return on Sunday out of a sense of loyalty must now pass sullen neighbors who, despite living in close proximity to the church, do not feel that it is "their" church. Old Firsts seem

4. Schaller, *Center City Churches*, 13.

forgotten by the wealthy and expendable to the men and women in power – so unlike an earlier time when the powerful needed membership in Old Firsts as a part of their respectability.[5]

What has taken place in so many city center churches is that the neighborhood and demographics have radically changed since their formation. As new people moved in, the ethnic makeup of the community transitioned. People began commuting in from greater distances, and the church found itself still holding on to its past. This same story can be told of church after church in the city centers across North America regardless of denomination. The latest happenings of First Baptist Church Tucson found it leveraging its assets to fund a church planting effort in the far reaches of the suburban fringe. More than a church plant, it was a relocation. While the building was rooted in the city, the church was attempting to flee the city. While those may seem like strong words, how else can we make sense of it? In light of this scenario that has taken place over and over again, Bakke writes:

> The evangelicalism I grew up with had a theology of persons and programs, but it lacked a conscious theology of place. Protestants generally cut themselves off from "parish" thinking – an ongoing commitment to their *place* of ministry – so that when a church's location became "inconvenient" it simply relocated to a new place, often near a freeway (reflecting our society's shift from a walking to an automobile culture). Along the way, we abandoned real estate that had been prayed for fervently by Christians before us – and along with it abandoned any commitment to the neighborhoods we left behind.[6]

Developing a theology of place can indeed be a tricky and arduous task. What we desire to do is say no more and no less than what Scripture says. I have heard amazing lectures on this topic of a theology of place with varying starting points, such as being rooted in Trinitarian theology, the *missio Dei*, and so forth. Usually it is accompanied by quoting dead theologians of yesteryear with names that are hard to pronounce. My attempt here in this chapter is to simply broach the subject, make some observations, set forth some applications, and move on.

A cursory reading of the Old Testament reveals some interesting insights in regards to place and God's emphasis on it. We find a holy

---

5. Bakke and Roberts, *The Expanded Mission of City Center Churches*, 16–17.

6. Bakke, *A Theology as Big as the City*, 60.

land, a holy city, a holy temple, and a holy people—"holy" in the sense of being "set apart." Let's start with the holy people. God called Abram out and through him created a holy, set apart, people. "And I will make of you a great nation."[7] Throughout the rest of the Old Testament, we find this called-out people, which became the nation of Israel, struggling with what it means to live in covenantal relationship with God. Next we find that the holy people needed a home or a country to dwell in. God provided that as well. "Then the LORD appeared to Abram and said, 'To your offspring I will give this land.' So he built there an altar to the LORD, who had appeared to him."[8] God's called-out people would have a country of their own with cities to dwell in, where they were expected to live out their relationship with God before the nations. "The mission of God to the cities of the world was to be lived out in Israel's theocratic self-understanding. Covenantal commitment to Yahweh carried with it a rejection of loyalty to the gods of the city-states and empire and rejection, therefore, of how those urban societies were ordered"[9]

En route to the Promised Land, God instituted a system of worship, celebration, and sacrifices centered around the tabernacle. Years later under the leadership of Solomon, this temporary tent was set aside for a permanent structure, the temple. This temple was located in Jerusalem. The holy people had a holy land and in that land was a holy city with a holy temple. Place was most certainly central to the identity of Israel, their practice of worship, but it was not supposed to just exist within certain geographic and ethnic boundaries. "The Lord who reigned over Israel had global and universalistic intentions."[10]

Fast forward to the New Testament and the idea of place was completely uprooted. First of all, the identity of the holy people exploded beyond the boundaries of ethnicity and a geo-political identity. No longer was it tied to those of Jewish descent or relegated to the nation of Israel. The good news crossed all ethnic, linguistic, cultural, and political boundaries. The center of gravity shifted away from its Jewish origins to include the Gentiles and the rest of the world. Now the idea of a holy people referred to a spiritual identity in Christ rather than a bloodline.

7. Genesis 12:2.

8. Genesis 12:7.

9. Conn and Ortiz, *Urban Ministry*, 97.

10. Ibid.

This shift also radically altered God's relationship with both the nation of Israel and the city of Jerusalem. "The Jewish/Jerusalem-centered community, shaped so profoundly by its long narrative history of God's dealings with them, has been displaced."[11] Across the pages of the New Testament, a decisive geographic shift takes place. The locus of the story in the Gospels through the first part of Acts was rooted in Israel and the Jews. By the end of Acts, it was as if the camera had shifted and zoomed out. The location of the drama unfolding of the emerging first-century church, the new holy people, was now taking place in numerous other cities of the eastern Mediterranean, including Rome itself. Lastly, in A.D. 70, Roman legions destroyed the temple and indeed all of Jerusalem. Yet even before its destruction, Christ's death and resurrection had rendered the temple structure and the sacrificial system as no longer necessary for worshipping God. In fact, the temple as a physical entity in Jerusalem in Israel had been replaced by a new spiritual reality—that the followers of Jesus themselves are now God's holy people. "Or do you not know that your body is a temple of the Holy Spirit within you, whom you have from God?"[12]

Where does that leave us today in regard to the role or theology of place in the mission of God? Constructing a theology of place must consider the context of where the *missio Dei* is to take place. Today, that context is that over half of the world's population are urban dwellers. Yet the challenge is we often see ourselves as pilgrims, sojourners, or aliens. David Bosch aptly states, "The church is viewed as the *people of God* and, by implication then, as a *pilgrim* church."[13] This would seem to imply that we ought to have no attachment to place. The natural progression seems to short-cut or make irrelevant any concept of a theology of place beyond where we happen to live. However, Bosch also states: "The church is a pilgrim not simply for the practical reason that in the modern age it no longer calls the tune and is everywhere finding itself in a Diaspora situation; rather, to be a pilgrim in the world belongs intrinsically to the church's ex-centric position. It is *ek-klesia*, 'called out' out of the world, and sent back into the world."[14] This is a decisive shift! Called out and sent back. The very nature or definition of the church is that we are the

11. Roxburgh, *Missional*, 29.

12. 1 Corinthians 6:19.

13. Bosch, *Transforming Mission*, 373.

14. Ibid., 373–374.

"called out ones" which gets at the idea of what *ekklesia* means. However, the tables are turned in John 20:21, where Jesus tells his apostles, "As the Father has sent me, even so I am sending you." God calls his people out of the world, transforms them, and then sends them back into the world. In other words, place has missiological implications.

One of the challenges at hand in regard to place is its future dimensions. Many have written about certain eschatological doctrines of the twentieth century that took root in the imaginations of Western Christians.[15] This has led to a disregard of place and its importance. The assumption was that if in the end everything "burns," then why care for it and steward it now? Why care for the environment? Why seek to see cities redeemed? If everything will get burned up like useless trash at the end of time anyway, then why bother? Wayne Grudem asks, "But will earth simply be renewed, or will it be completely destroyed and replaced by another earth, newly created by God?"[16] He further points out the tension these questions cause, especially in Protestant circles. "Within the Protestant world, there has been disagreement as to whether the earth is to be destroyed completely and replaced, or just changed and renewed."[17] Depending on how we answer those questions may dictate not only our view on a theology of place, but even our degree of involvement today with such things as creation care and urban renewal. After weighing the various arguments, Grudem's own conclusion is that, "The Reformed position seems preferable here, for it is difficult to think that God would entirely annihilate his original creation, thereby seeming to give the devil the last word and scrapping the creation that was originally 'very good' (Gen. 1:31)."[18]

Place is redeemable. "Salvation and spirituality are to be found," Millard Erickson writes, "not by fleeing from or avoiding the material realm, but by sanctifying it."[19] Again, the scope of place is more than the natural environment, such as oceans, forests, plant and animal life, and so forth. It encompasses our cities. In other words, we're not to flee from cities, but rather to live in them and carry out our responsibility to care

15. For further reading around this theme look at the theological debates surrounding the Great Reversal.

16. Grudem, *Systematic Theology*, 1160.

17. Ibid.

18. Ibid.

19. Erickson, *Christian Theology*, 402.

for them, the people within them, and work towards renewal. We are God's agents of urban transformation.

More than what will happen to place at the end of time, a theology of place has direct bearing on our lives today. "There is a 'theology of place.' God calls us to a place to be present; totally immersed as His agents of transforming presence. We are called to commit to a location for time periods and serve whatever needs arise there."[20] Any construction of a theology of place necessitates that it is rooted in missiology, for without that focus, it is easy to wander down many side roads. Far from simply being a set of theological assumptions about place, in the context of this book, this offers the urban practitioner more impetus to love the place along with the people to which God has called them. "God often calls us to commit to a place. God often accompanies that call with an unusual curiosity—if not supernatural love—for that place."[21] Place is of crucial importance in urban contexts as the intensity of where one lives is more prevalent due to density and has wide-reaching implications than in other contexts. It is why where we choose to live, minister, and/or plant churches is paramount. A theology of place is more than a cognitive adherence; it has influence over our everyday lives. It propels us into the city. "People of biblical faith are called to live in the city, to raise their families there, and to share in the struggle for life and the things that make for peace."[22]

In *Metrospiritual*, I spent considerable time exploring some of the features of calling in terms of where church planters feel that God is leading them. In looking at place, and in this case the city, it was helpful to consider where church planters felt drawn to. In light of my research into where churches were being planted in the city and why, I posed some clarifying questions: "The first question to ask is: Is God calling me to this part of the city? Is the decision based upon preference or fear? Is cultural compatibility and geographic familiarity the most important factor that weighs the heaviest? My fear is that if we church planters only stick to the parts of the city that we like, love, and are full of people just like us, then there will be many parts of the city that will continue to be untouched."[23] Our theology of place has a direct bearing even on

20. Smith, *City Signals*, 127.

21. Ibid., 128.

22. Gornik, *To Live in Peace*, 115.

23. Benesh, *Metrospiritual*, 104.

where we are drawn to minister and plant churches. If in our theological schemas, place is undervalued, or in this case various parts of the city are neglected, then there is a high likelihood of avoidance. That does not necessarily mean that everyone needs to pool and collect in the same parts of the city, but to instead realize that where we choose to live can be in some ways reflective of our theological assumptions of place. Place leads into other doctrines as well, such as the Incarnation. Jesus was place-specific in that he was born into a specific time, place, culture, and among a specific group of people. As *The Message* renders John 1:14, "The Word became flesh and blood, and moved into the neighborhood." The calling for us is to go and do likewise.

> The call to a place is followed by a commitment, even a love and perhaps a supernatural mantle is *incarnational* ministry. The word usually applies to God the Spirit taking on the flesh of hu-mankind as Jesus Christ did. When applied to urban ministry, it means that a 'person becomes one of us.' It means moving into a neighborhood and taking on the same circumstances of joy and pain that everyone else is experiencing. It means connecting to the hopes and destinies of the people of the neighborhood. It is living life *among* and *with* those who were are ministering among and with.[24]

Again, the practical importance of place is that it dictates our involvement in our cities today and into the future. Do we have hope for our cities? Do we jump in to see community transformation take place or simply throw our hands up and wait for the Rapture? I will leave you with two questions about place and cities that Ray Bakke poses: "Does God care only about people, or does he also care about places, including cities? And if the Holy Spirit of Christ is in us, should we also care for both urban people and urban places?"[25]

24. *City Signals*, 131.
25. *A Theology as Big as the City*, 61.

13

Theology of the Built Environment

ONE OF THE FEATURES that drew us to Vancouver was the built environment of the city. We have lived in and visited many amazing cities prior to moving here, but nothing prepared us for Vancouver. I have great memories of exploring numerous cities both in North America and overseas. Each city is like a fingerprint or snowflake in that no two are alike, even though there have shared common traits. For example, I recall sitting in a coffee shop in Lafayette Park just outside of the central business district of St. Louis close to Busch Stadium. From my vantage point next to the window, the view was amazing as I soaked in the historical features of the streetscape. I was given a tour of the neighborhood by a church planter-friend, Josh Jones of August Gate Church, and was struck by the amazing architecture, the old brick buildings, and the cultural vibrancy of the area, including the Soulard Neighborhood—a prime example of the national trend to repopulate urban areas. "More and more families and individuals are eschewing the sterility of the suburbs and returning to redesigned urban centers where they can experience the vitality of city life."[1] For the most part, the city of Vancouver stands in stark contrast to the built environment of such cities as St. Louis. Replacing old historic brick buildings is a proliferation of concrete, glass, and steel towers that punctuate the skyline across the Lower Mainland. If one has seen postcards of the downtown core, it almost has a futuristic feel about it akin to what we are more likely to find in Asia than North America.

One of practices I attempt to do in my writings is to invite the reader into the story of my context. Whether I'm exploring a new part of the city or walking a couple blocks over to my neighborhood Starbucks,

1. Swanson and Williams, *To Transform a City*, 28.

139

the city always paints the backdrop as it does today. Out of the large windows of the coffee shop I'm visiting, I watch the auto traffic speed by as people make their way to work. Perched above the roadway is the Skytrain line taking passengers west towards the heart of the city or east and away from it. Surrounding me, like giant sentinels, are a cluster of high-rise residential towers. On this sunny day, I can look across part of the city of Burnaby from north to south and watch as the towers that make up Metrotown radiate in the early morning sun. The built environment defines metro Vancouver, Canada and the United States may be neighbors, but urban form here in Canada "has more in common with Australia than with the United States when it comes to managing growth and determining its final form and location."[2]

There is no escaping noticing a city's built environment, whether it is new or old, beautiful or dilapidated, or the genre of the architecture. There is a frequent misunderstanding regarding the nature of God's presence in the city. How often have we heard people talk about the location or type of setting where they feel the closest to God? Most often those locations are in the wilderness, whether clambering up a mountain's ridge line, sitting on a rocky cleft overlooking the ocean as the waves pound the coast, or simply taking a stroll in a forested park. Usually people do not refer to the city as a place where they really feel close to God. Why is that?

Robert Linthicum in *City of God City of Satan* makes an interesting and thought-provoking statement: Instead of the conventional wisdom of viewing the city as the place where God is not, we should see the city as the dwelling place of God.[3] We have created a dichotomy between the wilderness and cities. The wilderness is typically seen as the creative genius of God while the city was created by man. As I've stated previously in this book, I believe the city is indeed the pinnacle of man's creativity and innovation. It is the mother of all inventions. "Cities are cauldrons of creativity."[4] And yet we taint our view of the city and set it up in contrast or even opposition to God. On the other hand, we praise God's creativity in regards to trees, flowers, birds, fish, glaciers, mountains, canyons, and of course humankind. In other words, the manmade city is totally bad and the unspoiled natural wilderness (or creation) is totally good. So when city-dwellers who feel this way want to feel close

---

2. CanU, "About Canadian Urbanism."

3. See the section "The City as God's Creation" in chapter 1.

4. Florida, *Cities and the Creative Class*, 1.

to God, their impulse is to flee to the wilderness. It is in response to this false dichotomy that Linthicum writes:

> How would we feel about our city if we began walking its streets, admiring its buildings, and reviewing its exquisite architecture? And what a difference it would make if we could begin viewing our city, not through the eyes that saw only its dirt and deprivation, but through eyes that could recognize the handiwork of the Creator. God created the city even as he created the mountains and hills and trees and brooks. In the countryside God has used the forces of nature to carve and shape and mold. In the city God has used the creativity of human beings to carve and shape and mold! The city is to be celebrated and admired, not simply for itself, but because the city is the creation and primary abode of God.[5]

We need to see the city, the built environment, as the revealer of the glory of God. Just as a steep canyon wall reveals the glory of God, so does the built environment of the city. In one setting God creates *ex nihilo*, in the other, God creates by endowing mankind with the powers of imagination and ingenuity. Both reveal God's creative genius.

Before we journey together any farther, it'd be helpful to pause and clarify. What is a city's built environment and how am I using the phrase? For starters, the definition is: "The term built environment refers to the human-made surroundings that provide the setting for human activity, ranging in scale from personal shelter and buildings to neighborhoods and cities that can often include their supporting infrastructure, such as water supply or energy networks. The built environment is a material, spatial and cultural product of human labor that combines physical elements and energy in forms necessary for living, working and playing."[6] It is what we see that makes up a city, such as the architectural variances, the density of buildings, the layout of street patterns, monuments, and so forth. No two cities are alike. There are cities with rampant low-density sprawl like Los Angeles and Phoenix or ones with more compact downtown cores and other city centers like Vancouver or Manhattan. Architectural features vary greatly. Consider Quebec City or Montreal compared to San Diego or Miami. Transportation networks are another marker that sets cities apart; some are heavy-laden with freeways while others are not.

5. Linthicum, *City of God City of Satan*, 32–33.
6. Wikimedia Foundation Inc, "Built Environment."

Within the city itself there is *place* and also *plexus*. "*Place* refers to the land use patterns and the distribution of activities across space. The less familiar, *Plexus* refers to the complex of networks that connect people and places."[7] Each city has made and continues to make decisions accordingly. Ideas of the ways cities should look and feel in their built environment are often influenced through the grid or lens of the ones we call home, since we're familiar with them, or those cities that we've deemed as exemplary. Michael Dear in *From Chicago to L.A.: Making Sense of Urban Theory* writes, "Our theories of urban change and our beliefs about good urban policy are rooted in the experiences of particular cities, which may not be typical."[8] He then walks the reader through several city examples and points out what makes them distinct. "Chicago has long been the prototype for understanding the large industrial city in 20th century America."[9] Dear goes on to highlight what makes other cities like New York and Washington DC stand out as well, but then he turns the corner to talk about the prototypical city of the future, Los Angeles. To the chagrin of many, he writes, "Los Angeles has become, for many, not the exception but rather a prototype of the city of the future."[10]

Prototype of the future? "If we as Christians want to take the physical structures of our cities seriously, at some point we must deal with the thorny issue of the future prospects of our cities."[11] The question isn't as much about the spatial layout of a city as much as it is about the values that undergird it. This critique isn't aimed particularly at cities like the Los Angeles of today and the future or the Chicago of the twentieth century, but again to ask, what are the theological underpinnings? Is there even another way to view such things as dense cities or rampant suburban sprawl? "It is important to note that we have not backed into sprawl and standardization as the dominant mode of development because of poverty, national crisis, or other limiting factors. Instead, we have boldly and confidently marched toward these unsatisfying arrangements with no one to blame but ourselves. We have done so, I believe, because we have been worshipping false gods in the name of American values. These

7. Levinson and Krizek, *Planning for Place and Plexus*, 1.

8. Dear, *From Chicago to L.A.*, 27.

9. Ibid.

10. Ibid., vii.

11. Jacobsen, *Sidewalks in the Kingdom*, 70.

gods go by the name of individualism, independence, and freedom, but they take many forms in our daily experience."[12]

What then do architecture, density, suburban sprawl, cities of the past, cities of the future, and so forth have to do with a theology of the built environment? We're simply employing a theological lens with which to understand the physicality of the city. Does it have meaning? Are there surface-level as well as subterranean ramifications, values, and motivations for the way our cities are being built? What is communicated by the city as a whole when we look at it? "I would argue that the built environment, and in particular sacred spaces associated with and produced by a culture, provides one of the most significant windows into understanding that culture."[13] Cities are places. They are the contexts in which over half the world lives their lives. A theology of the built environment offers a theological reflection on place, as T. J. Gorringe writes: "To be human is to be placed: to be born in this house, hospital, stable (according to Luke), or even, as in the floods of Mozambique in 2000, in a tree. It is to live in this council house, semi-detached, tower block, farmhouse, mansion. It is to go to school through the streets or lanes, to play in the alley, park, garden; to shop in this market, that mall; to work in this factory, mine, office, farm. These facts are banal, but they form the fabric of our everyday lives, structuring our memories, determining our attitudes. How, as Christians, should we think of them? Are they a proper subject for theological reflection?"[14]

A theology of the built environment is an exploration and look at the foundations on which a city is built. It is the story behind what we see. "A culture cannot be understood or fully appreciated without consideration of the built environments within it. The reverse is also true; an appreciation of built environments cannot be acquired in the absence of an understanding of the culture in which they are situated."[15] Last night, Katie and I were walking around downtown Vancouver in the glow of a cool summer evening. The sight before us was absolutely breath-taking. To the north, we could see across to North Vancouver and the snow-capped mountains rising above it. And yet we were transfixed on the downtown. Across the plaza and spread before us was a stunning display

12. Ibid., 21.

13. McAlpine, *Sacred Space for the Missional Church*, 13.

14. Gorringe, *A Theology of the Built Environment*, 1.

15. *Sacred Space for the Missional Church*, 15.

of architectural wonder as we stood before the Olympic cauldron that was left in place from the 2010 Winter Olympics. It was hemmed in by a concentration of high-rise glass and steel towers of such a variety of shapes that they caused the city to look almost futuristic. It is most certainly one of the most amazing views in the downtown core with water and mountains on one side and the best that Vancouver has to offer on the other.

A theology of the built environment asks questions about what the city is communicating in terms of how it is built and laid out. What is immediately noticeable? What is seen? What is unseen? Again, what are the underlying values that form and shape what we see and encounter on a daily basis? This is where a theology of the built environment begins leaning heavily upon other disciplines to form a well-rounded view of the city.

The built environment of cities reflect their values, assumptions, and strategies. As Jeb Brugmann writes: "Cities, and specific groups within cities, design and use urban infrastructure to extend their strategies and forms of association (e.g., commerce, politics, and crime) across a network of cities. They combine the unique advantage of one city with others to create whole new strategies for advantage in the City. Globalization is this process of developing new advantage from the unique economics of an extended group of cities—from their spatial designs, infrastructures, cultures, and local markets. Local urban affairs, therefore, are more (not less) important in the global era. They define the potential and burdens of the expanding City."[16] The built environment of our cities communicates so much of an underlying value system. Vancouver values density, walkability, and being transit-oriented. This is reflected in compact, dense city centers that dot the metro area, as well as the Skytrain, Seabus, and a ubiquitous bus system that dominates the city and inner-ring suburbs. Here's how Brugmann reflects on Vancouver:

> The main tenet of metro Vancouver's urban practice is encompassed in the term *liveability*. Liveability has particular meaning in the Vancouver context. It reflects a cultural consensus in favor of dense, efficient, mixed-use buildings that preserve the special green spaces and natural scenery of the region. The region's growth strategies have been consistently linked to in-depth research on the values of the region's residents. The result is four main axioms

16. Brugmann, *Welcome to the Urban Revolution*, 28.

of Vancouver practice: first, to protect a designated green zone consisting of the agricultural and park lands, watersheds, and environmentally sensitive areas that make up two thirds of the region's total land area; second, to develop compact communities in order to achieve density and scale economies in targeted areas; third, to further build and leverage these economies by designing "complete communities," where people can work, live, and play without having to travel great distances; and fourth, to build a regional infrastructure for transit, cycling, and walking to provide nonautomobile options for living in and moving between these complete communities.[17]

However, a city's built environment can also communicate something more sinister and ugly. Matt Hern sees a different side of Vancouver's celebrated urbanism. "But density without community just sucks. Thousands and thousands of people jammed into faceless little boxes, trying to pay off exorbitant mortgages is not much of a city."[18] At times the built environment of the city can work favorably for its inhabitants, but often it can have a negative effect. An example from Toronto highlights this effect:

> The problems that immigrants face in their personal development in Toronto have exacerbated the widening spatial gap in the urban region as well. The central city's recovering neighborhood citysystem have been less and less able to serve them. Historically, central Toronto was the landing point for the region's, and indeed for most of Canada's, immigrants. First-generation immigrants still make up half of central Toronto's population and more than a million immigrants have established residence there since 1980. But increasing numbers, unable to find jobs and affordable housing, have settled in the edge suburbs. Now three of greater Toronto's edge cities have a higher concentration of immigrants than Toronto itself.[19]

Along with the influences of the local job market, it is the physical nature of the city that poses challenges to these residents. If a city overly favors sprawl, it can create a clear demarcation between the haves and the have-nots. This is seen throughout cities in the developed world and is even more pronounced in developing nations. "Current forms of ur-

---

17. Ibid., 180.
18. Hern, *Common Ground in a Liquid City*, 54.
19. *Welcome to the Urban Revolution*, 173.

banization are pushing the lowest-income people into locations that are prone to natural hazards, such that four out of every ten non-permanent houses in the developing world are now located in areas threatened by floods, landslides and other natural disasters."[20]

While metro Vancouver is a poster child for densification, it also has rampant sprawl on its edges that creates parallel worlds between areas that are transit-oriented versus those that are car-dependent. "Canada currently has three of the world's ten urban areas with the most extensive sprawl – Calgary, Vancouver and Toronto."[21] A city's built environment now all of a sudden takes on a greater gravitas. Not only does it shape significantly the lives of those who live there, it has wide-reaching influences and impact upon them as well. In light of global changes, many cities are beginning to attempt to plan and build accordingly. "Rethinking how we create our built environment is critical in lessening our dependence on oil and minimizing our carbon footprint."[22] A theology of the built environment is more than simply observing what a city looks like; it is understanding its spiritual overtones (and undertones). "Metrospirituality embraces the city. It sees that physical issues are spiritual and the spiritual has physical implications."[23]

A city's built environment is one feature of its overall urbanism. Hiller defines "urbanism" as "a focus on cities and urban areas, their geography, economies, politics, social characteristics, as well as the effects on, and caused by, the built environment."[24] What urbanism highlights is how so much that takes place in the city (geography, economics, politics, etc.) affects the built environment, and in turn, how the built environment influences all of those other areas. Thus the need for theological reflection on this topic. As I wrote earlier in this book, as Christians, we think mostly along the lines of the spiritual and even when it comes to issues such as sin, we understand mostly about individual sin. Corporate or systemic sin evades our understandings, and yet one of its battlegrounds is a city's built environment. One such issue is gentrification. On the one hand, it beautifies and revitalizes a neighborhood, but on the other, it displaces the poor. How can a city have revitalization with-

20. UN-HABITAT, *Global Report on Human Settlement 2009*, 5.

21. Ibid., 28.

22. Newman, Beatley, and Boyer, *Resilient Cities*, 5.

23. Benesh, *Metrospiritual*, 152.

24. Hiller, *Urban Canada*, xii.

out the negative social ramifications? "A socially just urban renaissance must seek to counter the negative aspects of gentrification."[25] Freeway construction has been used to promote racial segregation agendas, as pockets of people are purposely separated from others by an eight-lane interstate cutting through a city. The more we understand a city's built environment and overall urbanism, the better our grasp is of the city, its ailments, and dreams.

For me, I need to understand not only Vancouver's urbanism but Canadian urbanism as well. Canadian urbanism focuses on the unique features of the fabric of urban life in Canada, including the built environment, cultural distinctive, immigration, and other features that set it apart, especially from its American counterparts. As detailed on the Canadian Urbanism website, the concept of "Canadian Urbanism" came to be from a few key observations:

1. Canada is increasingly an urban country.

2. There is a distinct Canadian Urbanism, a shared approach and perspective to cities and city-building that has evolved over time within our Canadian constitutional, political, social and cultural history.

3. Canadian cities and city-regions share challenges and opportunities unique to our Country. At the same time, Canadian Urbanism shares characteristics and challenges in common with progressive urbanist movements in other countries and global regions.

4. Canada's cities and city-regions face significant challenges and urgently require a more progressive, creative form of urbanism, to become more sustainable, liveable, healthy, and resilient.[26]

Each city has its own unique fingerprint which is influenced by larger cultural norms. The values system of the United States influences cities in their built environment. The same is happening here in Canada, which is why there are noticeable characteristics of cities between the two neighboring nations. Glenn Smith writes:

> For years urbanologists spoke about the North American city, combining Canadian and American cities in their analysis. However, if one applies the urban method we propose, it be-

25. Lees, Slater, and Wyly, *Gentrification*, xxiv.

26. CanU, "About Canadian Urbanism."

comes obvious that Canadian cities are distinct. In our URBAN FORM, Canadian cities are more compact in size and therefore considerably denser in population. In TRANSPORTATION and TRAVEL, Canadian cities have four times fewer freeways, relying 2.5 times more per capita on public transportation. (Interestingly, Americans own and operate 50% more motor vehicles than Canadians.) URBAN POPULATIONS represent more ethnic diversity, higher incomes, and more "traditional family" units. Canadian middle-income families show more propensity to stay in the central city. In monetary terms of URBAN GROWTH and DECLINE, Canadian cities are more stable, perhaps because URBAN SAFETY is much more in evidence.[27]

As mentioned earlier, there are numerous dynamics at play affecting a city's built environment that in turn affect everything else, especially those who live there. If we assess and reflect upon the changes in the North American economy and the differing phases of industrialization, it comes as no surprise as to the impact and influence they have had and continue to have upon the city. Each shift and advancement in industrialization shapes the city anew.

The First Wave cities were traditional walking cities with some use of horses and carriages while new industries began to develop along rivers and canals using water power. The Second Wave cities spread out along the railways of the steel and steam era. European cities have retained much of this corridor form. The Third Wave of electricity and the internal combustion engine saw electric tramways built, especially in the burgeoning cities of America such as Los Angeles, which had the world's most extensive tramway system. These cities followed linear development patterns along the tramways. At the same time the first cars and buses were appearing though they did not begin to shape city form until the Fourth Wave, which was dominated by cheap oil and which enabled cities to spread and sprawl in every direction. Thus was created the automobile city that confronts us today with the challenge of fossil fuel reduction. The Fifth Wave of Internet and digital technologies has replaced the old industrial manufacturing centers of cities with knowledgeable jobs, thus helping minimize some of the sprawl and spur the renewal of these older industrial sites. However the Fifth Wave still had cheap oil enabling cars to further dominate cities.

27. Smith, "Community Development in Canadian Cities."

> The Sixth Wave coincides with the end of cheap oil. It is the
> beginning of an era of resource productivity and investment in
> a new series of sustainability technologies related to renewables
> and distributed, small-scale water, energy, and waste systems
> (building on clever control systems and Smart Grids now per-
> fected from the Fifth Wave) all of which are more local and re-
> quire less fuel to distribute.[28]

No longer is a city's built environment simply a collection of
brick, concrete, steel, and glass buildings or a transportation network;
it communicates not only economic realities, but even an underlying
value system or spirituality. A theology of the built environment reflects
theologically on the city. On the one hand, the city is a reflection of the
creative genius of God, who has endowed mankind with amazing in-
novative faculties. On the other hand, since man is fallen and in need
of redemption, this is also displayed in the injustices that a city's built
environment communicates. How do we learn to distinguish between
the two? Let's take the example of fences. A nice, white-picket fence in
a suburban neighborhood communicates warmth, small-town charm,
and a connection to the rural. A fence in the city can communicate the
opposite: stay out. Edmonds Town Centre, where we live, is anchored by
Highgate Village, which is a mixed-use development. There are high-rise
residential towers atop grocery stores, coffee shops, ethnic stores, and
so forth. The crown jewel is a wonderful green space in the middle of
the towers. However, fences keep most of the neighborhood out. Often
we would be walking by as a family and notice other families inside the
fence playing soccer or frisbee on the grass. The fence keeps us out. It
also keeps the homeless out who often loiter just on the other side of the
fence, drinking liquor and smoking. Since I walk through this neighborhood daily, I often ask myself, what are the value systems that I see communicated in front of me? I see a plethora of BMWs and Mercedes autos
parked on the street in front of the towers, while just across the road
are low-rise apartments inhabited by many refugees and lower-income
immigrants. The towers and fences communicate a separation that is not
only physical, but also socio-economic.

So what's the best way for us to get to really know our city? How
do we learn to view our neighborhoods and cities through a theological
lens that far surpasses merely the academic? How do we begin to see

---

28. *Resilient Cities*, 52.

the city the way God does? Robert Linthicum offers a simple and yet profound way to begin that he calls "living into God's love for our city." I've reduced it to bullet points:

1. Spend time in silence and in an open, prayerful spirit before the map.

2. Ask God to reveal to you seven sites in the city that are particularly precious to Him.

3. Writes those down as they come, whether in one sitting or over time.

4. Take a full day off and visit every one of those sites. (Or do this over time.)

5. Walk to each site. If you have to drive, park a few blocks away and walk to the site slowly in a reflective, relaxed manner. Look around. Take it all in. Let your eyes see and your ears hear and your nostrils smell.

6. Enjoy the city God has created.

7. Linger awhile.

8. Ask God why this site is precious to Him.

9. Open your Bible and read some passages where God talks about His love for the city.

10. Be silent and listen.

11. Move on to the next site and repeat.[29]

A theology of the built environment is more then merely an academic discipline. The end goal is not only for us to understand our cities, but to begin seeing them through a theological lens. That in turn leads us into exploring our cities further and ultimately to love them and see them the way God does. And that can lead to only one response: taking action.

---

29. *City of God City of Satan*, 37–38.

14

High-Density, Walkable, and Bike-Friendly Cities

THERE ARE PLACES I visit in the city where I feel like I just stepped into a North Face, REI, or MEC photo shoot. Young urban hipsters riding single-speed urban commuter bikes, dressed in the latest outdoor clothing (just in case a blizzard hits . . . in July), sipping on lattes, totting yoga mats, and all with matching Apple computers with TOMS shoes stickers adorning the covers. Most appearances of the area being a gritty and "authentic" neighborhood have largely been replaced by yoga studios, cafes, coffee shops both chain and local, trendy clothing stores, and the like. Welcome to gentrification. Somewhere behind it all, just a block off the main thoroughfare, is an immigrant family from the Philippines packing up their belongings as their tenement housing complex is soon to be razed. In its place will soon arise a new "loft living" multi-use condo development with more trendy shops and cafes at the bottom and faux industrial-looking apartment lofts up above.

"If I am not yet disenchanted, I too have been dismayed by the way the city has morphed from a lumbering modern giant to a smooth, sleek, more expensive replica of its former self,"[1] laments Brooklyn College Professor of Sociology Sharon Zukin, who sees this same type of phenomenon unfolding in New York City." She adds, "I do miss the look and feel of neighborhoods whose diversity was tangible in the smells and sounds of ethnic cooking, experimental art galleries and performance spaces, and faces and voices of men and women who came from everywhere to create the distinctive character of the streets."[2] Welcome to

1. Zukin, *Naked City*, x.
2. Ibid.

151

the rapidly changing landscape of the city, not only here in Canada and the United States, but globally as well. Cities continue to reinvent themselves. Some already claim prominent and influential status while others are like the mythological Phoenix rising up from the ashes.

In the past two chapters, we explored the lightly-trod and rarely-visited topics of a theology of place and the built environment. Now we've come to a fork in the trail. Right or left? To the right, the trail continues to meander below the ridge line and eventually empties out into a wide grassy meadow between two massive snow-capped peaks. To the left, the trail shoots straight up the ridge and quickly out of sight. According to the map, it is at best a faint trail and rarely used. What we can tell is that once on the razor-like rocky ridge, the trail follows the precipitous route until the explorer is overlooking a massive glacier down below on the left. Which trail should I take? Safe and secure or risky and adverse? As I continue to look at the city, that is where I feel I am at personally—at a fork in the trail. I suppose I don't feel any great notion of risk sitting in this coffee shop . . . maybe I could fall off my chair or my coffee might be a touch too hot. So what then is the risk I'm feeling? It is to begin envisioning a better city.

What is a better city and how do we quantify it? "Better," like beauty, is in the eye of the beholder. For many, the brief impression of the city that I just shared is a much desired outcome. To a large degree, I share that desire. For years, I pined for downtown Tucson to become fully revitalized. I greeted every new restaurant, coffee shop, or store opening with continued excitement. Once construction began on a new electric modern streetcar, I wondered if the city had finally reached the tipping point. Maybe, just maybe, the city would become a bastion of hipness, coolness, and we'd see the rise of the Creative Class. Years later, having lived in and among low-income international refugees and immigrants, I've begun to see the city in a different light. No longer is a sprawling desert city my lens or grid through which I view and interpret the city; it is instead a city in the Pacific Northwest that is sprawling and rapidly densifying at the same time. Gentrification and development are taking place in countless neighborhoods across the city in varying degrees of size and scope. "How development is defined may differ by scale and, in addition, the approaches to development may be similarly scale-dependent."[3]

---

3. Willis, *Theories and Practices of Development*, 8.

Context can de decisive. It informs our understanding for everything we see and experience. I see cities differently from when I lived in Tucson compared to now living in metro Vancouver. So much has happened to stimulate a deeper understanding of cities as well as provided me with ample tools to evaluate and assess the vital essentials of what makes cities great. As I've shared both in this book as well as in *Metrospiritual*, there are several events that took place that reoriented and transformed our lives in the way we think about and experience cities, both individually and as a family. First, we have experienced the city through the lens of public transportation and NMT (non-motorized transportation) since we're car-less in the city. Second, we have struggled to eke out a living in a city as a church planter who lacked the aptitude to raise the financial support we needed. Add to that mix living in a foreign country on a clergy work permit which restricts what I can and cannot do. All of a sudden we were thrust into a world and lifestyle that we were not prepared for. We quickly transitioned from an American middle-class suburban lifestyle with two SUVs in a sea of low-density sprawl, to finding ourselves in the same boat as many of our neighborhood friends who are refugees or immigrants from unstable or war-torn nations. We were not aiming at being a part of the current upswing of believers who are moving into the city to gather in intentional communities and live incarnationally in and among the poor or marginalized. To be quite honest, I was determined to move into a trendy gentrified neighborhood, cruise the streets on my single-speed bike, and sip lattes in the various cafes. But God had other plans.

Through this immersion-by-necessity, we were thrust into a new world that smacked up against our middle-class upbringing and inherent values system. Buying a lot of our groceries at the dollar store, purchasing all of our clothes at the thrift store, and walking, biking, longboarding, or getting everywhere on public transit became the new norm. Indeed God has been faithful and countless times we have been on the undeserving receiving end of his gifts and grace. Numerous times as we've contemplated heading over to the local food bank, because we had only $20 in our checking account and it was Monday (payday was Friday), we would all of a sudden get a check in the mail for $150 or something like it. We've learned God's grace, love, kindness, and favor is far more than we deserve. Compared to many other families we know who are crammed into smaller apartments, we feel incredibly blessed.

Compared to the reality of global poverty, we still live like kings. The reason behind bringing this up is that I was forced to look at the city with a completely new set of lenses. The concept of high-density, walkable, and bike-friendly cities is more than a preferred lifestyle choice for urban hipsters in trendy gentrified neighborhoods; it has become a necessity not only for me but for many who live here and in other similar districts and neighborhoods across the city.

I began to notice a growing awareness of consumption patterns in my life that had previously marked me. Like shackles, they began falling off and I started living freer than I had ever before in my life, despite struggling to keep afloat. At times, we sold furniture or the myriad of extra bikes and bike parts I had collected over the years, so we could buy groceries. At the same time, I continued immersing myself in books on the city; urban planning, architecture, car-free cities, bike-friendly cities, Canadian urbanism and so much more, as I put aside books on the missional church or church planting. I was on a mission to begin making sense of this strange new world I found myself in. As I walked my neighborhood or rode to other parts of the city, the question that haunted me was, "What makes a city great?" It must be more than simply a robust economy, a picturesque skyline, vibrant entertainment districts, and global notoriety. It has to include an infrastructure that does not exclude the poor or disadvantaged.

In their book *Resilient Cities*, authors Peter Newman, Timothy Beatley, and Heather Boyer offer a glimpse of the state of our cities and even begin envisioning their future: "What does a resilient city look like? Bike paths and virtually car-free streets that lead from solar homes to grocery stores, recreation areas, parks, or a free tram to reach places too far to walk or bike. A solar office block filled with new Sixth Wave businesses. Schools with parents lined up on bikes to pick up kids instead of waiting in idling cars. A local farmers' market for buying bioregional produce."[4] The contention and argument that they set forth is that as a society, we're too car-dependent. It is an admission that a portion of the ills that plague the city are derived from high auto usage and the ensuing effects on a city's inhabitants and built environment. An auto-dependent city is most often equated with low-density sprawl that hurtles the city's growth outwards. Among many people, there is now a push underway to reverse these trends. To stop outward sprawl, they advocate densify-

4. Newman, Beatley, and Boyer, *Resilient Cities*, 55.

ing cities in their built environment, expanding public transportation, and reducing dependence upon personal vehicles. There are practical ramifications for this switch. "The denser a city, the less its residents drive, the more they use transit, walk, and bike. This suggests that people drive mostly because they have no other alternative. Providing nearby density to support transit, walking, and bicycling is a critical component to lessening oil dependence and reducing greenhouse gas emissions."[5]

How did all of this come about? What were the transitions in urban form that got us to this point? Cities, like organisms, are constantly changing, morphing, and adapting. Detailed below are some of the major key changes in the fabric of cities based upon transportation patterns:

> *Walking Cities* were (and are) dense, mixed-use area of no more than five kilometers across. These were the major urban form for eight thousand years and in substantial parts of cities likeHo Chi Minh, Mumbai, and Hong Kong, the character of a walking city has been retained. Krakow is mostly a walking city. In wealthy cities like New York, San Francisco, Chicago, London, Vancouver, and Sydney, the central areas are mostly walking cities in character.
>
> *Transit Cities* from 1850 to 1950 were based on trains and trams, which meant they could spread twenty to thirty kilometers with dense centers and corridors following rail lines and stations. Most European and wealthy Asian cities retain this form, and the old U.S., Australian, and Canadian inner cities are also transit-oriented. Many developing cities in Asia, Africa, and Latin America have the dense corridors form of a transit city but don't always have the transit systems to support them; thus they become car-saturated.
>
> *Automobile Cities* from the early 1950s on; could spread fifty to eighty kilometers in all directions and at low density. U.S., Canadian, Australian, and New Zealand and many new parts of European cities began to develop in this way, but these new areas are reaching the limits of a half-hour car commute as they sprawl outward. These are the most vulnerable areas to the oil peak.[6]

As I've explained before, a city's urban form affects so much in terms of culture, accessibility, and the day-to-day lives of its inhabitants. What I mean is, when it comes to urban mission or church planting, our responsibility as missiologists is to adapt and form our practices,

5. Ibid., 84.
6. Ibid., 89.

methods and strategies around what the urban context presents. It is imperative to keep in mind that "Cities are the epicenter of God's earth-shaking movements today, and it's important that any model for starting new churches takes into account the unique nuances of ministry in an urban context."[7] The challenge comes when there is a disregard for the profound influence that built environment and transportation infrastructure have on the city. We talk at length about "impacting our neighborhood," but how is that possible when most of the congregation lives miles away and commutes in for worship? "If the church wants to be the 'body of Christ' by including every member in its life, shouldn't the church advocate communal life that can fully include all members of the society as well?"[8]

Transportation affects more than the fabric of church life; it can have an enormous impact on a city economically as well. "A speedy and efficient transportation system may be more important than ever in the context of today's globally competitive, information-based service economy."[9] It influences church life, the local economy, and everything in between. What does all of this mean, then? Transportation is more than light rail trains, buses, or bike paths, in that it plays a massive shaping influence on those who live in these settings. Unfortunately, this is a conversation that most Evangelical Protestants are unaware of or don't engage in. We Americans have wrapped the gospel in the American flag and deal in middle-class values and politics. Often when I talk to others about favoring urban densification, bike-friendly cities, and public transportation, they smack up against these value systems. In particular, the US is "the home of the free" which we've equated to having the "right" for ample space and our own vehicles, thereby making it the underlying value system for suburbia. Far from being simply low-density in its built environment, various parts of the city do indeed communicate the values of its inhabitants whether we realize it or not. "Values underlie almost every decision in urban design and exert large influences on the organization of space."[10] To begin asking people to park their cars, walk more, bike more, live in higher-density neighborhoods then becomes a personal assault on this value system.

7. Patrick and Carter, *For the City*, 26.

8. Jacobsen, *Sidewalks in the Kingdom*, 27.

9. Staley and Moore, *Mobility First*, 38.

10. Crawford, *Carfree Design Manual*, 33.

Don't get me wrong. It's not all fun and games or simply a trendy neo-hippie way to live. Taking public transportation or calling a cab to get to the hospital is not fun. Standing in near-horizontally pouring rain waiting for a bus at 6:00 AM makes one call into question many things. There are times when the reality of bussing or biking for an hour to get somewhere knowing it would take only 20 minutes by car causes consternation. However, it is worth it. Many are waking up to the reality that the auto has altered their lifestyle in unhealthy ways. In his book, *Pedaling Revolution: How Cyclists Are Changing American Cities*, Jeff Mapes watches this trend unfold: "For the first time since the car became the dominant form of American transportation after World War II, there is now a grassroots movement to seize at least a part of the street back from motorists. A growing number of Americans, mounted on their bicycles like some new kind of urban cowboy, are mixing it up with swift, two-ton motor vehicles as they create a new society on the streets. They're finding physical fitness, low-cost transportation, environmental purity – and, still all too often, Wild West risks of sudden death or injury."[11] It should be noted that not all cities are created equally and that some are better equipped and oriented for this than other cities. I am fortunate to live in the Pacific Northwest with cities like Vancouver and Portland leading the way in terms of bike-friendly cities, public transportation infrastructure, or walkable neighborhoods. "Portland has been celebrated in urban planning circles and routinely lands at the top of various rankings of livability, walkability, and environmental sustainability."[12] This doesn't necessarily happen in Dallas, Orlando or Phoenix. With that said, though, how much can we change individually? Are our cities even favorable in this way? Many have seen the statistic that reveals "40 percent of U.S. trips are two miles or less."[13] I believe it was statistics like this combined with the emerging battle over value systems that prompted Mapes to ask, "Can Americans really be seduced out of their cars in large numbers, at least for short trips?"[14]

This gets to the heart of the earlier analogy of the fork in the trail and choosing the more adventurous route. Due to lifestyle changes (whether forced upon us or not), I've grown over time to become an advocate

11. Mapes, *Pedaling Revolution*, 7–8.
12. Ibid., 146.
13. Ibid., 14.
14. Ibid., 10.

for densification, walkable neighborhoods, a better and more ubiquitous public transportation infrastructure, and bike-friendly cities. I believe that there are numerous benefits that can reorient our cities and provide the soil for new churches to take root in. In terms of fertile environs for new churches, it does not get any better than this. As I've detailed in this book already, if our goal is city transformation, then we need a new approach and a different trajectory than the one we're on. We've narrowed the scope of God's activity in the city to the salvation of individuals taking place in the context of our worship gatherings. Responding to this mindset, Robert Linthicum writes, "We cannot simply save individuals in the city and expect that the city will get saved. If the church does not deal with the systems and structures of evil in the city, then it will not effectively transform the lives of that city's individuals."[15] What is needed is more thinking about the city's systems.

What role should the church or followers of Jesus play in a city's built environment? When it comes to dense walkable neighborhoods, there seems to be much that is congruent with the values of the Kingdom of God. On the other hand, low-density sprawl can have an adverse affect on people and the church. "The retreat of many well-to-do Americans behind the walls of gated communities, where they are seldom exposed to people from a different social class (except service personnel), has had a pernicious effect on American society and the maintenance of the social glue that binds the nation together."[16] Rather than only tackling it on a purely "spiritual" plane, what about churches seeing the development of the city and its various neighborhoods as part of their ministry? Since the built environment affects (or affirms) people's values systems, then why not play a role in shaping it? We do know that a city's urban form influences the health of its residents. "In the last decade, new studies have suggested that people who live in the cities are thinner than suburbanites, in part because they walk more instead of being constantly delivered from front door to front door by car."[17] As a result, I would affirm that "Non-motorized transport (NMT)—bikes and walking—need to be given priority over motorized vehicles, especially in dense

---

15. Linthicum, *City of God City of Satan*, 46–47.

16. *Carfree Design Manual*, 33.

17. *Pedaling Revolution*, 21.

centers."[18] Dense walkable neighborhoods and bike-friendly cities have been proven to promote health and reduce health care costs:

> Denmark used the City of Odense to test out various cycling programs, and a study found that savings in health care costs and sick leave were more than 50 percent greater than the investments in cycling. Since then, the government has continued to devote additional spending – and road space – to cyclists. Denmark now rivals the Netherlands in its use of the bicycle as a form of transportation. European health experts have also been influenced by a Finnish study that recruited previously sedentary adults to walk and bike to work, and found that both produced pronounced improvements in cardiovascular fitness but that the greatest gains were among those who cycled.[19]

Where is the church in this conversation? In our push to constantly grow larger in attendance, we have often (perhaps unknowingly) adopted a commuter value system that not only clogs our roadways but which can also as a consequence do the same to our hearts by promoting inactivity and a sedentary lifestyle. I told you that this fork in the trail was lightly used.

There are practical benefits to density. "Higher and more compact city design conserves valuable land resources, reduces transport distance and, thus, the energy needed, and the density makes public transport more viable."[20] Some even advocate removing cars altogether from urban neighborhoods. In his book, *Carfree Cities*, J. H. Crawford writes, "If we are to improve the form of our cities, we must first remove cars from urban areas, so that other needs can regain the primacy they once had."[21] That's a strong statement, but I understand the point that he is trying to make. I'm not one who longingly dreams of the cities of yesteryear before the advent of the car. However, there are benefits that the built environment in those pre-auto cities reveal today, primarily in dense, mixed-use, and walkable neighborhoods. It is these cities that Chye Kiang Heng and Lai Choo Malone-Lee write about: "Many now see the pre-industrial traditional cities as offering viable models of urban development, whose size was decided by comfortable walking distance,

18. *Resilient* Cities, 98.

19. *Pedaling Revolution*, 237.

20. Ng, *Designing High-Density* Cities, xxxi.

21. Crawford, *Carfree Cities*, 53.

urban forms organized in fine grain networks composed of narrower streets and public spaces, and urban life richly intertwined in an organic way across a relatively dense and compact urban fabric."[22]

When it comes to envisioning the future realities of the city, what voice do the church and the followers of Jesus have? Are we so preoccupied with church growth that we'll take it at any cost while the city exists simply for our utilitarian purposes? Are we no better than spiritual Vikings, pillaging the city for what we need and casting it aside when it no longer serves our needs? Why should we not envision a better future of our cities? Why should we defer to urban planners, realtors, developers, and politicians? What if we could catch just a glimpse of how dense walkable neighborhoods, bike-friendly cities, and thoroughly public transportation could indeed increase the impact and influence of the church and at the same time promote values that are more Kingdom-minded than consumer-oriented. What if, indeed?

Ponder with me the "Seven Elements of a Vision for More Resilient Transport" from the book *Resilient Cities*:

1. A transit system that is faster than traffic in all major corridors.

2. Viable centers along the corridors that are dense enough to service a good transit system.

3. Walkable areas and cycling facilities that can mean easy access by nonmotorized means, especially in these centers.

4. Services and connectivity that can guarantee access at most times of the day or night without time wasted.

5. Phasing out freeways and phasing in congestion taxes that are directed back into the funding of transit and walk/cycle facilities as well as traffic-calming measures.

6. Continual improvement of vehicle engines to ensure emissions, noise, and fuel consumption are reduced, especially a move to electric vehicles.

7. Regional and local governance that can enable visionary green transport plans and funding schemes to be introduced.[23]

22. *Designing High-Density Cities*, 42.
23. *Resilient Cities*, 90–91.

In reflecting on Kingdom values, how does this affirm and uphold the poor and marginalized that are close to the heart of God? It is scary to realize that urban form can continue to marginalize the marginalized. Not only would the poor and disabled benefit from these types of dense walkable neighborhoods, but it would also provide much traction for church planting and ministry in the city. There is so much going on in the city today that whether our focus is urban ministries or church planting, we need to understand better its influence on our lives and the way it shapes our ministry.

15

Pedestrian-Oriented Church Planting

SINCE MOVING TO VANCOUVER, my mind has been churning continuously over the practical implications of how to do ministry and
church planting based upon the city's built environment. As I shared in
the previous chapter, a major component is viewing the city through the
grid of it being pedestrian-oriented or transit-friendly. How does this
impact and influence ministry in these contexts? Do we blindly ignore
urban realities and plant churches as we would anywhere else, whether it
be suburban Dallas, Regina, Manhattan, Sherbrooke, or Boise? There are
indeed similar and shared commonalities to church planting from coast
to coast. But too often we have cultural blind spots. I find churches on
the west coast that are culturally no different from rural Arkansas, and I
know of small-town church plants that emulate the culture, imagery, and
strategy of urban churches that are in hip, gentrified neighborhoods in
large cities. Church planting and ministry run the temptation of simply
being a widget factory, in that the end product looks the same from context to context. As we as a family became more and more embedded in
our neighborhood, I realized quickly that church planting in this context
has to look different from the typical norms. It is along this theme that
authors Mark Driscoll and Gerry Breshears write, "A missional church
goes to great lengths to understand the people God has sent them to. It
seeks to know the culture and people better than any other organization,
even businesses, so that Jesus can be most effectively, persuasively, and
winsomely introduced."[1]

The topic of perspectives, lenses, or layers of the city continues to
crop up, because the dominant lens that we choose affects and influences
the way in which we view the city. Ministry or church planting then ends

---

1. Driscoll and Breshears, *Vintage Church*, 224.

up being shaped by this lens. Since I pay particular attention to urban form, my logical next step is to build and adapt strategies based upon it. In the same way that it would be absurd to plant a walkable church in rural Iowa, why do we then plant churches in cities that are devoid of context in relation to its urbanism? Based upon our life circumstances as I detailed previously, combined with the current realities across my city, I began thinking, "What if?" What if we started churches across the city with the pedestrian in mind? What would happen if we viewed the car as an obstacle that could potentially hinder people's access to the life of a church, and therefore removed it? For many of our friends in our neighborhood, the car is viewed as a luxury that is beyond their reach, anyway.

This past semester, I taught a class for the Canadian Southern Baptist Seminary and College called *Community Transformation in the City*. We spent considerable time exploring not only Canadian urbanism but Vancouver's urbanism as well and its affects and influence on community development or transformation. As I continued mulling over these themes, I ran some ideas by my friend Stephen Harper[2] who I was working with to coordinate, set up, and teach courses here locally through the seminary in Cochrane, Alberta. We began talking through different ideas to spread the word about the opportunity for people in metro Vancouver to take courses for credit and what we're doing overall. Somewhere along the way we decided to hold a public lecture or discussion to explore various themes we've been looking at in our classes. The theme we decided on was *the walkable church*. Soon we linked up with Paul Sparks and Tim Soerens who started the Parish Collective[3] in Seattle-Tacoma. This partnership proved to be invaluable since the Parish Collective defines itself as "a growing collective of churches, missional groups, faith-based orgs, and community development associations which are rooted in the neighborhood and linked across cities."[4] This was a perfect fit for exploring the walkable church and pedestrian-oriented church planting rooted in the neighborhood.

We set a date for the event and then began spreading the word. When the day arrived, Tim and Paul came up from Seattle. One of the fun features was that we held the lecture at Southside Church just a few

2. Not to be mistaken for the Canadian Prime Minister.

3. www.parishcollective.org

4. Ibid.

blocks away from where I live. The night proved to be invaluable as we kicked around and discussed topics related to a theology of place as well as pedestrian-oriented church planting and the walkable church. Tim did a masterful job of traversing through a theology of place that is rooted in a Trinitarian theology. I then shared about pedestrian-oriented church planting. What follows in the rest of this chapter are some of the specifics that I taught on that night. My desire is to begin laying a foundation for a walkable church as well as pedestrian-oriented church planting. As I track and follow church planting in the contexts of the future development of cities with more high-density environs, this is an attempt to set forth a course correction on the trajectory of church planting in cities.

So what if we started churches with the pedestrian in mind? Church planting lore is sprinkled with successful commuter churches. But what if we reduced the scale to those who live within a walkable proximity of where a church engages in body life, whether day-to-day interactions or worship gatherings? While this was more of the norm in cities before the advent of the car, most cities today have a definitive outward sprawl pattern which from the onset makes this idea of pedestrian-oriented church planting challenging. "In contrast, other cities, such as Chicago, Montreal, and various European cities were built and developed in their central cities before the rise of the automobile. With that in mind, urban planners had to think through issues of ease of access for people as they were on foot or horse. If that is how typical city dwellers got around town, there's no trekking six miles to one's 'local' Starbucks."[5] Cities in North America are simply different now from the way they were then. "The contemporary urban area is more dynamic and travel patterns more complex, than in the nineteenth and twentieth centuries when the current 'DNA' of the transportation system was established."[6] My intention is not to set forth some purely inapplicable neo-hippie purist ideal where we simply walk everywhere in Birkenstock sandals, use McDonald's french fry grease to power biodiesel mopeds, and make our own hemp clothing, but rather let urban realities shape our strategies and methodologies for ministry and church planting. Not only that, but our desire for healthy churches to be woven into the fabric of the city also means that we collectively envision a better future for our cities as well. "A century during which the vast majority of the world's population

5. Benesh, *Metrospiritual*, 44.

6. Staley and Moore, *Mobility First*, 26.

will have to live in urban environments cries out for images of the good city."[7] Are we responding to changes in the city as well as forging a path towards this notion of a "good" or "great" city in ways that align with the values of the Kingdom and God's blueprint for urban life?

Does how we get to church matter? What do a church's commuting patterns communicate? What would happen to a church if oil prices escalated to the point where many simply opted not to drive at all or at least only for work? The trends in our cities reveal that traffic congestion is an ever-growing reality that does not seem to abate. "What does this mean for everyday travel? Traffic delays will double over the next 25 years in 16 of the 20 most congested areas even though they already face severe congestion. The exceptions are the most congested cities in the nation: Los Angeles, Chicago, Washington, and San Francisco; their congestion is already so severe that doubling it is statistically difficult."[8] In reflecting on questions related to these issues, I've developed a working definition of pedestrian-oriented church planting. "Pedestrian-Oriented Church Planting is starting walkable churches in dense neighborhoods that are accessible by foot, available for all local inhabitants (rich, poor, young, old, and different ethnicities), rooted in the community, and acts as lead catalysts in community transformation."[9] That definition immediately raises other questions. How does this differ from the church planting norm? What are some of the differences in values and assumptions between pedestrian-oriented church planting and conventional commuter-based church planting? Doing ministry and church planting in this manner acknowledges three foundational realities; the built environment plays a shaping role (density), transportation influences the body life of a church (mobility), and theology of place is valued (city care).

I believe there are significant benefits to pedestrian-oriented church planting that are worthy of exploration. One such benefit is that it is accessible to all. Those who live in higher-density neighborhoods have more accessibility to your church and its body life. Socio-economics no longer is a dividing line, because people are not excluded because they can't drive to any of the gatherings. While in some cities that are transit-friendly there is the reality of being able to use transit to stay connected to the life of a body, but that is not always easy. Here's an example from

7. Friedman, *Insurgencies: Essays in Planning Theory*, 149.

8. Ibid., 18.

9. I first shared this at *The Walkable Church* lecture on March 23, 2011.

my own life. We live about two miles from a discount grocery store with great cost-saving prices that is helpful for a family of five. While the distance is relatively close, the fact that the only way for us to get there is via public transit makes the journey more of a challenge. That two-mile trek takes roughly about a half an hour. That includes walking to the bus stop, waiting for the next bus, cramming into this usually crowded bus with a pull-along grocery cart, getting lurched around on the mad dash from city center to city center, only to hop off the bus and wade through an ocean of people who are also seeking to save on groceries. Then the process is repeated on the way home. Also, since the grocery store is at a very busy shopping mall, it is not uncommon that the bus you're waiting for simply cruises past you and the other would-be riders since it is full from the previous stop. Then you're stuck there in the rain, holding an umbrella, with a packed pull-along cart full of food and toiletries wondering if the next bus will also be too full to pick you up. After the second bus passes by, you give up and walk across to the other side of the mall to take the Skytrain back home, which means upon arrival waiting for another bus to deliver us somewhat close to home. That "simple" trip to the grocery store just took about three hours. On the other hand, it is so much easier to pull your grocery cart three blocks to the neighborhood grocery store. And while the prices are not the best, the round-trip shopping excursion takes thirty minutes, and we save the cost of bus fare. All along the way to and from the store as well as inside it, you see the same familiar faces that you see on a daily basis. How is this similar to asking people who don't have cars to "just transit" to engage in the life of your church?

The scope of the city is almost terrifying to take in when we think of church planting, let alone pedestrian-oriented church planting. The needs are overwhelming. There is no denying that what I'm advocating for has a definitive bias towards the more marginalized as evidenced by this local statistic: "For the fifth-straight recorded year, British Columbia has the highest child poverty rate in Canada. The poverty rate for B.C. children living in families headed by lone-parent mothers was 50.3 percent in 2006, while the poverty rate for two-parent families was 16.3 percent."[10] What are we communicating about God's love and concern for the widow, the orphan, and the foreigner when so much of our church planting efforts are focused on the powerful, the middle class, the urban

10. Hern, *Common Ground in a Liquid City*, 159.

hipster, or the upper crust? "With church planting emphases still leaning towards a suburban bias, the trends for where to start churches are still slow to shift back to the city."[11] This has a shaping effect on who we plant churches among and where. Pedestrian-oriented church planting has an aim to remove obstacles or barriers that may hinder various segments of society and make church life accessible to all.

A second benefit to this mode of church planting is that it creates a natural rootedness in the neighborhood. If one of the identifying markers of a church is its auto-dependent commuting patterns, that can pose some serious threats to local involvement on the neighborhood scale. "Whereas it was once commonplace for people to worship with others in their neighborhood, the commuter mentality catapulted the church growth movement. Churches became regional and it is not uncommon for people to drive an hour to worship with others throughout the city. One of the challenges is the lack of ties and connections to the neighborhood."[12] Many already struggle with living fragmented and chaotic lives in the frenetic pace of the city. Long commutes to and from work, homework and extracurricular activities for school-age children and much more, plague many families. So often people spend hours each and every day in their cars. "The car-dominated culture of the city demands highways that slice it up, segmenting communities and threatening pedestrian activity, which drives us even further into our metal boxes and away from each other."[13] Does this mean that the life of a church should follow suit? Moving away from over-dependency on automobiles has many practical implications. "There are many reasons—environmental, economic, health, and social—to overcome car dependence."[14] We could add spiritual as well. Not just simply spiritual in the sense of our own individual walk with God, but the overall life of our local churches as well.

Another benefit of pedestrian-oriented church planting and walkable churches in denser urban environments is that the foundation of community is found in the communal. This builds off the second point in elevating rootedness in place. Although the church is in an era where the whole neo-monastic, communal-living way of church life is gaining

11. *Metrospiritual*, xxi.
12. Ibid., 157.
13. Wood and Landry, *The Intercultural City*, 4.
14. Newman, Beatley, and Bower, *Resilient Cities*, 87.

momentum, this is not necessarily what I'm advocating. For the majority of believers, that way of living is either not doable or desirable. For sure, there is a lot of value in communal living, especially in urban environments. However, what I am highlighting is that a walkable church means that people are living within proximity of one another. When that is the case, then church life takes on a more communal element as there is a greater chance of spontaneous run-ins whether at the coffee shop, grocery store, library, and so forth. Also it begins to eradicate any notion of "Sunday Christian" versus "Monday Christian." As we live in community and proximity with one another in a neighborhood, we can no longer hide or pretend. "An urban setting doesn't allow for as much space between people as the suburbs do, creating an urban mind-set that doesn't allow people to retreat and reappear with masks. Authenticity is not optional since fakery is too easily uncovered. Life is raw and fast, not allowing time for collected wits or subdued emotions."[15]

When there are long commute times for churchgoers, whether for worship or gathering with others during the week, distance becomes a hindrance. I think there is something amiss in the city when one commutes 20 miles one way to connect and worship with a group of believers. This is more a way of life in rural areas, but it does not have to be so in the city. I wonder out loud as to how much of this is really reflective of our consumptive patterns. Why else would one want to commute five, 10, 15, 20, or 30 miles to go to church? Most often we will hear such responses as, "It's because I like the preaching," or "They have great music," or "I really connect with them." The focus seems to be on what *we* desire rather than seeking God's heart and vision for our neighborhood and its overall health and transformation. In light of this, what we most often do is conflate *community* with *uniformity*. We like to hang out with and be around people most like us . . . and we will drive to get it. A communal neighborhood-rooted element to church life forces us to deal with what community is all about. We're also forced to even be in community with people not like us or who we may not even like. The following story was a painful teachable moment in our own lives.

When we first moved to Vancouver, we moved into a building with three different apartment units. We lived on the second storey and under us lived Tony. Tony was in his late 60's, lived alone, and was estranged from his family. Since we lived right above him, both of our doors, front

15. Smith, *City Signals*, 168.

and back, came out next to each of his, so we'd see him numerous times during the week. For the first few weeks of our living above him, the relationship was cordial, but that soon began to wear off. The building was a good 50 years old with no insulation in the walls or the floor. In other words, sound carried upstairs and downstairs, and having three boys meant we made a lot more noise than most. Unfortunately, the person living below us could hear every footstep, jump, dropped object, fumbled longboard, and so forth. I've even had conversations with Tony through the floor/ceiling. This is where things began to take a turn for the worse.

Tony worked downtown until after midnight and by the time he got home it was 1:00 a.m. He'd stay up for another hour before going to sleep. We rarely heard him come home, but in the morning he certainly heard us. He struggled with arthritis, so he took a concoction of medications that would keep him in bed until around noon. Our family would usually be up around 7:00, as the boys would be getting ready for school. Whoever designed the building thought it must be brilliant to put our kitchen with no carpeting or insulation right above the downstairs master bedroom. As we would be cooking, scooting chairs to and from the table, and clanking dishes around, inevitably it would wake Tony up. In a medicated fog he'd pound on the wall. When I heard it the first time I could hardly believe what I was hearing. "Is he really shushing us?" I thought. How could we get ready for the day? In the weeks that followed, tensions began building to a flashpoint. Soon the light tap on the wall turned into him pounding and sometimes yelling. We'd notify the landlord and there'd be a three-way conversation in which Tony, then fully awake, was amicable and cooperative. Then it would start all over the next day and get ugly. I remember one day Katie calling me in tears, because when she walked across the kitchen floor around 10:30 in the morning, Tony banged on the walls and swore at her through the floor telling her to take her shoes off. I immediately came home for another three-way conversation.

What were we to do? We were at our wit's end, so we decided to simply love him. We'd make him cookies, bring him coffee, and just talk with him. On his birthday, when his family didn't bother coming over, Katie made him a birthday cake. Over time we began a friendship that was almost Jekyll-and-Hyde because during the afternoons we'd have great conversations and the next morning he'd pound on the walls.

However, we learned of Tony's brokenness and his estrangement for his family. I began praying for him and then I began praying with him. Whenever we'd get together and chat he'd always finish the time by asking me to pray for him. I shared often of God's love for him and prayed that he would be reconciled with his family. This all went on for the first six months we lived in Vancouver. Then one day Tony left. Government housing opened up downtown and within a week he was gone.

While we were immensely relieved in that we could finally breathe again as a family, I'll never forget what I learned about community. When community is about uniformity, we get to pick and choose who we hang out with; but when community is found in the communal, we have no choice but to learn to get along despite our differences. It is easy to be flakey and just leave. Trust me, for six months we desperately tried moving into another apartment elsewhere but nothing worked out. When that did not happen we had to simply deal with it, and it was really painful for all of us. But God was kind and gracious and I pray that Tony saw that in us. When church is done and lived out in the neighborhood, it is done so publicly seven days a week. People will see the way we live, how we treat our kids, how we treat the cashiers and the baristas, and so much more

A church that is rooted in a neighborhood has the opportunity to act as a lead catalyst in community transformation. When churches are walkable and neighborhood-focused, they can begin forming the backbone of transformation endeavors. We live here, we value the neighborhood, we know what is going on, we have a vested interest, and we have the good news of the Kingdom of God that provides a great template for community transformation. Simultaneously, we can demonstrate a return to simplicity and a healthier way of life. Pedestrian-oriented church planting does simplify and slow down the life of the church. We become less frenetic since it cuts down on commuting. There's nothing more enjoyable than walking or longboarding to a worship gathering. This allows for simple, non-programmatic, relational ways of church life to become part of everyday life. Relationships are elevated and that has a reciprocal affect on a neighborhood.

A pedestrian-oriented church can also act as the glue that holds together the social capital in a neighborhood. Again, social capital is "The good will, sympathy, and connections created by social interaction within and between social networks."[16] What role does or should the church play in strengthening the social capital in neighborhoods across the city? Are we only concerned with spiritual activities like worship and Bible study to the point where we're disconnected from the rhythms of our neighborhood? As I've shared before, it is not an either/or but a both/and. When churches are rooted, they are able to sense the pulse of the neighborhood, knowing where the people and community are hurting and where they are healthy and thriving. The church has the powerful potential to step in as mouthpieces for the Kingdom, proclaim and live out the good news, point people to the King (Jesus), and demonstrate what life is like under him.

There most certainly is a significant amount of cultural adaptation that needs to take place when we think of church planting along this vein. Resiliency is key whether personally or as a church that seeks to be embedded physically and relationally in a neighborhood. Given the diversity of cities, there is a massive cultural shift at hand both on the individual level and collectively as a church. Authors Phil Wood and Charles Landry lay out the decisions one must face in this new cultural milieu:

> Typically when cultures meet there are four responses, whether this is for a Briton moving to Spain, a Costa Rican to Canada or a Hong Kong Chinese moving to Australia: to stay monocultural and become chauvinist by rejecting new influences as alien so retreating and entrenching within one's own culture and at the extreme to become militant nationalists; to assimilate to the host's culture and "pass off" as part of the new, so rejecting one's origins; to marginalize oneself by identifying with neither culture or to vacillate between the two and feel at home in neither; to synthesize elements of one's culture or origin and that of the host, which is equivalent of integration at the personal level. The result is to acquire a genuine bicultural or multicultural personality. These people can code switch—they are like a hyphenated person. They have flexibility and a relatively high degree of resilience.[17]

Will Christians individually or collectively as the church stay monocultural, marginalize themselves, reject the city and prevailing urban form, or seek to synthesize our methods and strategies to adapt to high-

---

16. Wikimedia Foundation Inc., "Social Capital."

17. *The Intercultural City*, 52.

density walkable neighborhoods? Are the Kingdom and the spiritual health of our cities worth it?

This chapter serves simply as a primer on this overall topic of pedestrian-oriented church planting and the concept of a walkable church. Again, this whole idea simply builds off the notion of adapting church life around urban form. The goal is not to do something unique or new as a novelty, but instead, to ensure our models and strategies are reflective of the cities we live in.

16

Authentic Neighborhoods
and a Transformed City

BECOMING EMBEDDED IN A community is a long-term process. Lots of simple acts of kindness, smiles, and being courteous repeated countless times do not produce immediate measurable results. If the end goal is to quickly plant a church, therein lies the rub, in that this posture does not quickly amass a group of disenfranchised Christians who are looking for a hipper and trendier version of the church they now belong to or which they left some time ago. The impulse to be missional through and through is more than a pragmatic difference in approach or methodology; rather it becomes a complete reorientation of a way of life that seeks to live as a church (individually and collectively) with an outward trajectory. William McAlpine plainly states that, "Any church that is not missional is not a church in the biblical sense. The very essence of the church demands mission. Therefore, mission is not solely or primarily what we *do* as the church; it is what we *are*. The church *is* mission."[1]

It is this identity which is marked by an outward impulse that identifies the church, and as McAlpine boldly states, to do otherwise ends up compromising even the notion of calling oneself the church. He goes on to write:

> The missional church operates on the wavelength of God's overarching redemptive purposes in the world for the glory and honor of his name. It is not solely concerned with activity, that is, what we do; it is concerned with being, that is, who and what we are. Let me put it this way: the missional quality of the church reflects both our identity (who we are) and our purpose (what we are called to do). We cannot separate identity from purpose. One

1. McAlpine, *Sacred Space for the Missional Church*, 3.

does not trump the other, since being the missional church will irresistibly manifest itself in doing, and that doing will be carried out in the particularity of identifiable contexts.[2]

One of the questions that I have wrestled through in the framework of this book has to do with the scope of God's redemptive purposes that McAlpine mentions. What are God's redemptive purposes in terms of the city? Does redemption encompass more than simply the salvation of individuals, or is the scope much larger than we realize? Does redemption cover not only urban *people* but urban *place* as well?

I've shared on numerous occasions my simple daily act of walking over to the neighborhood Starbucks. It's not that I even care much for Starbucks coffee, but the location is a true hub in the community that acts as a great intersection for the lives of many who call this area home. This idea of the thrust of the missional church, God's redemptive purposes, and transformation of urban people and places has been at the forefront of my thinking of late. My relationship with Drago, one of the eastern European patriarchs, a particular Starbucks patron whom I've mentioned earlier in the book, has continued to strengthen and grow. I've had the privilege of introducing my family and other friends to him. Drago's a common fixture in the corner of this Starbucks even more so than I am. Recently I noticed for about a two-week stretch that I did not see him in his usual spot. Since it was summertime, I had simply assumed he had gone on holiday somewhere or back to one of the Balkan nations to visit family. One day as I was immersed in my laptop, I looked up and there he was standing right in front of me. I was glad to see him and even a little worried, hoping his health was all right. Instead, Drago told me the tragic news that his son, who is my age, had been gunned down and killed. I was speechless and didn't know what to say. I listened to him, tried my best to console and comfort, and in all sincerity gave him that familiar pastoral response, "I will pray for you and I mean it." That was not a flippant statement either. I prayed for Drago, and continue to do so whenever he comes to mind, for comfort, healing, and even the healing only that a Savior can bring.

The next day when I walked in, I saw him in his usual spot, so I went over to see how he was doing. He was still reeling, because he had not been sleeping well. I assured him again that I was praying for him and that I was glad to see him. Then the following day, as I rolled into

2. Ibid., 4.

Starbucks before 7:00 in the morning, I saw him standing in line getting his morning tea. We chatted again and then he turned around and bought my coffee. I was pleasantly surprised—not for the free coffee, since I only buy a short, but in his reciprocity. A breakthrough. For an introvert like me, it takes seemingly extra time to get to know people and see the relationship grow deeper. I have been praying for Drago off and on for almost a year and a half. The relationship has slowly developed and unfolded. This week. it took a sharp turn in terms of depth, and I was grateful that he was able to talk with me and share. In a neighborhood full of immigrants, the common theme is that it takes time to see relationships strengthen. But that is what we love about Vancouver and our neighborhood. Author and sociology professor Sharon Zukin calls these "authentic places" as I will soon explain.

Having lived in the suburbs of Phoenix and Tucson, over time I began to crave these urban "authentic places" that became a refuge from the assumed safety and sterility of the suburbs. Many others have been on this same journey and it is not a new phenomenon in North American cities. "The desire for authentic urban experience began as a reaction to the urban crisis of the 1960s, when American cities were routinely described as hopeless victims of a fatal disease. They were losing their more affluent and ethnically whiter families to the suburbs."[3] This movement was buttressed in the 1970s by a growing new group of people. "In a curious and unexpected way, the counterculture's pursuit of origins—by loosening the authentic self and bonding with the poor and underprivileged—opened a new beginning for urban redevelopment in the 1970s, alongside gentrification and gay and lesbian communities. The allure of newly hip neighborhoods spread through the power of alternative media."[4] However, somewhere along the way, after these early gentrifiers embedded themselves in these various urban communities, things began to change. As gentrification became more mainstream, these urban neighborhoods became more desirable and safe. The next wave of people moved in, followed by another wave. However, the changes brought on by this "resettlement" began to reconfigure these neighborhoods on many fronts. Zukin describes this process: "In the areas where hipsters and gentrifiers live there's a new cosmopolitanism in the air: tolerant, hip, casual. And that isn't bad. But little by little the old ethnic neighborhoods they have moved into are dying, along with

3. Zukin, *Naked City*, 4–5.
4. Ibid., 16.

the factories where longtime residents plied their trades and the Irish bars, Latino bodegas, and black soul food restaurants where they made their homes away from home. The people who seemed so rooted in the neighborhoods are disappearing."[5]

The challenge which arises is that often these authentic places transition into *faux* authentic places—all planned and scripted like a movie set. What is an authentic urban neighborhood? Usually we conjure up words like *gritty, earthy, organic, raw,* and so forth. But in an age where many are pursuing lives in these numerous urban authentic neighborhoods, something then begins to change: we long for authenticity, but the problem is that when too many desire it, a neighborhood morphs into something altogether different. "How many shopping streets have been transformed by cafes, bars, and gourmet cheese stores for people who want to consume differently from mainstream culture? Who go for better coffee not to Dunkin' Donuts but to Starbucks, which tries to live down the fact that it's a chain, or, even better, to an anti-Starbucks, a dark little cafe where the tattooed barista knows how to foam the milk just right, the beans are organically grown on bird-friendly trees and purchased through fair trade, and you can connect to Wi-Fi with other customers who share your tastes?"[6]

What constitutes an authentic neighborhood and at what point does it transition to *not authentic,* where it simply becomes a fancy facade of its former self? Do we really long for what a neighborhood was or what it is? Where does holistic transformation come in? Twenty years ago, my neighborhood was classic urban blight (Vancouver-style), run-down, distressed, with low-quality stores, ugly strip malls, and so forth. Now I find it in a world that straddles the past and the future. Half the neighborhood is now sleek glass and concrete towers, Starbucks, sushi places, and the like. While maybe 20 years ago, it was more "authentic," I don't know of anyone who wants the neighborhood to return to that era with ugly buildings not worth preserving, drugs, and crime. When we clamor for authenticity, what are we really longing for? Do we really want raw, gritty, and rundown? I don't find too many hipsters moving into the many inner-city neighborhoods across the continent that are wastelands due to neglect. We desire a sanitized version of the past . . . myself included. The neighborhoods that I'm drawn to throughout the city are somewhere on the gentrification continuum. Take it too far and

5. Ibid., 7–8.
6. Ibid., 19.

I'm not interested. But somewhere in the middle of this process is the social environment that I enjoy the most. However, in five, 10, 20 years from now, it will more than likely look very different. Then what?

"Authenticity speaks of the right of a city, and a neighborhood, to offer residents, workers, store owners, and street vendors the opportunity to put down roots—to represent, paradoxically, both origins and new beginning."[7] Based upon that definition (strictly speaking), Vancouver is not a very authentic place. Sure, we purport authenticity to tourists, but how authentic are we really? Is everything simply a massive marketing or branding scheme to attract foreign investments? I hear from numerous lower-income immigrants and refugees of how difficult life in Vancouver is. In many ways, they don't have much hope for a better life for themselves, although they're more hopeful for their children. But returning to where they came from is not an option. We certainly have the multicultural thing down. We have a picturesque and stunning natural landscape. Our built environment is new and sleek. But are we authentic? Whenever that moniker gets applied to a neighborhood, then begins the progression towards hipness and coolness. Then all of the cool people will want to live there and any semblance of authenticity begins to diminish. Church planters are no different. I'm not sure what to think about this next reality: all the cool places in every city are occupied by a proliferation of church planters. Either in the far-flung suburbs or gentrified neighborhoods, that is where we're seeing a bumper crop of church plants.

Recently I had a friend up from a west coast city visiting and we were talking about this very same topic. Neighborhood by neighborhood, he told me that all of the church plants in the city are predominantly in the cool urban-hipster neighborhoods. I wonder if God is either an urban hipster or a suburbanite, because almost all church planters are "called" to such spots. The reality is that most church planters make the decision on where to live based on the criteria that almost everyone else uses. That is why the more desirous places get the most planters, plain and simple. No one really wants to live in a run-down and degraded neighborhood that is bland, without character, and an eyesore. So we skip over them to the cooler spots and voila! . . . church planting in North America.

My intention is not to be cynical or critical because here is the reality: I am holding up a mirror and looking into my own soul. I am held captive by market influences and the desire for hip and trendy neighbor-

7. Ibid., 26.

hoods, great cafes, and the like. These are the places in the city that hold the most appeal for me without a doubt. And yet I do question my own motives, tastes, and desires. I wonder how often I have confused personal preferences with "God's calling?" We need more churches in these types of neighborhoods, not less. Also, we're not being disobedient or in sin if we do indeed plant in these kinds of neighborhoods. When I look into my own soul, what I constantly need to ask is, what are my motives? Am I driven by Kingdom values or the allure of a certain type of lifestyle? This highlights the tension we face by desiring to be in the world and not of it. We are to become embedded and incarnational, and yet as Michael Frost points out, we're also exiles who "cannot pitch their tents in this host empire and settle down as if they belong here. Exiles know that this is not where they belong, and the levels of corruption, abuse, persecution, violence, oppression, and greed are a constant reminder of their own foreignness. But neither can exiles return to sleepy, middle-class Christianity that seems unconcerned about such manifestations of evil in our world. Being *in* this world but not *of* this world means an ongoing commitment to walking a less traveled road—the road of injustice, compassion, generosity."[8]

Are we even authentic? Or are we just as much pushed and pulled by lifestyle choices, a city's branding mechanisms, and so forth? Most of us want a *faux authenticity* in that not too many people (myself included) *really* want to live in an "authentic" neighborhood where instead of Starbucks there's cheap coffee at 7-Eleven. Instead of trendy boutique shops, there's a Thrift Store. And instead of chic yoga-mat-totting pedestrians, there are bag ladies pushing shopping carts and drinking liquor at nine in the morning. Do we really want authenticity or the commercialized and sanitized version of it?

This is all to paint the backdrop of this chapter as well as the trajectory of this book. What is a good city? What makes a city great? What constitutes a healthy and vibrant neighborhood? What roles as followers of Jesus do we play in a neighborhood's and city's transformation? Again, what does that even look like? Certainly it must look different than the norm of gentrification and revitalization, although there will be some commonalities. As followers of Jesus, we're called to jump into the midst of city life and seek transformation. My desire throughout this book has been to call forth the church to embrace the city, love it, and understand

8. Frost, *Exiles*, 227.

it. The apostle Paul wrote in a similar vein when he penned his letters to the urban churches of the day. "One of Paul's primary concerns was to enable these urban churches to act rather than react to their city, province, and empire. If they could not be assertive in undertaking ministry in their city and as part of the Roman Empire, they would eventually die. To be effective in ministry was necessary for Paul's churches to understand their urban and international context."[9]

The subtitle of this book, *Developing a Theological Framework for Understanding the City*, points to the path we've been on as well as where we're going. Being a pragmatist, I believe our theological reflection should move us to action as we embrace our cities with the good news of the Kingdom. Our desire and longing is to see our cities transformed. "I would suggest that a transformed place is that kind of city that pursues fundamental changes, a stable future and the sustaining and enhancing of all of life rooted in a vision bigger than mere urban politics."[10] This hits especially close to home. Since we moved into our neighborhood, our aspiration has been to see community transformation develop and unfold. Knowing that this is a long-term process, we began the slow work of embedding our lives here and weaving them into the people of this community. In longing for life and community transformation to take place in others, it has instead been taking place in our lives. We left everything to come and give our lives here regardless of the personal cost. Just last week, Grant, our oldest son, said to me, "Dad, we're a lot like my other friends. Before they moved to Canada, they were well-off and now that they're here, they are poorer. That happened to us too." As I bring this book to a close, we're in the midst of immigration issues where there's a good chance we may have to make a hasty transition back to the States. Such is the nature of the push-and-pull effects of global immigration, as we know of many people in our neighborhood who moved to Canada leave only one year later for some other country or city. Maybe it was precisely these dynamics that I needed to be immersed in, as they provided the backdrop of this book. Theology needs to be grounded in the ordinariness of everyday life. Welcome to the global urban village.

The end goal for our endeavors here as a family is more than simply planting a church or even a cluster of churches. Instead, it is to see a city transformed. As I've laid out already in this book, that entails more

9. Linthicum, *City of God City of Satan*, 66.
10. Smith, "Urban Mission Methodology," 6.

than the foundational elements of evangelism, church planting, and local church ministry as a whole. Pining for a transformed city is more comprehensive in scope. Too often as followers of Jesus, we're preoccupied with our own activities, whether church planting or our specific ministries. We dream dreams about larger church attendance or more impact and influence in our ministries. Again, while these are foundational, sometimes they have the effect of causing the way we view the city to become myopic or parochial. We're certainly not the only ones who have a vision or dream of a better city. At times it seems as though our dreams of a transformed city pale compared to those "outside of the faith."

An example is found in the Millennium Development Goals (MDG). These "are eight international development goals that all 193 United Nations member states and at least 23 international organizations have agreed to achieve by the year 2015. They include eradicating extreme poverty, reducing child mortality rates, fighting disease epidemics such as AIDS, and developing a global partnership for development."[11] I wonder how or why that it is that national governments are able to cooperate towards these crucial goals, while it seems sometimes as though the church has a difficult time even cooperating within one city, let alone display common grace. God cares for humanity and, as we explored earlier, he will seek to care for, protect, and redeem humanity with or without us. The Millennium Development Goals lay out some key components for transformation in a city:

1. Eradicate extreme poverty and hunger

2. Achieve universal primary education

3. Promote gender equality and empower women

4. Reduce child mortality rates

5. Improve maternal health

6. Combat HIV/AIDS, malaria, and other diseases

7. Ensure environmental sustainability

8. Develop a global partnership for development[12]

"These goals have been widely used by multilateral agencies, governments and non-governmental organizations (NGOs), in framing development policies in order to achieve the associated targets by 2015.

11. Wikimedia Foundation Inc., "Millennium Development Goals."
12. Ibid.

Such clearly stated goals suggest that defining 'development' is easy and that what is important is the end point that a society gets to, not how those goals are achieved."[13] While these are indeed great goals and are very foundational, they overlook the spiritual dynamics which are precisely what the church is poised to provide. That does not diminish the magnitude or importance of something like the MDG, but we need to acknowledge that the ultimate transformation for now and for eternity is found in Christ and Christ alone.[14] "In a world with overcrowded prisons, millions of addicts, an epidemic of HIV/AIDS and unprecedented levels of people trafficking, Christ could be far more credible than we have allowed him to be."[15] I have seen too many well-meaning programs that do a wonderful job in attempting to rehabilitate people, but which stop short of full transformation. Life in Christ is transformative. Darkness turns to light, as sinners become saints, sealed with the Holy Spirit as temples of the living God.

What then does this mean for the city and our involvement in it? What is needed is a synthesis that holds the "physical" and the "spiritual" together, because God does indeed care for both. Common grace and saving grace. Or putting it another way, we're to be engaged in doing the physical as a demonstration of the transformative effects of the spiritual. "Whether we like it or not, we carry the burden of having to live out the truth in such a way as to establish its viability among those who are watching."[16] We can embody the good news of the Kingdom. "When evangelicals deliver multi-million dollar relief and development projects or feed the hungry in their neighborhoods, they become the good news."[17]

> Following Jesus in the city means getting serious about issues like good schools, responsible government, sanitation and clean streets, fairness in the marketplace and justice in the courts. It means working to eliminate squalor slums and every depressing condition that dishonours God by degrading human life. Once urban disciples see the big picture of what it means to be citizens

13. Willis, *Theories and Practices of Development*, 1.

14. See *To Transform a City* about the discussion between "ulterior" and "ultimate" motives.

15. Edwards, *An Agenda for Change*, 30–31.

16. Frost and Hirsch, *ReJesus*, 53.

17. *An Agenda for Change*, 87.

of the Kingdom in the cities as they are, they begin to work from a new and enlarged perspective. Obedience to King Jesus takes them to every nook and cranny of city life. They find the challenges innumerable and the cost often high. But they know that while the dark powers are awesome, God's rule is greater and its advance is worth every sacrifice.[18]

In many ways, this assumed dichotomy between physical and spiritual dynamics does not or should not have to exist. It is the product of our own thinking. Rather, we need to ask, along with authors Eric Swanson and Sam Williams, "As we consider city transformation, what clearly is the end we have in mind? What would it look like for our city to be transformed?"[19] Glenn Smith of Christian Direction in Montreal has laid out a vision for city transformation based on key indicators that are in turn the outflow of a highly contextualized process that is indigenous to the host city. In contrast, he writes, "Far too many practitioners, especially church planters, are using American paradigms. The unending debates about the usefulness of 'seeker-sensitive' models, 'purpose-driven initiatives,' and 'Christ and our culture forums' are examples of this. We are not taking the time to think biblically so as to act contextually."[20] Christian Direction's twelve indicators, which they use in the cities of Quebec and La Francophonie (the world's French-speaking nations) are as follows:

1. An increasing number of churches involved in spiritual transformation of their city regions.

2. The people of God animated by a passionate spirituality involved in concrete acts of reconciliation and justice for the welfare of the city.

3. Leaders desirous to see the people of God use their gifts (in partnership with other churches) to demonstrate the Good News in all aspects of the city.

4. Equality (equity) in economics, social policy, language acquisition possibilities, infrastructure, housing, public transportation and education.

5. Happy and well-developed children and youth living in peace with God, themselves and others, guided by good spiritual values that

18. Smith, "Key Indicators to a Transformed City," 7.

19. Swanson and Williams, *To Transform a* City, 41.

20. "Key Indicators to a Transformed City," 7.

enrich their life and allow them to reach their full potential and the welfare of the city.

6. A decline in the rate of suicide.

7. Healthy adults, great marriages, vibrant families (AIDS prevention decreasing number of people contracting the virus).

8. Multiple institutional opportunities for the most vulnerable to re-connect joyfully with city that cares for all its populations.

9. City/regions as places where violence is in decline.

10. A decline in sexual abuse against women and children.

11. Beautiful cities and regions as artistic expressions and the heritage of the community are more deeply valued.

12. Reduction of pollution for a better and more wholesome environment.[21]

This is not to diminish the commonalities that are found across all cities, whether they be in developed or developing countries. The overarching goal is or should be about seeing cities transformed with followers of Jesus playing a pivotal role.

The vision of authentic neighborhoods and transformed cities is paramount to our work in cities. This forms the culmination of my de-sire for developing a theological framework for understanding the city. We pray, we care, we love, we serve and give our lives to the city and its inhabitants. Far from mere theological speculation or academic mental gymnastics, we're to be compelled and propelled into action. God has a heart for the city. It is a beautiful vision. We noted that from the outset, beginning in the Garden of Eden, man's trajectory has been urban. We traced in the pages of the Old Testament a definitive blueprint for urban life which offers us an understanding of God's intent for the city. The early church was birthed in the city and found its home there. Today, with over half the world living in cities, including over 80 per cent of Americans and Canadians, we must adjust our lenses, which have for so long been so tightly focused on local church ministries, and instead pan the camera back to include the city—its people, the built environ-ment, transportation infrastructure, economy, and all its various other layers, lenses, and perspectives. These all matter to God. Yet the question remains, do they matter to us?

21. http://www.direction.ca/

Afterword

FALL IS FAST APPROACHING. Here above the 49th Parallel, the recognition of the changing seasons comes earlier than in other places. Already the morning has a refreshing coolness to it. Changing weather and temperature mark transitions in the calendar year that remind us of the movement of time brought about by these seasons. And what is true of the seasons is also true of life. To everything, there is indeed a season.

This morning I quietly slipped out of our home to walk over to the neighborhood Starbucks to reflect and collect myself. Half of our home is already filled with moving boxes as we count down the days, five to be exact, before we load up the moving truck and transition back south of the border to the States. Portland, Oregon, to be exact. Roughly two years have come and gone since we first arrived here in metro Vancouver. In many ways it feels like a lifetime and in other ways it is as if only a week has passed. Seasons. Changes.

There's no denying that context has played a vital role in the formation of this book. Vancouver was the lens through which I viewed and interpreted the city. The question I must now ask myself is, how will this inform and shape my view of cities when we leave? What insights will I glean from the context of Portland? Where are my blind spots? What will I see? What have I missed?

Like most missionaries or church planters, when we respond to God's callings and promptings in our lives we gladly respond regardless of the personal cost. We envision great happenings; churches birthed, peoples' lives transformed, movements, and the beginnings of seeing a city redeemed. Instead, what took place was on one level more mundane than we had imagined, but on another level, more profound than we could ever have imagined. We came to see a city transformed, but instead our lives were transformed.

Bibliography

Abrahamson, Mark. *Global Cities*. Don Mills: Oxford University Press, 2004.

Aikman, David. *Jesus in Beijing: How Christianity is Transforming China and Changing the Global Balance of Power*. Washington: Regnery, 2006.

Bakke, Ray. *A Theology as Big as the City*. Downers Grove: IVP Academic, 1997.

———, and Sam Roberts. *The Expanded Mission of City Center Churches*. Chicago: International Urban Associates, 1998.

———, and Jon Sharpe. *Street Signs: A New Direction in Urban Ministry*. Birmingham: New Hope, 2006.

BBC, "King Herod," http://www.bbc.co.uk/religion/religions/christianity/history/herod .shtml.

Benesh, Sean. *Metrospiritual: The Geography of Church Planting*. Eugene: Resource Publications, 2011.

Berelowitz, Lance. *Dream City: Vancouver and the Global Imagination*. Vancouver: Douglas & McIntyre, 2005.

Bergquist, Linda, and Allan Karr. *Church Turned Inside Out: A Guide for Designers, Refiners, and Re-Aligners*. San Francisco: Jossey-Bass, 2009.

Bosch, David. *Transforming Mission: Paradigm Shifts in Theology of Mission*. Maryknoll: Orbis, 1991.

Boyce, Ron. "The Nature of Cities." Class notes from The Nature of Cities class at Bakke Graduate University, Seattle, Washington.

Brugmann, Jeb. *Welcome to the Urban Revolution: How Cities are Changing the World*. Toronto: Viking Canada, 2009.

Cairns, Earle. *Christianity Through the Centuries: A History of the Christian Church*. Grand Rapids: Zondervan, 1996.

Conn, Harvie and Manuel Ortiz, *Urban Ministry: The Kingdom, the City & the People of God*. Downers Grover, InterVarsity, 2010.

Council for Canadian Urbanism, "About Canadian Urbanism," http://www .canadianurbanism.ca/en/about.

Crawford, J.H. *Carfree Cities*. Utrecht: International, 2002.

———. *Carfree Design Manual*. Utrecht: International, 2009.

Davis, John, *Paradise to Prison*. Grand Rapids: Baker, 1975.

Dear, Michael J. *From Chicago to L.A.: Making Sense of Urban Theory*. Thousand Oaks: Sage, 2002.

Deloria, Vine. *God is Red: A Native View of Religion*. Golden: Fulcrum, 1994.

Dictionary.com, LLC. "Urbane," http://dictionary.reference.com/browse/urbane.

———. "Control," http://dictionary.reference.com/browse/control.

———. "Temporal," http://dictionary.reference.com/browse/temporal.

Dodd, Philip, and Ben Donald. *The Book of Cities*. New York: MJF, 2006.

Dorrell, Jimmy. *Trolls and Truth: 14 Realities About Today's Church That We Don't Want to See*. Birmingham: New Hope, 2006.

Driscoll, Mark, and Gerry Breshears. *Vintage Church: Timeless Truths and Timely Methods*. Wheaton: Crossway, 2008.

Edwards, Joel. *An Agenda for Change: A Global Call for Spiritual and Social Transformation*. Grand Rapids: Zondervan, 2008.

Ellul, Jacques. *The Meaning of the City*. Grand Rapids: Eerdmans, 1970.

Erickson, Millard. *Christian Theology*. Grand Rapids: Baker, 1998.

Florida, Richard. *Cities and the Creative Class*. New York: Routledge, 2005.

———. *Who's Your City? How the Creative Economy Is Making Where You Live the Most Important Decision in Your Life*. New York: Basic, 2008.

Friedman, John. *Insurgencies: Essays in Planning Theory*. New York: Routledge, 2011.

Friedman, Thomas L. *The World Is Flat: A Brief History of the Twenty-First Century*. New York: Farrar, Straus and Giroux, 2006.

Frost, Michael. *Exiles: Living Missionally in a Post-Christian Culture*. Peabody: Hendrickson, 2006.

———, and Alan Hirsch. *ReJesus: A Wild Messiah for the Missional Church*. Grand Rapids: Baker, 2008.

Gornik, Mark. *To Live in Peace: Biblical Faith and the Changing Inner City*. Grand Rapids: Eerdmans, 2002.

Gorringe, T.J. *A Theology of the Built Environment: Justice, Empowerment, Redemption*. Cambridge: Cambridge University Press, 2002.

Grudem, Wayne. *Systematic Theology: An Introduction to Biblical Doctrine*. Grand Rapids: Zondervan, 1994.

Guder, Darrell, and Lois Barrett. *Missional Church: A Vision for the Sending of the Church in North America*. Grand Rapids: Eerdmans, 1998.

Guthrie, Donald. *New Testament Introduction*. Downers Grove: IVP Academic, 1990.

Harper, Stephen. *They're Just Not That Into: The Church's Struggle For Relevancy in the 21st Century*. Calgary: Cougarstone, 2011. Kindle edition.

Hayes, John B. *Sub-Merge: Living Deep in a Shallow World: Service, Justice, and Contemplation Among the World's Poor*. Venture: Regal, 2006.

Hern, Matt. *Common Ground in a Liquid City: Essays in Defense of an Urban Future*. Oakland: AK Press, 2010.

Hiller, Harry. *Urban Canada*. Don Mills: Oxford University Press, 2010.

Hirsch, Alan. *The Forgotten Ways: Reactivating the Missional Church*. Grand Rapids: Brazos Press, 2006.

Hjalmarson, Leonard. *An Emerging Dictionary for the Gospel and Culture: A Conversation from Augustine to Zizek*. Eugene: Resource Publications, 2010.

———, and Brent Toderash. *Fresh and Refresh: Church Planting and Urban Mission in Post Christendom Canada*. Eagle: Allelon, 2009.

Jacobsen, Eric. *Sidewalks in the Kingdom: New Urbanism and the Christian Faith*. Grand Rapids: Brazos Press, 2003.

Jenkins, Philip. *The Next Christendom: The Coming of Global Christianity*. Don Mills: Oxford University Press, 2007.

Kotkin, Joel. *The City: A Global History*. New York: Modern Library, 2006.

Ladd, George, *A Theology of the New Testament*. Grand Rapids: Eerdmans, 1993.

Lees, Loretta, et al. *Gentrification*. New York: Routledge, 2008.

Levinson, David, and Kevin Krizek. *Planning for Place and Plexus: Metropolitan Land Use and Transport.* New York: Routledge, 2008.

Linthicum, *City of God City of Satan: A Biblical Theology of the Urban Church.* Grand Rapids: Zondervan, 1991.

———. *Transforming Power: Building Strategies for Making a Difference in Your Community.* Downers Grove: IVP Academic, 2003.

Lupton, Robert D. *Renewing the City: Reflections on Community Development and Urban Renewal.* Downers Grove: InterVarsity Press, 2005.

Mapes, Jeff. *Pedaling Revolution: How Cyclists Are Changing American Cities.* Corvallis: Oregon State University Press, 2009.

McAlpine, William. *Sacred Space for the Missional Church: Engaging the Culture Through the Built Environment.* Eugene: Wipf and Stock, 2011.

Newman, Peter et al. *Resilient Cities: Responding to Peak Oil and Climate Change.* Washington: Island Press, 2009.

Ng, Edward. *Designing High-Density Cities: For Social and Environmental Sustainability.* London: Earthscan, 2010.

Olson, Roger. *The Story of Christian Theology: Twenty Centuries of Tradition and Reform.* Downers Grove: IVP Academic, 1999.

Ott, Craig, and Harold Netland. *Globalizing Theology: Belief and Practice in an Era of World Christianity.* Grand Rapids: Baker Academic, 2006.

Patrick, Darrin, and Matt Carter. *For the City: Proclaiming and Living Out the Gospel.* Grand Rapids: Zondervan, 2011.

Roberts Jr., Bob. *Glocalization: How Followers of Jesus Engage a Flat World.* Grand Rapids: Zondervan, 2007.

Roxburgh, Alan. *Missional: Joining God in the Neighborhood.* Grand Rapids: Baker, 2011.

Schaller, Lyle. *Center City Churches: The New Urban Frontier.* Nashville: Abingdon, 1993.

Smith, Brad. *City Signals: Principles and Practices for Ministering in Today's Global Communities.* Birmingham: New Hope, 2008.

Smith, Glenn. "Community Development in Canadian Cities." Paper from Christian Direction website, http://www.direction.ca.

———. "Key Indicators to a Transformed City." Paper from Christian Direction website, http://www.direction.ca.

———. "Urban Mission Methodology." Paper from Christian Direction website, http://www.direction.ca.

Staley, Sam, and Adrian Moore, *Mobility First: A New Vision for Transportation in a Globally Competitive Twenty-First Century.* Lanham: Rowman & Littlefield, 2009.

Swanson, Eric, and Sam Williams. *To Transform a City: Whole Church, Whole Gospel, Whole City.* Grand Rapids: Zondervan, 2010.

Uhalley, Stephen, and Xiaoxin Wu. *China and Christianity: Burdened Past, Hopeful Future.* Armonk: M.E. Sharpe, 2001.

Urban Dictionary, LLC. "Urban," http://www.urbandictionary.com/define.php?term=urban.

UN-Habitat. *Global Report on Human Settlement 2009: Planning Sustainable Cities.* London: Earthscan, 2010.

Walvoord, John, and Roy Zuck. *The Bible Knowledge Commentary: Old Testament.* Wheaton: Victor, 1985.

Wikimedia Foundation, Inc. "Built Environment," Wikipedia, http://en.wikipedia.org /wiki/Built_environment.

———. "City," Wikipedia, http://en.wikipedia.org/wiki/City.

———. "Civitas," Wiktionary, http://en.wiktionary.org/wiki/civitas.

———. "Conurbation," Wikipedia, http://en.wikipedia.org/wiki/Conurbation.

———. "Megaregions of the United States," Wikipedia, http://en.wikipedia.org/wiki /Megaregions_of_the_United_States.

———. "Metropolis," Wikipedia, http://en.wikipedia.org/wiki/Metropolis

———. "Nazareth," Wikipedia, http://en.wikipedia.org/wiki/Nazareth#Early_Christian _era.

———. "Polis," Wikipedia, http://en.wikipedia.org/wiki/Polis.

———. "Town," Wikipedia, http://en.wikipedia.org/wiki/Town.

———. "Xi'an," Wikipedia, http://en.wikipedia.org/wiki/Xi'n.

Willis, Katie. *Theories and Practices of Development*. New York: Routledge, 2011.

Winter, Bruce. *Seek the Welfare of the City: Christians as Benefactors and Citizens*. Grand Rapids: Eerdmans, 1994.

Wood, Phil, and Charles Landry. *The Intercultural City: Planning for Diversity Challenge*. London: Earthscan, 2008.

WordIQ. "Polis," http://www.wordiq.com/definition/Polis.

Zukin, Sharon. *Naked City: The Death and Life and Authentic Urban Places*. New York: Oxford University Press, 2010.